THE CRAZY-MAKING WORKPLACE

The Crazy-Making Workplace

Dr. Archibald D. Hart

VINE
BOOKS

Servant Publications
Ann Arbor, Michigan

Vine Books is an imprint of Servant Publications especially
designed to serve Evangelical Christians.

Published by Servant Publications
P.O. Box 8617
Ann Arbor, Michigan 48107

Cover design by Gerald Gawronski / The Look

93 94 95 96 97 10 9 8 7 6 5 4 3 2 1

Printed in the United States of America

ISBN 0-89283-828-0

Library of Congress Cataloging-in-Publication Data

Hart, Archibald D.

   The crazy-making workplace / Archibald Hart.
      p.   cm.
   Includes bibliographical references.
   ISBN 0-89283-828-0
   1. Job stress.   I. Title.
HF5548.85.H38   1993
158.7—dc20   93-30809

94-0915

Dedication
to
Richard, Rick, and Russ
Great sons-in-law and very special friends

Contents

Acknowledgments / 9
Preface / 11

1. Can a Workplace Be Toxic? / 15
2. What Makes a Workplace Dysfunctional? / 35
3. How to Keep Work from Killing You / 59
4. Are *You* Poisoning Your Workplace? / 79
5. Toxic Bosses / 99
6. Dealing with the Crazy-Makers / 119
7. Your Job, the Pressure Cooker, and Occupational Stress / 139
8. Burnout on the Job / 159
9. Women at Risk / 181
10. Sex, Power, and the Workplace / 205
11. Changing Your Job / 223
12. Crazy-Making Work and Your Family / 245

Afterword / 265
Notes / 275

ACKNOWLEDGMENTS

I AM PROFOUNDLY INDEBTED to several important people in my life for helping me complete this manuscript:

- As always I am indebted to my wife, Kathleen, who has always been a source of great encouragement and inspiration to me. Without her forbearance I doubt if I would ever get any task accomplished, let alone write a book.
- I am particularly indebted to my executive secretary, Nova Hutchins, who has persisted with me through many book projects already. Nevertheless, she seems to have boundless energy and great endurance, qualities that I very much appreciate. Her enthusiasm and dedication, not to mention her many hours in front of a temperamental computer, have once again supported me beyond my anticipation.
- I am also indebted to David McMartin who helped with the typing and my other office staff, headed by Bertha Jacklitch, who have inspired me to believe that dedicated employees can be models of healthiness that can easily offset and pardon a boss's many blunders.
- Finally, my deepest appreciation goes to Pat Springle who first suggested that I might consider writing a book such as this, and to my very special friends at Servant Publications, Ann Spangler, Beth Feia, and Don Cooper, for their continued support for the project and patience with my tardiness. I value all your friendships greatly.

Archibald D. Hart

Preface

THIS BOOK IS NOT ABOUT LEADERSHIP or management style directly. It's about how the quality of work life can enhance or diminish overall feelings of well-being and happiness. Indirectly, however, it raises vital questions about leadership and management style.

This is a book for all workers—from top level CEOs to factory apprentices and the most junior office clerks.

This book is for all who work, from the rank and file to top management in industry, banking, government bureaus, insurance, ministry, the professions, and even the military. If you work within an organization, no matter how large or small, you are caught up in a system of relationships, interactions, and obligations that will influence whether you feel fulfilled, contented, cheerful, and significant. Your work, too, can affect how fast you age, how often you become ill, the emotional pain and adversity you may face, and even when you will die. Furthermore, your workplace's influence does not stop at your life, but radiates to that of your family. It is a factor in whether you have a satisfying marriage, well-adjusted children, and even whether you or your spouse gets ulcers.

Working can be risky business. You may be thrust into an environment for five (or more) days a week, fifty-two weeks a year, forty (or more) years, which will subject you to strains that may erode your confidence so that you become less than the person you intended.

I describe such a workplace as "crazy-making." It could also be called "toxic," since it produces emotional and physical toxins that slowly poison your mind, health, and spirit. A "crazy-making" workplace can injure your psyche, making you feel unbalanced, when you are not.

Why do workers put up with such unwholesome workplaces? Why don't they just quit a dysfunctional office or an abusive factory? For the same reason, I suppose, that many spouses and children tolerate dysfunctional and abusive homes. It's called "learned helplessness." Such victims learn to be helpless through exposure that proceeds so slowly and insidiously that they don't perceive what's going on and in time feel powerless to leave, avoid, change, or control.

Thank God, alongside the many toxic workplaces, there are many healthy workplaces, where workers are treated with respect and consideration. Employees there are contented and effective, physically, mentally, and spiritually. Thank God for such a workplace if it be yours.

When a worker is unhappy it may not be the workplace's fault at all. Many troubled and disturbed employees are toxins. They may blame the boss or their work, but the craziness is in themselves. Pity their supervisors! Many bosses suffer from unduly angry, rebellious, and maladjusted workers, and are themselves the victims of helplessness, feeling powerless to take corrective action, demote or dismiss these troubled workers.

My sympathy goes out to such managers. Often they are not supported from above and are left to their own devices to make the best of a bad job scene. They are frequently the victims of toxicity that flows downward from the top of a crazy-making organization.

How can you tell whether the workplace or an individual worker is creating the craziness? The answer is not always clear-cut. As we proceed I will provide guidelines for you to differentiate your personal toxicity from that of your workplace.

I envision this book being used individually and in groups— even by work groups over lunch or during special staff training workshops. To facilitate group use, discussion questions are provided at the end of each chapter, as well as questionnaires and individual exercises. Whether you are a leader or a follower, a manager or managed, my hope is that this book will help you create the work life that you deserve. Change is always hard to achieve because it challenges the existing system of authority, which feels criticized by demands for improvement. Don't be put off by the reality that existing systems *always* resist change. Your worklife is a major investment and you owe it to yourself, and those near and dear to you, to try to achieve a better and healthier workplace.

Archibald D. Hart, Ph.D.
Pasadena, California

1 || Can a Workplace Be Toxic?

I do not like work even when someone else does it. **Mark Twain**

If you have a job without aggravations, you don't have a job. **Malcom Forbes**

I MET HER ON A PLANE TO CHICAGO. Late thirties, divorced and unattached. Obviously very intelligent and career-oriented. And she wanted to talk—especially when she discovered I was a clinical psychologist.

She was in sales and worked for a large medical equipment supply company. She made good money, which is why she stayed in her job. But as she began to tell me about her work environment tears filled her eyes. Like so many others I have met, she loves her work but hates her job environment. Her immediate boss "is a little crazy," she said. This is how she described him:

"When I return to the office after a long sales trip, I go straight to my desk in a large office that we all share, greet everyone as pleasantly as I can—and wait. I know it's coming. It happens every time. My boss eventually comes up to me and says, 'What's wrong with you? How come you don't have a smile on your face for me?'—or something like that.

"I start to boil but I do my best to remain polite. I reply, 'I'm fine, Bill. Everything's fine!'

"'You've really got an attitude, haven't you?' he will shout back at me. 'You're a real bitch, you know that? No one can say anything to you without you bitching up.'

"He just won't let up on his attacks. I admit I've had to stand up to him at times, but he's so unreasonable in his demands. No matter how well I do or how much I sell, it isn't ever good enough. He never praises my work but always finds something to pick on me about. But I'm the best salesperson they've got. I win all the sales awards, or nearly all of them, and yet he's always on my case."

"Can you recall any incident where you might have embarrassed him?" I asked, suspecting that he may be harboring a grudge against her.

"Well, yes, I suppose so," she replied tentatively, "but surely he doesn't harbor grudges that long."

"Tell me about it anyway."

"Well, when I first started working for the company about eight years ago, he was just a fellow salesman. He tried to date me. I told him I don't go out with married men. For a while he left me alone —and then suddenly one day I began to sense that he's picking on me, finding fault wherever he can or just making life hard for me."

I got the picture. Our short flight was nearly over. The best I could do was to encourage her to see a psychotherapist. "You're not emotionally disturbed and you're certainly not crazy," I assured her, "but you certainly need an objective outsider, preferably someone who is trained to understand the innermost mysteries of people like your boss, to give you sound advice on how you should proceed."

She thanked me profusely. She had never shared concerns about her job problems with anyone before. "It feels good," she commented, "just to talk about my problems."

We said our goodbyes as we strolled through the Chicago terminal and I began to wonder: how many other people are there out there who feel like she does? She must be one of millions of Americans who are unhappy in their work, not because what they do in their work is so disagreeable, but because their work atmosphere or climate is abusive or dysfunctional. For them work is a living hell because their job connections drive them crazy.

ALL IN A DAY'S WORK

Everybody has to work. And the vast majority of us have to work under someone else's direction. A lot has been written about "leadership"—but in truth most of us are followers. Someone is always in charge ahead of us, from whom we take our lead. Only a select few are in the "ultimate" leadership position, a role I personally would not relish. And because someone else always has some influence over us we cannot control everything that happens to us.

Not much has been written about the workplace and how it contributes to the well-being of the worker and determines whether a person experiences fulfillment. Yet I estimate that at least 50 percent, if not higher, of the workplaces in our nation are significantly dysfunctional. Practices, behaviors, attitudes and systems in the environment undermine the well-being and spirit of workers to such an extent that they can destroy homes, hopes and happiness. Whatever happens at work can affect not only the worker but his or her spouse, children, and even the pets!

Why is the influence of the workplace so profound? The answer is simple: we spend between forty and seventy hours a week (or even more) for forty to fifty years of our life working. This is a big chunk of our existence. Anything that takes that much of our life is bound to have a major influence on how we experience living. If what goes on in the workplace is crazy-making it will tend to make us a little kooky also.

IS IT THE PLACE OR THE PEOPLE?

Step inside the corporate offices of the ABC-Whatever Company. Walk down a corridor and enter the large general office. Row upon row of neat cubicles. Desks with computers. Desks with typewriters. Desks with just writing pads. Trays of files, filing cabinets, a water cooler and a copy machine stuck away in a corner. It's still too early for anyone to be working—except the janitors. They've done their early morning sweep, emptying trash baskets and rearranging chairs. Everything is neat and tidy and ready for the army of workers that will invade the premises in just a few minutes.

Nothing is crazy here—yet! A crazy-making workplace has nothing to do with cluttered desks, files piled high, untidy premises or even prefabricated buildings. It has nothing to do with uncomfortable chairs, out-of-date computers or how well-organized the flow of work is—even though these are all important to the effectiveness of the organization's activity.

A crazy-making workplace is about people—the warm-blooded

human beings that do the work, the breathing and emoting machines who toil and labor in the place. Soon these workers desiring to earn their livelihood will begin streaming through the company's doors. Men and women of all ages. Clerks, accountants, bookkeepers, auditors, typists, computer analysts, line managers, equipment operators. Imperfect people. Troubled people. Hurting people. Even dying people trying to make the most of what's left of their lives. People with unmet needs and unfulfilled dreams. They will occupy the desks, work the machines, file the papers, and do what's necessary (or even unnecessary) to keep the corporate machine ticking. Whether the workplace will be crazy-making or not is determined by these people.

But are business offices the only crazy-making workplaces? Not at all. Step inside the machine shop of a small engineering company. Lathes and drill machines line the walls here. Music plays continuously in the background because the work can be repetitive and monotonous and one can go crazy without some distraction. The smell of machine oil and cooling lubricant fills the air. Metal cuttings litter this space and must be swept up and collected for recycling at least twice a day. While noise, oil, and metal particles can make this workplace hazardous, so can the people who work the machines.

Don't misunderstand me. We all know that the physical conditions of the work environment can be extremely perilous. Many health problems can result from bad working conditions. But my focus here is on the psychological environment and the emotional damage that the workplace can inflict on unsuspecting employees. A crazy-making workplace can make people feel powerless, emotionally blackmailed, sexually harassed, manipulated, and overstressed. In short, a crazy-making workplace can make you believe you yourself are crazy. The psychological environment is determined by what goes on behind the closed doors of big companies, little machine shops, and wherever people gather to work, that is usually kept politely hidden.

How many of us who want to be good workers deserving fair wages feel crazed by our workplaces? No one really knows. Very little research has been done. Work is a major part of everyone's life. It should provide satisfaction, fulfillment, and meaning to existence. It should be more than earning money to put food on your table. Work should uplift your character and give you a sense of purpose. But how often does it? Vern Bengston, professor of sociology at the University of Southern California, conducts research on cross-general relationships. He is particularly interested in how work satisfaction has declined over time. Studying 2000 people from 328 families, he has found that while people in their late thirties and forties seem to be more devoted to work—putting in six hours a week longer than their fifty- and sixty-year-old parents—they are less satisfied.[1]

The fact that your job can make you sick, emotionally and physically, is a fact I will come back to several times, but let me provide some evidence for this assertion at the outset so you can better appreciate how important it is to ensure that work contributes to your well-being and does not undermine it.

Let's suppose you feel lousy. You've tried to take better care of yourself, you've changed your eating habits, you exercise and get sufficient rest. Still, you're crabby and quick to anger. You feel profoundly tired a lot of the time. You think you must have the flu or are allergic to something, except neither is the case. What's going on? What you may have used to be labeled the "sick-building syndrome," because some felt it was caused by air-tight, closed-up modern buildings where stale air, with its load of germs and viruses, is recycled. But that idea had a very short life.

According to Cornell University psychologist Alan Hedge, it may not be a closed-up building with its recycled air that is making you sick, but your job. You are not the victim of a "sick-building syndrome" but a "sick-job syndrome." His research convincingly shows that often job dissatisfaction and stress make employees suffer from vague and undefinable maladies.[2]

For his study, Dr. Hedge and his colleagues surveyed 3,155 workers in eight different office buildings. Nothing unusual or toxic was found in the air quality. What they did find was that workers who were least satisfied with their work were more likely to suffer from the "sick-building syndrome." The problem, it seems, is not in the building, its air-conditioning, or the work itself. It is in the work environment, its emotional atmosphere and its operational system.

Do you feel irritable and fatigued a lot of the time? Are you performing below par? Do you feel dissatisfied with your work life? Perhaps you are in the wrong job. Perhaps you have a boss who hates your guts or is driving you crazy. Perhaps you feel like a misfit in your work, or perhaps the place where you work is full of un-happy people who in turn make your life unhappy. Whatever the reason, your job can be hazardous to your physical and emotional health. Fortunately, with a little bit of understanding and help you can change this and restore balance and sanity to your work life. You can, in fact, turn your workplace around and make it healthier and more functional. And I say this no matter where you stand in your organization's hierarchy. I know from personal experience that even someone way down on the totem pole can have a signifi-cant sobering and healing effect both upward and downward in the work environment. So before you rush to blame your boss or coworkers for all your problems, pause and consider whether you are trying your best to be healthy yourself. You have the power to exert an influence on your job. With the right heart, attitude and a plan that you can develop as you read through this book, you can make a difference. All it takes is one person to start behaving healthfully in a toxic work system and you begin to see a change in the rest of the system as well. If I didn't believe this I wouldn't bother to write this book because there is no way you can change a whole system without beginning with a few individuals. What does it take? A friendly word spoken regularly to a lonely or shy person. A kind deed done to someone who has snubbed you. A moment of time taken to encourage a member of your team who has failed. This is the stuff of which healthiness is made. Every little contribu-tion erodes the toxicity of unfriendliness, jealousy and isolation.

Sometimes, I hope rarely, there is nothing anyone can do to im-prove a bad job situation. The best you can do in these extremely bad circumstances is leave the job before it kills you. But how can you know when a crazy-making job is beyond salvaging? What signs indicate that you are unable to turn things around? And then, if you decide to change your job or even your career, how can you be sure that you are not going from the frying pan into the fire in your next job?—By trying to understand as much as you can why and how your present employment is crazy-making. Whether you stay and try to turn things around or leave so you can start afresh somewhere else you need to take a penetrating look at your present workplace and try to understand, to the best of your ability, why it is dysfunctional. You can only make a difference if you understand what is going on. And if you can't turn things around, at least understanding the unhealthy stresses of your workplace should help you in selecting a healthier environment for your next job.

So this book is about the workplace: how dysfunction occurs and can be changed; how an organization's leaders can pass dysfunction "from generation to generation" without recognizing their own dysfunctional management styles, and finally, how you can help fix the problem starting at the bottom and working up.

The impact of turning your workplace into a healthy environment is far-reaching. Not only will your health improve (because stress depletes the immune system and makes you more prone to illness), your level of happiness and general satisfaction with life will rise also.

WHAT POISONS A WORKPLACE?

No one person or characteristic makes a workplace toxic. Usually several factors combine to create the dysfunctionality that underlies toxicity. There are four major players that contribute to the toxicity:

- coworkers,
- bosses,
- upper-managers, and
- the workplace atmosphere.

Coworkers. Do you like the people you work with? Do your peers and subordinates treat you with respect? Do you clash with certain types of personalities? If you don't like your coworkers, feel disrespected or clash with certain personalities, chances are that your job is toxic for you. The workplace is not just a place where you work or where you meet professional needs. It is also a place where social needs are met as well. The caliber of your coworkers determines the quality of your social relationships at work. Crummy people don't help to make the enormous amount of time you spend at work very pleasurable. And the extent to which you feel you have fulfilling relationships at work is probably as sound an indicator you will get of the healthiness of your workplace.

How can coworkers contribute to the craziness of your workplace? In several ways. Top of the list for me is a *lack of group cohesion*. We all need to feel a part of a larger group. We need to feel that we are surrounded by people who are friendly, supportive and committed to our success as a group or team. This is true for our private lives and it is certainly true for our work lives. When you are not made to feel a part of the larger group at work, when there is insufficient group cohesiveness or when coworkers function in a highly individualized way where most are just looking out for themselves, you have the potential for crazy-making. In such a workplace people won't share ideas, no one has a clear sense of the group's goals, so one or two will try to dominate the activities and force social interactions to revolve around them. Communication is usually poor or nonexistent and the group lacks a feeling of togetherness. Work efficiency is compromised and everyone feels unhappy.

Without cohesiveness, people become suspicious, distrustful, and defensive. New ideas are suppressed, creativity discouraged. Constructive suggestions are taken as personal criticisms or attempts to control. Paranoia develops in the group.

Prejudice and discrimination are particularly toxic in the workplace. Wherever strong racial, sexual, age, disability or religious biases exist, so does the potential for crazy-making because some are allowed to feel "in," but others are forced to feel "out" of the group. Cliques and favorites develop. Only if you dress, behave, and believe in a certain way are you accepted. Individuality is stifled and prejudice fostered.

Wherever a strong personality dominates the workplace and takes control you can have trouble—and lots of it! Such a person, usually without authority to do so, "rules the roost" by dominating, monopolizing, controlling, manipulating and bullying everyone else, or just you. Only in the natural world is it necessary for the strong to run the show and dominate the weak. The survival of the species depends on the fittest winning out. But in a civilized society this is not only unnecessary but inhuman. We all have a right to survive, weak or strong. Yet animal instincts often still control us. Primitive patterns of intimidation create fear and insecurity. Of course, modern-day dominant types don't use biting, scratching or fang-baring. They resort to sarcasm, biting wit, innuendo, criticism and verbal threat to intimidate. The corporate jungle is much more sophisticated than Tarzan's, and more dangerous!

Finally, a less obvious but nevertheless significant source of coworker crazy-making can be found when the work environment is unresponsive and emotionless. In such a place there is no tolerance for any expression of feelings. If you are happy, you dare not show it because others will scoff at you. If you are sad, you hide it because you don't want to be seen as weak. Fellow workers are cold, stoic and unfeeling, so you have to be someone other than yourself. Where does this coldness come from? Sometimes it is a cold-fish boss who is so afraid of emotions that he avoids them like the plague and suppresses them in others. Sometimes it is a coworker who is trying to avoid the pain of severe abuse as a child so that she has no tolerance for feelings and has become insensitive to the hurts of others as a way of avoiding her own. Whatever the reason, a cold, unfeeling work environment can be demoralizing. It forces you to suppress your deep feelings and there is always an emotional penalty to be paid when you are not allowed to be a real person.

Bosses. At the end of a workday, much of how an employee feels is determined by the type and quality of interaction with a boss. Some managers want their workers to be afraid of them. Some want their followers to like them. Problems can arise at both extremes.

Whoever supervises you probably has the most important influence on your work health, because this person has the most power over you. Your boss can make or break your spirit just as readily as he or she can make or break your day.

The workplace is chock-full of bad bosses. They roam the corridors of our offices and aisles of our factories wreaking havoc on people's lives. They intimidate, lie to support their distorted views of themselves, harass and insult. I heard of a boss recently who makes a female employee raise the flag in front of the company building. So what's wrong with raising the flag? He makes her do it even when it is pouring rain. Another boss has his motto framed in large letters on the wall behind him. It reads: "People are animals." Can you imagine what it must be like to work for him?

I will devote a whole chapter later on to a discussion of bad bosses. Here I merely want to give an overview of the problem for the sake of completeness. What are the characteristics of a bad boss? How can you tell if your boss is just tough (and don't knock this because a tough boss, in the long run, is better than a weak one) or really toxic? Here are a few features to look for. Your boss is toxic if:

1. Your boss loves power. Nothing corrupts more than power in the wrong hands. It corrupts the workplace and it corrupts your well-being. A power-hungry boss loves to dominate others. Orders must be obeyed without question. Any resistance even to the most outrageous commands is met with severe discipline. This means you have constantly to be on guard against making mistakes that could be interpreted as disobedience. You dare not question a decision or instruction so you are doomed. If you obey and something goes wrong, you will be blamed for not questioning the command if you knew it was wrong. If you refuse to obey you will be disciplined or even fired. Definitely the stuff of which headaches, ulcers and high blood pressure are made!

2. Your boss never takes responsibility for mistakes. I don't know about you, but I want my boss to take responsibility for his mistakes. Not for mine—I'm willing to do that—but for his or hers. When those around get blamed or, even worse, when those vague and undefined administrators above get indicted, I become very nervous. This doesn't feed my confidence. I begin to suspect dishonesty. I become all tense, not knowing when I'm going to be blamed for something.

3. Your boss can't make decisions in a timely manner. Wiffle-waffle, double-talk, and technical jargon are used to rationalize delays. Someone "upstairs" is holding up the agreement or balking at the proposal. Such a boss is often insecure and unable to take responsibility for the job. Sure, occasionally it is crazy-making upper management that promotes this insecurity and makes it difficult for middle-level supervisors to do their job, but more often than not it is a boss who is out of her or his depth or just plain indecisive. Good bosses use good judgment, but they are also decisive. Otherwise everyone suffers.

4. Your boss does not maintain appropriate boundaries. It can be helpful to imagine that there is an invisible circle that surrounds your private life, just as there is one that surrounds your work life. When a boss steps out of the work circle and intrudes into your private circle, he or she is violating your boundary. If he doesn't respect your privacy or tells you when to get a haircut, he is overstepping the boundary of your private life. If she offers advice on raising your kids, tells you to get a divorce or where you should invest your money (little that it is) she is going too far. Any interference outside of your work is a clear violation of your boundaries and should never be encouraged or even tolerated. We all need to be better "gatekeepers" to ensure that our rights are protected. Sometimes boundary problems arise because a boss interferes with the imaginary circle around someone else's department. Perhaps he runs to complain to upper management about a worker in the other department or tries to tell another supervisor how to do her job. The varieties of boundary violations is endless and the larger the organization the greater are the number of infringements. Bosses who make a habit of trespassing on the territory of others create stress for everyone in the workplace.

5. Your boss is overly ambitious. One doesn't usually think of too much ambition as being a problem. Those above don't usually think it is. They like ambition. They get more for their buck out of the aspiring zealots. Ambitious people appear to work harder and longer. But coworkers usually suffer. Now don't misunderstand me. I'm all for enthusiastic ambition. I like to be surrounded by go-getters and energized people. Working with deadbeats is depressing, to say the least. But preserve me from those who must win at my expense or who are so status-obsessed that they pout if they don't win in the business game. Pathological ambition is a sickness. It is so selfish as to cause great hardship for everyone else.

How does an overly ambitious boss behave? He takes credit for all your accomplishments. If he can't take the credit he downplays your contribution. She insists on signing all the reports so it appears that she did the work. She insists on making all the presentations so she is always in the spotlight. The contributions of others are minimized to superiors. Yuk! The end result is always the same. Everyone else is merely a stepping stone to success.

6. Your boss is a very angry person. Now let's be honest. Some anger is inevitable in a boss. I know because I sometimes feel it. There are moments when you just can't contain it. Workers are not always right. They don't always see the whole picture. Often they are too caught up personally in an issue to be objective. So you get mad at them! You can't help it. A display of anger is the only language that speaks to some people. This doesn't make it right, but it is inevitable. So don't hold it against bosses because they sometimes blow their stacks.

But then again there is the angry boss. He's angry a lot of the time. Sometimes it is "passive-aggressive"; it comes out as criticism, put-downs, pouting or unfriendliness, not as thunder-rolls, fist-banging or calculator-throwing. This "active aggression" is a little more dangerous but it is not as destructive as the passive kind. I'd rather work for an upfront angry boss than a passive one. I remember a boss I had in my engineering days who was the passive-aggressive kind. I was his second in command. But he could never talk out his anger. He'd go silent. When I tried to get him to talk about his anger he'd withdraw further and the anger would last longer. For three or four days he would avoid talking to me, on the average. Sometimes it was more than a week. When he was angry at something, seldom at me directly, I just did not exist even though we shared an office. Finally, I requested that a glass divider be built to separate us. I told him it would give him more privacy. The glass barrier didn't change his behavior, but I felt better not having to put up with the sound of his silence!

The outwardly angry boss, of course, can also be a source of much toxicity. Direct attacks, assassination of your character, yelling and even physical threats are not that uncommon.

I heard of one boss (an ex-military type) who "playfully" (so he says) goes around choking and biting his employees. You don't have to be a psychologist to interpret the meaning of such symbolic behaviors! Any company that tolerates supervisors like this deserves to be sued.

Whether a boss expresses high levels of anger directly or passively it is always dangerous to be around and crazy-making in the extreme. I have seen patients who have developed severe patterns of regular nightmares over a boss who is terrorizing them. These nightmares don't always stop when you change a job. They can haunt you the rest of your life.

Upper-managers. Most workers don't usually have direct access to "upper management." But a profound toxic influence can come down to you simply because they have so much influence over you. I would include here those who occupy positions of power in the "head office" (all large companies seem to keep the real power in some such remote place): vice-presidents, chief executive officers, boards of directors and trustees. All wield power over you. Unless you are in a very healthy workplace they are beyond your reach and seem like strangers. If you are an ordinary worker, somewhere "up there" one or more upper management persons is making decisions that can make or break your work life. Do they always make decisions that serve your best interests? The answer depends on whom you work for.

Here are some of the ways upper-managers can turn a job into a nightmare:

- They create bad policies by making decisions without consulting those affected. No upper management person should make critical policy decisions without talking to those who will have to live with the consequences of those decisions. Plain and simple!
- They tend to be inflexible. For instance, having made a bad decision they stick with it just on principle. Since they don't have the courage to own up to their mistakes bad policies are never reversed even when they are known to be bad.
- They tend not to establish adequate personnel policies to protect workers from abuse; abusers are tolerated without accountability.
- They remain as inaccessible as possible, preferring to be aloof from the workers, and hence out of touch with the workplace and worker needs.
- Because they are out of touch, they do not respond adequately or in timely fashion to worker complaints. This erodes worker motivation and produces low morale.
- They tolerate incompetence in middle level managers, perpetuating bad working conditions and undermining worker confidence in management.
- They fail to establish clear lines of authority or to delegate authority appropriately, creating an organization which is chaotic and unstable.
- They fail to balance the needs of the organization against those of the worker and integrate this balance into the goals of the organization.

This last point needs to be underscored. Any organization that fails to take into account the personal needs of workers or allows the goals of the company (usually, profit, but often to serve the power needs of a few) to override these personal needs is destined to create a toxic workplace. Worker loyalty will be undermined, motivation will be eroded, and, saddest of all, *everyone* from top to bottom will feel unfulfilled in their work.

Workplace atmosphere. By "atmosphere" I mean the overall emotional climate of a workplace. Every place has an atmosphere. I remember when I first visited New York. Around midnight I stood in front of my hotel and watched the passing scene. It was electric. I could feel the atmosphere. I also felt special emotions when I first visited London, Paris and a little town in Bavaria whose name I have forgotten. Atmosphere. Sometimes a good atmosphere. Sometimes a bad atmosphere. Dachau, the infamous concentration camp where many were gassed to death, was a bad atmosphere. I will never forget it. Total silence. Scores of tourists, but no one uttered a word. An eerie silence that expressed evil. The atmosphere spoke volumes.

I find that workplaces also have their atmospheres. You can "feel" what a job-place is like. No two feel the same. Not only do the individuals who make up the workplace have their own personalities, with unique quirks and prejudices, but together they form a personality that is distinctive. The effect of this is to create a very distinctive emotional atmosphere that is different for each workplace.

When is the corporate atmosphere toxic? I will briefly discuss two representative characteristics that can pollute the emotional atmosphere of a workplace:

1. Distrust of newcomers and outsiders. This is called xenophobia. It is a built-in fear of strangers or anything foreign. You take a new job with a company that looks promising. Their product is highly respected. But the day you start work you realize you've made a mistake. Newcomers are distrusted. You just don't measure up to other worker expectations. From the beginning someone takes it upon himself to prove to you that you are not as good as they are. Often there is a dominant group (usually ethnic) that sets the atmosphere and resents anyone who doesn't match the group in race, color, social standing, age, or sex. If everyone is male then women are resented. If everyone is old then youth is resented. The dominant group sets out to prove that the newcomer can't make it with them. You are kept in the category of "outsider." Perhaps, after a long period of being ostracized, the intruder may finally earn the right to be an "insider."

Xenophobia is particularly damaging to societal minority groups. It is not always ethnic- or gender-focused. Religious groups, the physically challenged, and even emotionally or mentally challenged persons are often the targets of xenophobia. People just don't like to be reminded of the frailties of the human condition.

Certain occupations are particularly prone to xenophobia. Security services like to use men of "a certain sort," meaning they can only trust someone who fits the "Rambo" image. Ladies not welcomed! Medicine, fire services, airline pilots and many trades are at high risk for xenophobia because they have been dominated by particular groups, usually white males. And while the presence of other groups is increasing, the xenophobia still persists.

Members of minority groups who attempt to enter elite disciplines are subjected to offensive treatments designed to prove that only the dominant group is capable of doing the work. Unreasonably high standards are invoked and malicious behaviors are carried out toward those who try to penetrate the established dominance. These groups become "closed," professionally and socially, and self-protecting. Often a wall of secrecy is built around such a closed system. Members hide their dirty linen so as to prove to outsiders that they are as near perfect as a group can get.

2. Distrust of change. Xenophobia does not stop at newcomers, strangers or minority groups. It also means fear of change, new ideas and procedures. It even causes people to object to new equipment, furniture, or a change of offices.

To put this phenomenon into perspective, I should point out that all people basically fear change because it undermines their security. Change breaks with tradition and introduces new rules for playing the work-game. It becomes a problem because everyone fears that in some way they will lose out in the change. People would rather keep things the same than risk losing something. This is why the process of change is helped when those who are affected are allowed to participate in the planning for change. It helps them understand why change is necessary and establishes their security in the transition.

TOXIC WORKPLACE OR TOXIC WORKER?

I want to close this chapter by posing the question: Is it always the workplace that is toxic? Are there not times when the problem is the worker? I've been around long enough to know that every now and then the problem is not entirely the fault of the job. We cannot always blame the work environment, the boss, or other workers for creating a crazy-making workplace or making a particular worker unhappy. We may not want to admit it but sometimes the problem is mostly with ourselves. I say "mostly" because you can never categorically blame any one side in these matters. There are times, however, when *you* may be the virus that is making an otherwise healthy workplace sick. *Your* pathology may be poisoning the system, y*our* irritability may be putting everyone else on edge. *You* may be the unreasonable one, the negative influence making it difficult for others to function healthily.

Each of us has a circle of influence in a workplace. You may supervise a hundred or only be responsible for yourself. You may be in a position where you constantly interact with others, both inside and outside, or you may never see, touch, or have anyone to disagree with. It's this circle of personal influence you need to look at and ask yourself: "Am I part of the problem or of the solution? Am I behaving in such a way that I cause someone else emotional pain, hurt or anger?" If you are, you need to face up to it.

Honest self-examination is the most significant gift we can give ourselves. We are often blind to our own deficiencies. Also, the more disturbed we are and the more negative our influence, the more likely it is that we don't realize just how hurtful our behavior can be. We stay sick because we won't accept that we are part of the problem. We are always the victims, never the victimizers. And the more people try to get us to see how we are the source of the problems, the more defensive we become and the more resistant we are to change.

How can you tell if you are such a person? Below are questions you can ask yourself. Write each question on the top of a small card (leaving some space where you can write) so that you can carry the set around with you for a day or two. Put the cards in your purse, jacket pocket, overalls, or briefcase. Keep them close to your stethoscope, calculator, tax manual, or reference books. Periodically throughout the day, take out a card, read its question and write the answer down on the card. If you feel comfortable doing so, discuss the questions with a close friend. Talking about the issues will help you to be more honest and insightful.

1. Do I feel resentment or anger toward someone whom I cannot bring myself to forgive?

2. In my work environment, do I dislike someone intensely or am I alienated from someone?

3. Am I critical of others? Am I constantly condemning or criticizing?

4. Have I been told (or do I believe) that I am insensitive, unfeeling or careless about how I treat the feelings of others?

5. Do I overreact to the actions of others? Do I become angry or depressed because I cannot get my way or because others don't see things my way?

6. Do I avoid taking responsibility for my mistakes, blame others, or refuse to cooperate when I feel blamed?

7. Do I react or behave without understanding my motives or causes of what I do?

8. Is it difficult for me to celebrate the successes of others or to affirm them?

9. Am I a loner, sticking to myself so much that others believe I am standoffish?

10. Am I so gregarious, boisterous, overbearing, or dominant that others feel overpowered by me?

It takes guts to work through these questions and face up to your weaknesses honestly. But self-awareness is always the first step to growth and change. Awareness precedes change, not the other way around. Don't become too discouraged at what you discover here about yourself. I will help you take a more in-depth look at yourself in chapter 4 and provide some practical suggestions for change.

In this first chapter I have tried to present an overview of what makes a workplace crazy-making. Several of the issues I have raised will be dealt with in greater depth later in the book. A major theme will follow me throughout. It is that unless we each take responsibility for our own workplace relationships we will never bring about the improvements that can help us to be more productive and fulfilled in our work. We need to learn how to nurture and take care of ourselves in the workplace, but we must also take control and assist our employers in creating a healthier work environment. It is a collaborative endeavor. When the organization is insensitive to our needs, then our response should be to help raise consciousness. When the organization calls for greater collaboration in creating a better workplace, then our response should be to cooperate. What is best for the workers is ultimately what is best for the company or organization. So get involved. Tell your employers that you are 100 percent behind them in their desire to build a better company. The right spirit coupled to the right vision can overcome all obstacles.

Ten Symptoms of a Dysfunctional Workplace

1. You are constantly subjected to unwarranted stress that slowly erodes your self-confidence so that you become less and less the person you want to be.

2. Supervisors are unable or unwilling to affirm your job performance, or set such high and unreasonable standards that you constantly feel unappreciated.

3. You are made to feel that you have no rights, that you cannot avoid or change the way the organization functions.

4. Communication is poor or nonexistent. You are never sure exactly what is expected of you or whether you have achieved a goal.

5. New ideas are suppressed, creativity is discouraged, and constructive suggestions are taken as personal criticisms.

6. Racial, sexual, or religious prejudices are evident and management does not take adequate steps to eliminate discrimination of any sort.

7. A strong or angry personality dominates the workplace. He or she creates fear by abusing power, threatening, or making personal attacks.

8. Your boss is unstable, overreactive, or emotionally disturbed and is unaware of the forces that drive him or her.

9. Your coworkers remain aloof, distrust newcomers, lack cohesion, and compete for strokes from above.

10. Management neglects to deal with incompetent supervisors and remains inaccessible and aloof from workers.

CHAPTER

2

What Makes a Workplace Dysfunctional?

In my experience, there are two great motivators in life. One is fear. The other is love. You can manage an organization by fear, but if you do you will ensure that people won't perform up to their real capabilities.

Jan Carlzon
Chairman and CEO
Scandinavian Airlines

BEHIND EVERY CRAZY-MAKING WORKPLACE is a dysfunctional system. "Dysfunctional," now a popular word, means abnormal, impaired, or incomplete in its functioning. It used to be a medical term reserved for a body organ that didn't work properly. But family therapy and psychotherapy have taken it over and use it to describe social or psychological mechanisms that go wrong. When a group like the family or workplace is not functioning in a healthy way, such that it hurts its members, we label it dysfunctional.

What models will help us understand the nature of the dysfunctional workplace? Basically there are three. They each have some helpful factors but none of them is a perfect model.

1. The Individual model emphasizes the importance of each individual employee in shaping his or her workplace. In this model your work is your job, little else matters. You go to work, do what you are supposed to do, go home, watch television and go to bed. You do not connect your work with the rest of your world. Nor does who you are and what you do affect other workers much. Each worker is in a cocoon by him or herself. Clearly this way of looking at your job has severe limitations. It cannot adequately describe your work experience. It certainly doesn't call for any changes to improve your work environment.

2. The Family model views the workplace and those who work there as a "family." It can be a big family, but the way it functions has many parallels with the way a household functions. You, in effect, are a part of two family units, one at home and one at work. While this model takes into account the social context of work, it also has limitations because it sees the work family as primary and separates it from home life. It is inadequate because while there are some similarities the people you interact with at work are not family members in the most intimate sense of meaning. There is no blood tie. In a family you can put up with stuff you should never tolerate at work. Furthermore, the two entities (or families if you will) are not seen as overlapping in any significant way.

3. The Systems model is the one I prefer because it extends the model to emphasize the interdependence between the workplace and the home family. Work life and home life are linked. You cannot understand crazy-making without seeing how they are connected. Both settings operate as a "system" of which the individual is a part. While the interrelatedness is complex, it nevertheless can be analyzed and understood. What happens at work clearly impacts what goes on at home and vice versa.

To illustrate how work and family overlap let us examine a profession where you would think there was no connection. The surgeon (and what I have to say could equally apply to the truck driver as well) has a very specific job to perform. The surgeon's work in the operating room does not *directly* affect how her children behave at home. A surgical procedure does not require a family consultation and the outcome of the surgery does not directly impact how the children perform at school. Indirectly, however, *all work impacts one's personal life*. If the surgeon fails in an operation because the disease is too advanced and a patient dies, that surgeon may have great difficulty relaxing over dinner and being communicative that evening. The last thing she would want to do is play games with the kids or read a nursery rhyme. A surgeon would be extremely callous not to feel some pain over the loss of a patient. While the sadness might not intrude into conversation during dinner, it will unconsciously affect how the doctor reacts to family frustrations or misbehavior. Hubby may have great difficulty getting any meaningful conversation going. It will be a long evening for all.

Similarly, the truck driver who gets a speeding ticket on the freeway or dozes off for a moment and rear-ends a new sports car cannot be expected to turn off feelings when he is putting his kids to bed and they're pleading for "just one more story, please...." Work and family life cannot be separated. I sometimes wonder how many divorces are the result of workplace dysfunction. A lot more than we give credit for. I know from personal experience that some of the most difficult times in my own marriage have centered around major work problems.

Work impacts family life in other significant ways also, which is why a systems approach is so important. A patient once proved to me by doing some rapid calculations on the back of his pay slip that he spent more hours with other women in his workplace than at home with his wife. Work takes up so much of our time that we spend less at other activities. He was not proud of this but just tried to make the point that sometimes coworkers felt more like family to him than his own family. My response? "No matter how close people may feel because they work together," I told him, "they still do not constitute a family." The family analogy, applied to the workplace, has many limitations. Members of families have certain privileges that outsiders do not. Families are permitted certain behaviors that other social units are not. While the workplace may take up a large portion of our lives, coworkers do not constitute another "family" and it can lead to many erroneous consequences if you think this way.

Conceptualizing the workplace as a family unit has many flaws, but still remains popular. Those in charge are seen as parents, and workers are the children. Relationships are spelled out in terms of these analogies. And while some are helpful in clarifying labor-management hassles, much of this way of thinking only muddies the water and I don't find it helpful. Families can tolerate much more "give and take" than the workplace. Bosses are not parents and supervision is not synonymous with parenting.

The systems model focuses exclusively on the workplace as a "system" of connected entities, as well as how it is connected to the rest of a worker's life, including the family. Systems thinking is a fairly recent development in our understanding of how groups function and impact individuals. Systems thinking deals less with the content of our interaction and more with the *process*. For instance, let us suppose you are my supervisor. You give me the wrong information I need to complete a project. I spend hours working out a contract for a client only to find that my time was all wasted. I get into trouble with the boss who wants to know why I went off on a tangent. We can analyze your contribution to my failure in two ways: we can look at what was wrong with the information you gave me. Perhaps it was out-of-date. Perhaps you were just incompetent. Or we can look at why you gave me wrong information. Perhaps you wanted to sabotage my efforts. You don't like me, or perhaps you want to take revenge for something I said a week ago that you felt was a put-down. It is this last aspect that systems thinking emphasizes. It wants to know *why* you gave me the misleading information more than it wants to know *what* the information was. And this distinction is important because it is what helps us decipher what makes a workplace dysfunctional.

The systems approach, then, emphasizes several important issues. It emphasizes that whenever you get more than two people interacting, the interaction becomes very complex. Imagine three design engineers working on a project together. The first one believes he has the answer to the design, but he is only the junior. The senior engineer is very defensive. He doesn't want to be seen to be the less competent, especially since his engineering skills are a little out-of-date. He sometimes feels younger engineers mock him. The middle person is a woman. She's smart enough to know that she can easily get trapped in a battle between the two males. She doesn't care for the younger guy, yet knows he is probably right in his design. What does she do? Side with the younger and risk alienating the older? Stay neutral and appear not to know what she is doing? If she's not careful she can easily be triangled between them. Dilemma upon dilemma. People always create dilemmas. And the greater the number of people trying to work together the more complex is the interaction.

Take another example. Imagine trying to interpret what is going on in a large real estate sales office full of high-pressured, live-wired, competitive sales people. Joe likes Peter but has an ongoing conflict with Cedric. Cedric is upset at Pete, whom he considers to be his best friend, for having beaten him out of a sale, so he complains to Sheila who is a second cousin of Joe's. But Sonya overhears Cedric ventilating to Sheila and because she has a crush on Joe and has dated him several times, she tells Joe hoping she will score a few points in his favor. Joe, however, gets angry at Sheila. The bearer of bad news always ends up losing a head. This has been true since the dawn of time. Now Joe and Sheila aren't talking—and my head is spinning, as it was when I tried to help Sheila understand what was going on in her workplace.

Can you imagine trying to figure out the complex interplay in an enmeshed workplace full of high-strung and stressed-out sales people? Well, the systems approach provides the best tools for doing this. It looks at what is going on beneath the surface of interpersonal conflicts and tries to understand how people function together.

Perhaps the most important contribution of the systems approach to understanding the workplace is the realization that if you change one part of a system, you change *many* other parts also. The very meaning of the word "system" implies interconnectedness. The workplace is like a mobile—you know, those hanging, decorative, moving pieces of art that are balanced even though they don't look like they should be. They hang there perfectly poised, but if you change one part of the mobile, you change the other parts also. It is easy to understand, therefore, that a "system" goes beyond the worker to include family and other activities beyond the walls of the office or factory. Touch one part of a worker's life and you touch all of it!

HOW DOES THE SYSTEMS APPROACH WORK?

My goal here is not to teach my reader all there is to know about the systems approach. But unless you understand a few key concepts you will not benefit from the rest of this book. There are three key concepts that I believe we can all benefit from knowing. They are important in helping us to design a healthy workplace and understand a dysfunctional one.

1. Every worker has a large family. Every person is a member of several "families." Coming after the family of origin (grandparents,

parents, brothers, and sisters) is the extended immediate family (aunts, uncles, cousins), followed by others close enough to function as a social group (church, social groups, work groups). Together they form the extended family field. The influence of this larger network is very significant in everyone's life. Again, the mobile is probably the best analogy of this extended field. One piece of a mobile can be seen as representing the immediate family, another the grandparents, another cousins, another social or church groups, and even the workplace might be represented by several components. *Figure one* represents a mobile that describes a typical extended family field.

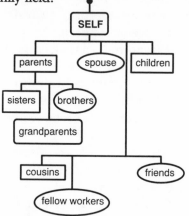

Figure one

Each person's network of interconnected relationships is important to him, since each component affects his overall life. One never fully understands how a person functions, whether healthy or ill, without taking his extended family field into account. Those parts of the larger field that are healthy can be the source of strength, encouragement, and support. Those parts that are unhealthy can be the source of aggravation and irritation.

Dysfunction, then, doesn't usually operate in all the components of the extended field at the same time. Work relationships may be dysfunctional while immediate family components are supportive, or vice versa.

2. Every worker is doing a balancing act. The way a system maintains balance and internal stability is called homeostasis. In the body, for instance, organs respond in a coordinated way to automatically compensate for changes. If you step outside into the cold, blood vessels close down on the surface of the skin to avoid excessive heat loss. If you step back inside, they open up again. The body is full of homeostatic mechanisms. It's what keeps us alive!

Social groups also operate homeostatically. The mobile representing the family field is a perfect analogy. It is self-correcting and tries to keep the system in balance. If you lose your job and a part of the field falls away, the system quickly readjusts so as to restore the balance. Family and friends will gather round (if it's a healthy field, of course) and compensate for what is lost. The primary goal is always to preserve the balance in the system. Whenever there is an imbalance that can't be corrected, a state of disequilibrium follows that puts a terrible amount of stress on the primary person. You are really twisted out of shape as you try to cope with the imbalance. If there is a family feud, in your extended family for instance, it unsettles the system and begins to unbalance you. In order to maintain the equilibrium you might try to shift things around a bit, make conciliatory moves to an offended party, and restore balance. However, while a system always tries to maintain balance, sometimes a healthier response, as we will see, may be to give up trying to force this balance.

Systems are highly resistant to change precisely because of this homeostatic or self-balancing tendency. Whereas it is healthy for a body to be this way, for systems it can be a problem. Hanging lopsided because some component has been added or removed to their extended field causes people too much anxiety. They prefer to be balanced. A healthy system, however, knows how to resist homeostasis creatively when appropriate. It facilitates change by helping individuals in the system face up to their anxiety.

The workplace also functions to maintain the homeostasis, not always for the good of the worker. Work systems often try to stabilize themselves too quickly. Just like family systems, they close in to protect the person and maintain homeostasis. They may force "togetherness" at all costs and will often tolerate and even "adapt to trouble makers, complainers, and down-right incompetents" because they can't handle any imbalance.[1] This can be a major obstacle to change.

3. To find the problem, find the hurt. In family systems theory the person who hurts the most and is taken for help is called the "identified patient." In a dysfunctional family, the identified patient is the family member with the obvious symptoms. To the family this person is the "sick one." But is he or she the cause of the problem? Hardly ever. It may be that the bed-wetting child, the drug-addicted teenager, the juvenile delinquent, or the alcoholic wife is not really the "sick one." The problem could be elsewhere in the system.

Systems thinking prefers not to see the identified patient as the problem, in the sense of *causing* the problem, but rather as the one in whom the stress or pathology of the system has surfaced. No single person can account for the turmoil in a family. Many factors contribute to every dysfunctional system.

The value of this approach to understanding workplace problems is obvious. A particular worker may be causing a lot of trouble—interfering with another worker's job, angry and negative, making mistakes, or even sabotaging the company's activities. Everyone sees that worker as the "identified patient," but is that assessment correct? Not necessarily. The system may be so dysfunctional that the worker has become the unfortunate victim on whom the stress or pathology has settled. The problem could be the way work is processed, complaints ignored, procedures enforced, or toxic managers tolerated. The identified patient may not be the real problem at all, just as the "rebellious" teenage kid brought to therapy by angry parents may not be the real problem in that family either. A systemic problem has to be treated systems-wide.

The identified person or problem, not just in families but in all systems, is often a convenient scapegoat who can be blamed so that other members of the system don't have to face up to their part in the problem. It's a lot easier for mom and dad to take a child for help than to confront their dysfunctional marriage. So it is with the workplace. A manager can easily put all the blame on a particular worker, when in reality, the problem is elsewhere—even with the manager.

If we are to create healthy workplaces we will have to replace our individualistic approach and way of thinking about problems with a systems approach. Every worker is a part of a system, and the system has to be healthy if the worker is going to be healthy.

THE INGREDIENTS OF DYSFUNCTION

I have tried to show that the systems model is clearly the preferred way of understanding the workplace. This model emphasizes that no worker is an island. Every employee is connected to other employees as well as to the extended family field outside of the immediate workplace. While this extended field always tries to maintain balance, this balance can sometimes be detrimental to the worker because it aids in maintaining status quo and builds resistance to change. An identified problem, therefore, is not necessarily the cause of the dysfunction—it can be the symptom rather than the cause.

Now let us examine the *ingredients* of dysfunction as they are found in the workplace. What components of the system cause or perpetuate dysfunctional patterns?

Dysfunctional leadership. In examining how a workplace can be dysfunctional, we must start at the top. While concepts of leadership have changed in recent years, leaders by and large have not. Many remain entrenched in out-of-date leadership styles.

What makes for a healthy leader? The preferred style of leadership these days is less autocratic and more democratic. Vertical hierarchies are being replaced by "team" concepts where everyone is equally responsible for a particular project or aspect of work. There may be a team leader, but that leader is democratic rather than authoritarian. So the effective new leader must share power. This is more effective than hogging it. The effective leader builds teamwork, both inside and outside the boundaries of his or her department or unit, and learns to celebrate success with others. Above all, this leader pays attention to human needs.

A leader who fails to grow toward this style of leadership is walking close to the edge of dysfunction and is likely to be the cause of significant disruption or unhappiness in the workplace. How to be such a healthy leader is such an important topic that I will deal with it in a separate chapter. Here I want to focus on the personal characteristics of the leader who contributes to the formation of a dysfunctional workplace. What are the characteristics to look out for? There are four: The leader's personality, the leader's pathology, the leader's behavior, and the leader's competence.

The leader's personality. It is easy to like some leaders and to hate others. Leaders, like all humans, have distinctive personalities. Personality types that function well possess patience, flexibility, an ability to listen, a sense of justice and fairness, an ability to appreciate the value of others, and demonstrated respect for others. It's easy to like such leaders. They make you feel good about yourself and your work. Dysfunctional personalities are characterized by fault-finding, blaming, scapegoating, and disregard of the opinions of others. They usually also have a strong need to dominate or control. One comes to dislike and even hate such leaders. They don't make you feel valuable to the company and leave you without any sense of value or purpose in your work.

The leader's pathology. Some leaders are emotionally troubled or unstable. They may not have always been this way. Sometimes pathology comes on later in life, after being promoted to a position of power. By then it's difficult to get rid of them and companies find themselves stuck with a serious source of aggravation. Pity you if you are stuck under such a leader. Early in my engineering career, while still in training, I got stuck this way. For more than two years I suffered under a most disturbed supervisor who made life a hell for several of us trainees. I think I had nightmares every night and then lived them through the day. When that man died suddenly I wasn't at all sad. While I didn't have the skills then to really know what his pathology was, I knew he was sick!

Now while there can be some pretty disturbed people in places of power, let me hasten to add that none of us is perfectly healthy. We are all a little neurotic—it goes with being imperfect human beings. We all have some flaws. There are insecurities, hurts, bad habits, and ineffective ways of dealing with difficult situations. But while none of us is perfectly healthy, I also know that there is a huge gap between the so-called "normal" neurotic, a little of which includes all of us, and the person who is pathologically disturbed. Trouble arises when the disturbance is in the area of the emotions (severely depressed, excessively anxious, or borderline manic) or in the area of personality disorder (excessively paranoid, schizoid, or narcissistic). My purpose here is not to train you in psychodiagnosis (although we could all benefit from being able to tell the normal neurotic from the severely disturbed leader), but merely to point out that somewhere in a dysfunctional system there is sometimes a disturbed person of influence. He or she is passing on the craziness to others. Such persons need to be identified and either helped to change or removed.

The leader's behavior. Let's face it. A leader can have a fairly normal personality but have some bad behaviors or habits. He or she may be capable of listening but choose not to. A lifetime of bad habits may prevent a leader from being flexible. Bad behavior can be just as crazy-making as psychopathology.

The leader's competence. Sometimes people are promoted because they are family or because they have friends in authority. Sometimes people are given leadership roles because of long service or because no one more competent is available. Every so often people grasp power and force themselves into positions of leadership. Such people land in top positions without the competence to support their status. The result? Dysfunctional leadership. They make a lot of mistakes. They act impulsively and without adequate information. Wherever you have an incompetent leader you will have a crazy-making workplace and workers will be the casualties.

Dysfunctional workers. A dysfunctional work environment is not always the direct result of bad leadership. While ultimately all workplace dysfunction is the responsibility of those in charge, sometimes the problem lies much deeper in the organizational system. Personality conflicts, lack of worker empowerment, or inadequate communication can all contribute their share of the problem. A dysfunctional work environment tends to treat workers as children: workers must be seen but not heard!

But let's be fair here. Often the dysfunction is not fostered from above downward, but from below upward. It is not so much a leader problem as it is a worker problem. Here are some examples of *upward* bound attitudes and behaviors that can create chaos on the job:

- Workers are encouraged by other workers not to respect authority. An environment of rebellion is created and maintained by insubordinate or mutinous attitudes.
- Instructions are sabotaged to make management look incompetent. Mistakes are deliberately made to create chaos or disruption to normal production.
- One group of workers fosters their self-interests above the interests of other groups. The "tyranny of the majority" often operates here to put other groups at a disadvantage. For instance, one particular work group may outnumber another group and then use their vote to resist changes that might benefit a smaller group more.
- Any worker who excels is cut down so as to keep productivity

minimal and prevent management from raising its expectations for other workers.

- All workers are made paranoid and suspicious toward all authority by rumors that are untrue or exaggerated. These rumors include stories of firings, plant closures or dishonesty in the company.

The list could continue for several pages. There are literally scores of ways that workers can sabotage the integrity of a company and the security and comfort of its employees. I know from personal experience how easy it is for employees to foster a dysfunctional workplace and how difficult, even impossible, it can be for managers to counteract their influence. Sometimes the only way to eradicate such dysfunction once it has taken deep root is to close down the enterprise and start afresh.

In the systems way of thinking, the tendency of a workforce to sabotage its own workplace is part of the homeostatic phenomenon described earlier. As soon as something happens to change the balance, forces kick in that try to resist and remove the change. If the force for change is bad, then this resistance is good. Who would want a change that is clearly damaging? But if the force is good and the change is necessary and strongly desired by the majority, resistance is tantamount to sabotage.

Take, for example, a medium sized, privately owned, production machine shop that produces, say, a particular type of plumbing tool. For years the workers have become used to a certain volume of production. All of the workers understand what constitutes a "fair day's work" and the shop has an unwritten rule that workers don't try to exceed this. Nowhere is this rule written down. It is just "understood." Everyone knows how hard and how fast to work. Then, one day, a young eager beaver shows up. He immediately sees a way to shorten production time, and his box of finished tools is full in half the time of the other workers. His employer is pleased, praises him, and gives him a raise. Eager beaver's superior performance, however, has not pleased his workmates. He has raised their anxiety level because they now fear that the boss will demand that they match the young upstart's standard of production. Even more, they fear that since the boss has been shown a faster way to produce the tool, he might even do a more foolish thing than to listen to a young upstart; he might consider bringing in those workshop-dreaded "Time and Motion Study" experts to really shake up the production. The workers immediately rebel and make all sorts of threats. What was a peaceful, easy-going work environment is now beginning to feel high-pressured. Everyone, except the boss, is unhappy.

What has happened? The "balance" of the system has been disturbed. Homeostasis within the system now kicks in and forces come into play that try to restore things where they were before eager beaver arrived on the scene.

One of the ways a system tries to stay in balance is through workers who try to sabotage the change. Over lunch, then, one of the workers slips a few faulty tools into the young upstart's box, hoping the boss will find them and criticize the young man for his shoddy workmanship. Surely this will prove that when production is too fast mistakes will increase. They hope that everything will go back to where it was before.

Since this is only a hypothetical scenario you can make up your own ending to the story. It has real soap opera possibilities if you can introduce some romance somewhere. When the boss discovers the botched tools, does the upstart get fired so the factory can go back to its old ways? Does another loyal worker accidentally observe the sabotage and reveal the deception? What if the boss discovers the sabotage because he has some secret coding system that can tell what section produces a particular unit, and it wasn't eager beaver's? Whatever the outcome, I can assure you that sabotage like this goes on in many workplaces. Sometimes it's subtle, like derogatory comments made at a party in front of the boss about a new worker. Sometimes it's blatant, like drumming up a false accusation and organizing a petition against a worker who threatens the status quo. Whatever the method, that workplace becomes dysfunctional. It resists change to the extent it not only destroys some workers, but ultimately it destroys the company or organization itself.

How dysfunction "works." Every company or organization has its own "culture." It has ideas, customs, behaviors, practices, procedures, and even beliefs that are unique to itself. When you change a job one of the first things you have to do is learn the "culture" of your new place of work.

It's not unlike changing countries. New customs and behaviors must be learned so that you can exist comfortably in your new land. Some years ago my wife, three daughters, and I moved to the

United States from South Africa. While both cultures speak English and have a few similarities, there is much that is different.

Our initial reaction was one of "culture shock." I didn't expect it. I thought I knew what to expect but it took us by surprise. It was more of a shock to us as parents than to our children mainly because so much of the new culture fostered a level of freedom and value confusion that seemed to us to be unsatisfactory. Our biggest struggle as parents was the absence of peer support for our children that would reinforce the values we were trying to teach. If the only friends you know are into drugs or inappropriate sexual behaviors it is going to be mighty difficult to resist their pressures to do the same. Slowly we settled down and discovered that we didn't have to let what we didn't like get to us. As a family we could withstand the negative influences of what was bad and enjoy what was good. It put more pressure on us as parents, but having laid a good foundation we were able to reap what we had sown.

Changing a job is similar to moving to another country. There is always an adjustment that must be made to new people, habits, and procedures. You may first experience some culture shock. People in your new workplace may have different values than those you are accustomed to. Some may be into drugs. You may clash with some personality types you haven't had to work with before. Their ways of behaving will be foreign to you. Sooner or later, fortunately, you adjust to the new work culture and find your level of comfort as you set limits on what you do and don't accept.

Not only does an organization have a unique culture, it also has a distinctive "personality." I call this the "corporate personality." While it is partly made up of all the current personalities in the organization, it is heavily influenced by the personalities of its significant leaders from times past who have helped to shape the company. The company's vision, its way of thinking, and its definition of itself are all expressions of the "corporate personality." Whether the company is healthy or dysfunctional will depend on whether or not the corporate personality is healthy. Often, dysfunction can be traced back to the company's founding. It was there at the beginning and never went away.

How do corporate personalities vary? The personality of one company may be "quiet" and respectful. Everyone tends to be reserved and polite. For another, the personality may be "loud" and gregarious. Everyone shouts and blows off at the slightest provocation. Sometimes the personality is happy and upbeat. Sometimes it's pessimistic and melancholic, or paranoid and suspicious. One can almost apply the same descriptions to the company personality that apply to individuals. They are as varied as human nature, and sometimes as perverse.

Because a workplace often has an entrenched dysfunctional personality it can be extremely difficult to bring about a healthy change quickly. It may take a change in upper management or a radical turnover in the workforce, a feat that cannot always be accomplished abruptly. If you are willing to pay the price of change and have the patience to hang on in a job you like because you are beginning to see some hope of improvement, then take heart. Change is possible, even though it is slow. If your job is not very rewarding you may be better off beginning to look for something better now.

THE DYNAMICS OF DYSFUNCTION

When we are confronted with a work system that is dysfunctional it is helpful not only to ask the question *how* does a workplace become this way, as I already have, but also the *why* question. When we examine why a workplace becomes toxic we can get at the deeper causes of the dysfunction. The why question gets at the *dynamics* of a dysfunctional workplace.

There are three dynamic factors that contribute to dysfunction in the workplace, just as they contribute to problems in the family system. They are: open versus closed systems, unconscious forces, and the dependence of humans on motivation to achieve or accomplish anything. An understanding of each of these will help us to build healthier workplaces.

1. Open versus closed systems. In the book *Incest in the Organizational Family*, William White does an excellent job of analyzing how organizational systems can damage individual workers by creating and maintaining closed systems. He stresses the importance of openness in determining whether an organization is healthy or not.[2]

In physical and biological systems, being "closed" means that the system maintains its homeostasis or balance. The system is

"closed" because it doesn't need any input from the outside to do its job. This is normal and necessary in a biological system since it preserves life. In a psychological system, however, "closed-ended" may equal "unhealthy," because without input from the outside it resists needed change. Open-ended systems are essential for organizations. They permit exposure to outside influences in the struggle for growth, change, and ongoing evolution. Healthy change can only take place in a social system that is open.

Organizations that are closed to external feedback, isolated and cut off, are, in effect, committing incest. They breed within themselves and feed back into the system their bad genes. This recycling means they are not being rejuvenated by new ones. The result is not unlike that of physical inbreeding: deficiency of body and mind. The company becomes systemically handicapped, with emotional and personal defects. An incestuous organization is always dysfunctional.

The parallels between what happens within a closed family and a closed organization are striking. Take, for example, how a closed system fosters *enmeshment*. Enmeshment (first described by Menuchin in 1967)[3] refers to how family members, usually in a "closed family system," become caught in and interfere with each other's concerns. Each member becomes so wrapped up in the issues of other members that there is no autonomy, no individuation. Each one is in the other's hair. One can't move or make a decision without it upsetting another family member. In such families there is always someone not talking to another or a family feud.

In the organizational family, enmeshment represents the extreme of being a closed system. Some of the effects an enmeshed workplace can have on you as a worker are:

- You have little social or professional contact with groups similar to yours. You are cut off from and have no interaction with companies similar to your own.
- You find outsiders are treated with suspicion and even rejected. Everyone else is the enemy.
- Your individual rights are surrendered to the corporation's rights. Complete allegiance is demanded of you.
- Your managers, and in turn, fellow workers, perpetuate bad habits that have been passed on from worker generation to worker generation, due to dysfunctional inbreeding, from manager to manager, worker to worker.

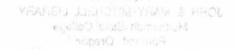

- As a worker you have no privacy; work intrudes into your personal life. Everyone seems to know what goes on in your private life. You begin to feel like you are living in a glass house.
- You are expected to surrender your personal and family life out of loyalty to the company.
- You are made to feel excess guilt if you step out of line. In fact, neurotic or false guilt is a very common feature of an incestuous organization.
- You come to depend solely on your job for social support, (rather than friends, church and so forth).

A closed organizational system, therefore, can be about as dysfunctional as it gets. Incest is not a bad label for it, and all the negative connotations we apply to family incest can equally be applied to organizational incest!

2. Unconscious forces. In the workplace, as elsewhere, much of what happens between people is influenced by unconscious forces. In other words, what you say or do may reflect something you are not consciously aware of. A workplace is dysfunctional to the extent that these unconscious forces are allowed to predominate in worker interactions, boss-worker relationships, or in leadership decisions. Too much hidden beneath the surface can be bad for the job.

Now I know I am opening a Pandora's box here. If it is an unconscious force, some might be asking, then how on earth can we possibly know it exists? Doesn't the very term "unconscious" imply that it can't be felt, seen, or measured? To a certain extent, yes. But an unconscious force can be identified from the behavior that results from it. If you attack me after the boss has bawled you out, I don't have to be a genius to know that you are taking out your frustration on me because you are really mad at your boss but don't have the courage to tell the person what you think. You may not be aware of it because you are too angry. But I can see it. Unconscious forces are nearly always recognizable to those who aren't subject to them at the moment.

Let me emphasize that a lot of thoughts, feelings, and other mental processes go on without our full awareness. They are unconscious. We sometimes forget someone's name. Okay, so maybe we're getting older and memory is weakening. But sometimes our unconscious forgetting has to do with not liking a particular person or not wanting to remember an unhappy association.

But there is a more important aspect to the unconscious that we must recognize. We often say or do something without realizing *why*. Our motivations are unconscious. If we give someone advice on what model of car to buy, and don't realize that in fact we would like to have that particular car for ourselves, we are being controlled by a force hidden from our recognition.

Another unconscious process occurs when we react to someone in an inexplicable way. Let us suppose we have just gotten angry with someone without adequate cause. We know the person did not do anything to deserve our anger, yet we are irrationally angry. The reason may simply be that this person resembles someone from our past who has hurt us, but we are not conscious of this fact. Hidden forces like this operate all the time without our realization.

In the workplace unconsciously driven behaviors can be very puzzling and certainly destructive. Why was Joe fired? Why did I not get a raise? Why does my work partner hate my guts? Why am I being overlooked for promotion? One could easily be driven to paranoia!

In a healthy organization, every effort should be made to see to it that unconscious actions or motivations are brought out into the open. Let us suppose a boss points out that you have made a mistake. It's a petty mistake, yet he makes a lot of it. You react by becoming extremely angry, mainly because you don't feel it's a big deal. The boss can't understand why you make such a big deal of his minor criticism. Maybe you are still mad at your spouse for forgetting your wedding anniversary. Besides, the boss resembles your spouse. You can't explain why you overreact to the criticism, you just know his behavior infuriated you. Maybe you were criticized so much as a child that you have become insecure at every suggestion of weakness. Whatever it is, unconscious forces are controlling both you and your boss. Before you, or he, go any further you should call a halt and plead for some sanity and careful examination of the dynamics of what is going on. A third person as an impartial observer can often see the issues a lot better.

Can you discover unconscious forces within yourself? Typically they become accessible only with much effort. You will need to work at being honest with yourself to force unconscious factors *within yourself* into the open. Here are some suggestions on how you can do this:

- Don't take everything personally. Take some time to reflect on your behavior and the reasons for it.
- Don't become defensive too quickly. A person who jumps to the defense right away is almost certainly being driven by his or her own unconscious forces.
- Try to be as honest as you can with yourself and expose any unconscious forces (they can be motives or needs) by asking yourself: Do I have any reason to be defensive? Why am I acting this way?
- If possible, withdraw from the present interaction and find someone you trust to talk with about your feelings and reactions. The hidden motivation can be exposed more easily if you talk about your feelings immediately.
- Try not to be suspicious of someone else's motives, but focus on your own reaction first.
- When you are sure that you have owned up to your own unconscious motives, challenge the other person to do the same.

Just remember: You don't have a right to challenge someone else's unconscious forces until you have first examined your own. It's just possible that *you* are the one who is being driven by hidden forces, rather than the other person.

How can you compel unconscious forces in another person to come into the open? That is another story! If you are convinced that someone is being driven by a hidden need, then go right ahead and say so. Be prepared, however, to do battle because people resist being exposed. Stand your ground. Insist that a third party be brought in to arbitrate your different interpretations. And get your mind off "winning." You may leave the scene of a disagreement feeling that you haven't been heard or that your adversary hasn't faced reality. So be it! However, this doesn't mean that nothing good has happened. Most people will go away from an honest encounter and continue to process what has happened. The "healing" work may only come later that night or the next day. Most of us need some "processing" time before we can do any growing.

3. Motivation—the power within. The most powerful force I know within the human spirit is what psychologists call "motivation." We depend on it for all achievement, and much of the dynamic of a workplace revolves around the presence or absence of it. Motivation is what impels us to action. It is the force that energizes, directs, and sustains our behavior. While some motivation is self-generated (it comes from deep within yourself), a lot of it is created by the work environment. When a workplace kills motivation, it is clearly dysfunctional.

Every manager knows that while some people often work up to their capacity, many don't. In fact, studies have shown that the average person works somewhere between 20 percent and 80 percent of his or her work capacity.[4] Twenty percent is often the base minimum required to keep a job. To keep workers up at 80-90 percent of their work potential takes a unique style of leadership, especially if leaders don't want to stand over them all day. Motivation is needed to get someone to work well.

How many of us are highly motivated? Surprisingly few. While 52 percent of those surveyed by Public Agenda, a non-profit organization that studies public policy, were able to say, "I have an inner need to do the very best job I possibly can," only 23 percent felt they were performing up to their potential.[5] Forty-four percent admitted that they put in only the minimum required to keep their jobs.

This is a bleak picture. Why the huge gap between capability and performance? Seventy-five percent say it is because "management doesn't know how to motivate workers." Are they correct? To a large extent, yes. But another reason most managers inadequately motivate workers is that the most effective motivation comes from within the worker, not outside.

How can the dynamic of a workplace cultivate inner motivation, not kill it? Why do people behave the way they do? Why doesn't the average worker work consistently at full capacity? Why don't people understand things that seem so simple and clear? Why do some workers resist changes that could benefit them? I remember an illustration of a man sitting at a desk with a puzzled look on his face and staring at a toy man on top of his desk, about six inches tall with a wind-up key in his back. The toy was doffing his hat at him and asking the question, "What winds me up?" We all feel like that toy man at times, wondering what winds us up, what keeps us doing what we do. Where does our motivation for work come from? How can we create a higher level of motivation in both workers and the workplace? For the sake of brevity let me list some of the ways:

What aids motivation from within the worker?
- a sense of confidence that helps you believe you can do a job and do it well
- a sense of purpose that you can see in your work
- a sense of self-worth that you can derive from your work
- a sense of security that you can project into the future
- a degree of challenge that stretches your abilities
- honest and constructive feedback that is specific, immediate and more positive than negative

What aids motivation in the workplace?
- perceived support for meeting the personal needs of workers
- encouragement for workers to be ambitious and to set realistic personal goals for growth
- adequate rewards or reinforcements, not just monetary but social approval and affirmation as well
- adequate utilization of a worker's skills, abilities and knowledge
- adequate affirmation and confirmation to all workers so that they feel they are achieving what is expected of them
- the setting of goals and challenges that help energize the workers
- equitable and fair treatment of all workers
- challenges to improve workers' skills and knowledge by appropriate and timely feedback
- increased responsibility according to a given worker's increased competence
- the sense given to workers that they are succeeding more than they are failing

This last point is crucial, but often overlooked in some types of work. Motivation will never survive in a job where there are more failures than successes. For instance, if you are in sales and sell a product that has been superseded by another company's improved version of the same product, you are guaranteed to fail more often than you succeed and your motivation is diminished. If you are a social worker without adequate resources to help the needy people you encounter every day, you will feel that you fail more than you succeed and motivation will plummet. If you are a business manager and the company does not provide sufficient funds to keep the office running as it should so that you are always in the red, your motivation will be eroded. And where motivation is under attack rather than being encouraged, the potential for worker burnout increases dramatically.

A workplace that constantly or ignorantly exposes workers to more failures than successes is a dysfunctional workplace.

WHAT DO EMPLOYEES REALLY WANT?

When you have healthy supervisors and good working conditions, what more do workers look for? One way to answer this question is to ask yourself: What do I want more than anything else out of my work? There is really only one answer to this question. *Recognition*. Not just bonuses and plaques, privileged parking spaces or "worker of the week" announcements, though these are very important, but the type of recognition that affirms the value of your self at the deepest possible level.

Why is this important? Because deep down every one of us suspects that we are not really valuable. Our culture does not do a good job of raising us to value the self. We are too competitive, too preoccupied with pleasing parents and too vulnerable to damage by rejection. So as we grow and our sense of self develops, it develops with a pervasive self-rejection that forms the basis for self-esteem problems. We *all* feel deficient. We *all* struggle to achieve a sense of value. And we naturally turn to our work to help us recapture the sense of value needed to keep us healthy and energized. Unless our work gives meaning to our existence and builds our worth as persons, we will not function at our best.

This struggle to achieve a sense of our own worthwhileness is at the root of all motivation. It is also at the root of a lot of dysfunction in the workplace. When our work attacks or undermines our self-worth, it becomes toxic to our self-esteem and self-valuing. It robs us of the feedback we need to maintain any sense of value.

Recognition, then, not just of our competency or our profit value to the company, but of our true value as persons, is what we need and want above everything else. It is a very basic need of all humans. We need to feel that we are objects of primary value. We need to feel that we are the heroes of our own world (and I mean this in a positive and healthy sense), and that we have something valuable to contribute.

Unfortunately, we are seldom conscious of this need to be the hero of our own world. All we know is that we get angry or depressed when that need is thwarted. Ernest Becker suggests that if we all admitted this urge to be heroes,[6] we would be freed to stop playing games and ask for what we really want. We would all be a lot healthier. We could ask for our freedom and human dignity without feeling guilty about it.

What else do we want? We all want fair treatment and a square deal, job security, good working conditions, comfortable facilities, a chance to be heard, an opportunity to take pride in our work, clear direction and unambiguous instructions, an opportunity to help guide our future, competent and respectful leadership, a chance to prove ourselves, a sense of belonging, a challenge to be the best we can be. Too much? I don't believe so.

Our fundamental needs, therefore, are very basic: We need to feel valuable and that we are the heroes of our own world. Our work must help us meet these needs if it is going to be meaningful. If managers give high priority to helping employees feel that these needs are being met, they are going to be effective. They can do this by helping employees feel "in" on things, showing them appreciation for work well done, by being loyal and empathetic about personal problems. Above all they help employees become the heroes of their world by giving recognition to their value as persons. They can see beyond the job, behind the skills and abilities, to show that they value us not just for what we do but for who we are. Who wouldn't go the extra mile for such a company?

Diagnosing Your Workplace

Here are twenty signs that indicate a workplace is dysfunctional:

1. Workers are highly resistant to change.
2. Workers sabotage attempts to improve work effectiveness.
3. Workers often misunderstand or disregard instructions.
4. Workers tend to ignore organizational patterns of responsibility.
5. Workers are preoccupied with their own interests, not the interests of the organization as a whole.
6. Workers have no clear understanding of the organization's purposes or goals.
7. Communication of personal feelings is suppressed.
8. Workers do not share decision-making, which is confined to a select few.
9. The system stifles creativity.
10. The system "cuts down" anyone who excels.
11. Authoritarian leaders dominate the system.
12. The organization cannot face its problems openly, so it cannot modify its dysfunctions.
13. Leaders or supervisors are openly defensive and avoid confrontation.
14. At all levels, the organization resists change.
15. Workers feel anxious, insecure and tense most of the time.
16. Most workers hate or have love/hate feelings about their work.
17. Supervisors maintain an emotional distance from workers.
18. Supervisors are inaccessible to workers.
19. The workplace is full of "bad manners"—people are discourteous, requests are ignored, personal feelings are disregarded.
20. One or a few workers are repeatedly blamed for problems in the workplace.

How to
Keep Work
from Killing You

The power of people is perhaps the most potent force, for it reaches into all facets of all kinds of businesses, touching every stage of operations and every strategy, goal, or vision.... The new reality is that how people work, think, and feel dictates the direction and success of a business.

Robert Rosen, Ph.D.
The Healthy Company

W HAT MAKES A WORKPLACE healthy and functional is *more* than the opposite of what makes it dysfunctional, just as physical health is *more* than the opposite of sickness. The absence of sickness, while desirable, doesn't guarantee that you feel happy, strong, healthy, or fulfilled. All it indicates is that there is no disease present. Positive healthiness needs to include the presence of health-sustaining growth.

An analogy can be drawn from sailing—a passion which regrettably I don't get to indulge in much these days. The absence of stormy seas, gusting winds, and driving rain doesn't mean that you are having a good sail. If there is anything that a sailor hates more than turbulent seas it is dead stillness. No wind—no go! Dead in the water! You might as well be sitting in your favorite chair at home.

So a healthy workplace is more than the absence of stormy dysfunctions. It is the *presence* of a positive environment, where workers feel fulfilled, purposeful, and confident that survival in their workplace is in their own hands.

A HEALTHY WORKPLACE: PIPE DREAM OR REALITY?

Come with me as we visit an imaginary workplace. It's the beginning of the workday. You walk into the office (or workshop or factory) and everyone is upbeat. A new day is about to begin; the atmosphere is vibrant and stimulating. It's not yet starting time but every worker is on hand—not because the boss doesn't like tardiness or pay will be docked, but because everyone believes it's not fair to others not to be on time. Everyone's talking enthusiastically about an upcoming deadline, project, or work quota. Vision, strategy, and ideas are being shared and received graciously. No one is threatened by the competence of anyone else. Mutual respect prevails. A few banter lightheartedly; there's no trace of tension. The mood is energizing for all.

As you observe this hypothetical workplace, it's hard to tell if anyone is in charge. Everyone seems to assume responsibility naturally. Nobody seems to be goading others to keep their minds on their work. As the day progresses the pace of work quickens. Phones ring, copiers buzz, machines whir and the occasional crisis doesn't faze anyone. A few workers turn to supervisors for a consultation or with special requests. A group gathers around a desk with another work unit, and everyone quickly agrees on a creative solution and returns to work without bickering. The workers diligently look for ways to deliver productivity or service faster and better, without stress. They don't pass the buck; they see themselves as a part of a larger team; they go home feeling good about themselves and with a sense of accomplishment.

Fiction? A pipe dream? Unrealistic? Pie-in-the-sky? I hope not. It may sound farfetched if you now work in a crazy-making environment, but I do know of several companies and organizations which come pretty close to such an ideal.

In any event, my purpose here is to highlight the features of what I call a healthy company or organization. You may never achieve them all in the same place, but at least you can strive for some of them wherever you work.

Robert W. Reed, vice-president of the Intel Corporation, has said, "A healthy company is immediately noticeable." And I don't think he means that so few companies are really healthy that they stick out like a sore thumb. What he means is that the characteristics of healthiness are immediately apparent, especially on the faces and in the demeanor of the employees. It is apparent because the workers get out of their work what they really want. What is it they really want? Max De Pree, retired chairman and CEO of Herman Miller, Inc. and a friend of many years, says it is "... to find the most effective, most productive, most rewarding way of *working together*" (emphasis is mine).[1]

Working together is the key to developing a healthy company. Enabling people to work in harmony, mutual respect, and coopera- tion so that their deep need "for belonging, for contributing, for meaningful work,... for the opportunity to grow and be at least reasonably in control of [their] destinies" can be met.[2] Any work- place facilitating this has to be healthy.

What are the keys to creating a healthy workplace? I wish to address four: The "spirit" of a workplace, the unique type of leader- ship, the attitudes that prevail, and the behaviors that are encour- aged. While these factors overlap, there is value in examining each separately. The interrelationship between them is depicted in *figure two* on page 62. They form a loop that is continually evolving. Each factor depends on the others to reinforce it. If leadership begins to change for the better, attitudes and behaviors will begin to change and affect the "spirit" of the workplace. That, in turn, will help leadership to be more determined to change things. Such a loop is called "synergistic" because it works together, each part strengthening and growing from the other parts. Think of the loop, then, as starting small and gradually growing bigger as the organization becomes healthier.

The "spirit" of a healthy workplace. Dr. Robert Rosen, a well- known expert in management, reports that he has consulted with a number of healthy companies and has arrived at some significant conclusions.[3] The most important discovery is that every healthy company emanates a certain vitality. The spirit of which he speaks is not like a religious fervor or the mindless enthusiasm of a cheer- leader who jumps and shouts an allegiance just because he or she attends a certain school. Rather, a deep feeling of shared values exists at the core of the company.

Max De Pree says the same: "Healthy companies [are] about shared ideals, shared goals, shared respect, and a shared sense of values and mission."[4]

The unique spirit of a healthy company is not confined to the board of directors or the production line. Sharing extends vertically, from the bottom of the corporate ladder to the top, from the least important worker to the most important. For a workplace to be healthy, everyone must buy into the spirit-life that characterizes that place.

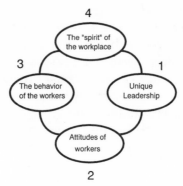

Figure two

The "spirit" of an organization is the glue that binds a healthy workplace together and ensures that employees are successful, healthy, and productive. It influences the way people think and act at all levels. It determines the degree of loyalty to the organization. Corporate policies and practices also reflect this spirit. The company has a soul—and it shows.

What characterizes the soul of a healthy organization?

- Workers exhibit vigor and enthusiasm.
- Workers take risks if necessary to change for the better.
- Workers endorse the organization's mission.
- All workers share the goals of the organization.
- Workers respect each member's contribution.
- Both workers and the organization share values rooted in integrity.

Shared values are perhaps the most important component of an organization; they are also the most difficult to generate and keep alive. Values have to do with those principles, goals, or standards accepted by a group. They are at the heart of an organization and determine how everyone will grow and renew themselves when the going gets tough. Those who don't accept them are better off working elsewhere. People are attracted to the company because they believe in the values that its workers share.

When the values of an organization are healthy, it is healthy, and its employees exhibit extraordinary commitment. The reason is simple: each worker has found expression for his or her own aspirations through the activities of the organization. This is why charitable or religious organizations are so effective in developing loyalty. Workers value what the organization values and will work longer hours for less money because their values are finding fulfillment.

But let me sound one word of caution here. Sadly, shared values can sometimes be abused when an employee's loyalty is taken advantage of. Religious and charitable institutions can unfairly capitalize on the generous spirit of workers who are strongly committed to the organization's mission.

Dr. Rosen has identified seven values at the heart of a healthy workplace:

- *A commitment to self-knowledge and development.* Managers inspire both personal and professional development in their employees. They seek the most fulfilling life for all they supervise.
- *A firm belief in decency and goodness.* This value is based on the belief that people work best when they are highly respected and appreciated.
- *Respect for individual differences.* All persons are treated with equal respect in hiring, promotion, and work schedules. Diversity is respected and tolerance for all enforced.
- *A spirit of partnership.* This value is based on a belief in the importance of community and the strength of shared effort. Teamwork prevails; strong relationships are built.
- *A high priority on health and well-being.* Workers are regarded as resources that must be maintained and protected. The power of work to make people sick or well is recognized, and every effort is made to create a desirable physical and psychological climate. Managers know that how people are managed directly affects their health.
- *Flexibility and resiliency.* Change is inevitable in a growing company. Flexible and resilient employees are valued because they can roll with the punches. They bounce back encouraged, not discouraged. They can stick with the job through hard times, yet quickly make changes when necessary.
- *A passion for products and process.* Workers care about what happens to their company. They have a high degree of per-

sonal involvement, and the company values this. But the passion for success is balanced by a passion for process—they care as much about how something is produced as about the quality of the product itself. So they respect relationships as well as work.

How do values like these become the life-blood of an organization? Teaching and rewarding these values is the key. The process must begin at the top. Those in charge need continually to manifest that they adhere to these values. Everyone is encouraged to apply these values to their work. Those who don't need to be removed. Healthy leadership is crucial, and this is the topic of the next section.

Unique leadership. Leadership is crucial to the synergistic growth that produces a healthy workplace (review *figure two* again). Every other component takes its cue from leadership. But the leadership that produces a healthy company is *unique* and is, therefore, nonconforming.

The styles that most of us are accustomed to have been around a long time—and still dominate the workplace. What characterizes them?

- *Personality-based:* The charisma or dominance of the leader is valued. If the personality is strong (a better word is perhaps stubborn), the more forceful the leadership will be. Such leaders give orders and expect obedience—if not worship!
- *Brilliance-based:* Here the smarter the person, the more likely he or she will assume leadership. Brains count because they enable the person to outsmart everyone else and thus take control. However, their smartness may not extend to people management.
- *Power-based:* It helps to be the owner's daughter or son. Or one can become favored by working into the good graces of the owner. Power, as the basis for leadership, can be inherited or earned. However, it is seldom respected when it leads by force and fear.

These types of leadership are all around us in banks, factories, churches, and government. Do any of them produce a healthy organization? Hardly ever. They usually have a debilitating effect because they emphasize leadership superiority and authority at the cost of worker autonomy and freedom. Company leaders, such as presidents, supervisors, and vice-presidents, do indeed have power. But how they use their power determines their effectiveness. If they take too much control, they take away the autonomy of workers. When they use *less* authority, group members take greater responsibility, become more self-managing, and gain greater freedom to make decisions that will improve productivity. The relationship between leader authority and worker freedom is depicted in *figure three*.

LEADER AUTHORITY

tells   sells   tests   consults   joins

WORKER FREEDOM

Figure three

On the left we have the worst case scenario, that of a leader who is highly authoritarian and commands or "tells" workers what to do. Workers have no freedom. They must do precisely what they are told. Leaders must use all their energy and power to control what people do. At this end of the continuum, therefore, not only do we see leaders burn out quickly, but we also see the highest degree of burnout in workers. To be constantly observed and corrected, to be criticized for every little mistake, is very stressful. Overcontrol of workers inevitably leads to a high degree of dysfunction. It is crazy-making.

As we move to the right on *figure three*, we see less authoritarian control and more worker freedom. It moves from "telling" to "selling" (convincing workers why they must perform a certain task), and then to "consulting" (making workers part of the decision-making process), and finally to "joining" (where the worker owns full responsibility for the work). The farther we move to the right, however, the less demanding is the leader's role in trying to get people to work. The leader can then focus energy on being a true leader, not a slave driver.

The most desirable style of leadership, therefore, enables the work force to participate in decision-making and goal-setting and encourages worker autonomy. It also creates the healthiest workplace. The two go hand in hand. As Max De Pree writes: "I believe that the most effective contemporary management process is *participative management* (emphasis is mine).[5]

In a collaborative process of achieving shared goals, the leader must believe in the potential of people to bring gifts that will contribute to the effectiveness of the company. Leaders who don't have such a conviction should be put in the back room as idea people and not allowed to manage. They will sabotage the creation of a healthy workplace and the profitability of an enterprise.

A leader who influences relationships to produce team-mindedness is a *functional leader* (as opposed to dysfunctional). Such a leader:

- is flexible, but not impulsive
- is aware of personal unconscious forces within self that might interfere with effectively leading others
- respects diversity
- understands that relationships come before procedures
- can discern forces within an organization that could sabotage the well-being of workers
- is honest and open in all dealings; engenders trust
- can balance short-term goals against long-term; knows when to choose which
- does not shirk responsibility or shrink from conflict
- ensures that, except for urgent matters, all decisions are given adequate time for processing and fact-finding by all those affected
- does not act precipitously

The characteristics of the *functional leader* can also be described in terms of what she or he does:

- identifies problems clearly for all to understand
- raises the level of motivation by involving as many workers as necessary in decision-making
- works at improving the quality of decisions made by all
- furthers the individual growth-needs of all workers
- works at making it easy for workers to change and become more effective
- takes care of him/herself, no matter how many demands are being made
- always says "thank you" for a job well done

Sometimes leaders serve as team leaders, not supervisors. They oversee group activities, not the work of individuals. If they are to be functional, they:

- regulate boundary transactions so that people know where their boundaries begin and end
- work at increasing cohesiveness and team spirit
- enhance access to outside sources of replenishment (in other words, they avoid creating a "closed system")
- avoid becoming the "high priest" or "high priestess" of their workplace
- decentralize power—give it away as much as they can
- help the decision-making process but don't force their opinions on others
- clarify roles for everybody—constantly (role confusion quickly degenerates into stress)
- know how to say, "I'm sorry," and "I don't know."
- keep in touch with the troops (the bigger the company, the more important that they stay in touch with the rank and file)

A CEO of a large company once said, "If you want to know what is really going on in most companies, you talk to the guy who sweeps the floors. Nine times out of ten, he knows more than the president. So I make a point of knowing what my floor sweepers know—even if it means sweeping the floors with them." Now there's a functional boss!

But being a functional leader goes further than just facilitating communication and being a participative manager. One must have a special concern for the well-being of people. During my first weeks on the job as a young engineer, I used a day off to visit a construction site for some exposure to the real action.

I introduced myself to the sun-hardened foreman, who courteously explained what was going on, pointing out the different rock formations they were excavating through. As I was about to leave a car drove up and out stepped a tall, handsome, middle-aged man in casual clothes, whom the foreman introduced to me as the "big boss."

"Where's Bill?" he asked. The foreman pointed to a nearby bulldozer struggling to get a foothold at the base of some large rocks. The boss strolled over to the machine, inviting me to go with him.

Bill shut down the bulldozer and climbed down as soon as he

saw who it was. He removed his wide-brimmed felt hat—the kind often used to keep the hot South African sun off the face—and smiled broadly.

"Pleased to see you, sir," he greeted.

"Happy birthday, Bill! You must be thirty-five today, is that right?"

Bill nodded happily and they continued talking a while about family matters. Bill had been expecting the big boss. Turned out that everyone got a birthday visit, come rain or sunshine, holiday or workday. Rarely have I seen a leader receive the respect I saw that day.

Attitudes of workers. The attitudes that prevail in a workplace promote or destroy a healthy work environment. Attitudes determine behavior. In a dysfunctional workplace attitudes are negative and destructive. It is common these days to hear, "You've got an attitude, man," meaning that the person's disposition is less than desirable.

Attitudes can take the form of hypercriticalness, cynicism, expressions of hopelessness and even depression. They can manifest themselves as resentment toward authority, or hostility toward a particular race or sex.

The problem with attitudes is that they are *contagious*—they spread through the system. In a workplace under high stress or one which is poorly-managed, bad attitudes can spread like wildfire. Low morale fuels the flames. A whole organization can be subverted by unchecked bad attitudes.

Just as negative attitudes are contagious, so positive ones are "caught" from the leadership, who must set the ball rolling. A supervisor who constantly complains that everything is screwed up teaches subordinates to think and feel the same way. Similarly, a supervisor whose attitude is positive and constructive will inculcate the same in subordinates.

I am not suggesting that supervisors should overlook poor working conditions and ignore dysfunction just so subordinates will feel good. That is not only denial—it lacks integrity. But even when a workplace is not perfect, a positive attitude is more likely to bring positive change.

Of all the attitudes that are good and helpful, the most important is *enthusiasm*, which is an amalgam of eagerness, optimism, and hope. In Max De Pree's book, *Leadership Is an Art*,[6] he discusses the work of Buckminster Fuller, the philosopher, engineer, inventor, and designer. If ever you see a huge dome covering a stadium or any other large space, chances are you are looking at one designed using Buckminster Fuller's ideas. He called them "geodesic domes," and when he first invented them traditional engineers pronounced that they would collapse.

When I was a young engineer, I spent a morning with Buckminster Fuller in South Africa, trying to comprehend his methods and glean whatever I could from his rapid-fire mind. I went away charged with creative ideas and experimented with geodesic domes for years afterward. But it wasn't Fuller's brilliance that left its mark on me so much as his *enthusiasm* for what he believed in. The opposition he was facing at that time had not fazed him. His enthusiasm led people to follow him, it was so contagious! Enthusiasm of Fuller's sort can help to create a healthy work environment. When leaders lack zeal for what a company is about, it is almost impossible to create a healthy work environment. Downbeat attitudes are even more contagious!

Behavior of workers. The behavior of the workers is a vital factor in whether a workplace is healthy. Worker behavior flows out of the spirit of a workplace, which has been created through the attitude-shaping influence of leadership. The workers' behavior then helps maintain the spirit at the core of a company or organization. The relationship between behavior and attitudes is important. Behavior is the "seal" that entrenches the attitudes and beliefs. I would even go so far as to assert that our behavior influences our feelings *more* than our feelings influence our behavior. For instance, if I don't like someone I work with, I can still *behave* toward that person with patience and give him or her respect. And what happens when I consistently behave *as if* I respect someone? I can come to like the person. My respect is reinforced by my behavior. In this way I can actually reshape my attitudes by behaving in the right way.

This principle is used extensively in family therapy. Let's suppose a husband complains that he doesn't "love" his wife anymore. What is my prescription? I recommend that he behave toward her "as if" he loves her. "Buy her flowers on your way home from work sometime," I suggest. "Treat her with kindness and resist becoming impatient, and let's see what happens." He is a little taken aback, but he goes away saying he will do what I tell him. Invariably, two or three weeks later, he is saying, "I'm quite surprised. I can actually begin to feel some of my love coming back! Just behaving as if I love my wife is changing how I feel about her." Yes, it's true. Acting with love builds love.

Now before you jump on my case with all sorts of exceptions, let me say that I know that a prescription for loving behavior won't fix every marriage, but it has turned quite a few around. Besides, do you know of any other way to rekindle love? It doesn't only help a marriage but it can restore a daughter's love for her father, a mother's love for her son, and innumerable friendships. It can also work wonders in a workplace. Right behavior will shape the right attitudes. Too many psychologists have overlooked the power of right behavior to repair damaged feelings.

Courtesy, sharing ideas, fostering trust, tolerance, flowers for a birthday, a card at holiday time, an encouraging word, a listening ear *are all behaviors* that change attitudes. They cost little but create a "spirit" of cooperation and mutual love. You just can't go to work without it!

MANAGEMENT STRATEGIES THAT HELP EMPLOYEES GIVE THEIR BEST

Most of what I have said about the healthy workplace has management implications. But let me summarize some basic management principles that are absolutely necessary if employees are to perform well.

Helping others succeed. For companies struggling to remain competitive, the ability to respond to change is the key to success. One critical change taking place in corporate America has to do with how people are managed. Everywhere organizations are drastically reorganizing and tossing away traditional corporate hierarchies in favor of smaller units, empowered workers and a "team" approach. Key to this change is the abandonment of the command-and-obey approach in which orders come from above and obedience from below. At long last the truth has finally dawned: unless workers buy into commands, they can easily sabotage them. You can give all the orders you like, but unless workers "own" the ideas they do not follow. The *real* power is at the bottom of an organization and success can be achieved only when this power is mobilized and turned to good.

Furthermore, bigness, with its never-ending hierarchy, is out. It tended to de-individualize workers over time; it led to high turnover, high accident rates and less efficient work. In very big companies the gap between the top and the bottom was too great. Now companies are going small, making a new style of management essential. Many smaller units, or teams, will make up the company of the future. The challenge for the new breed of manager will be how to foster creativity and overcome dissent in smaller groups. Thousands of these smaller units can make up a large company.

One key goal for managerial success, therefore, will be to help these teams succeed. No longer can those in charge get away with the manipulations of a few to succeed. Everyone has to be motivated or else no one succeeds. Bureaucracy will be the enemy in the company of the future. The empowerment of all workers is the ally of effective management.

How does a manager help a team succeed? By helping its individual members to succeed. The most common leadership pitfall is to use time and energy focusing on the weaker members of the team, leaving the stronger to fend for themselves. In the "old" days, problem workers sapped all the attention and many companies suffered as a consequence. Weaker workers may have improved marginally from this attention, but those who could have delivered the goods, being deprived of the leadership they needed, languished. So leaders are more effective if they lead the stronger and leave the team to deal with the weaker. This builds coresponsibility and creates a more productive work environment. Furthermore, pressure from peers is less threatening and more productive than pressure from a superior.

Managing diversity. Nothing destroys a healthy company more quickly than disrespect for those who don't fit the majority mold. Since we are a pluralistic culture, knowing how to manage diversity is crucial. Right at the outset let me say this: don't tolerate intolerance! Workers who are prejudiced need to be weeded out. Intolerance for diversity, if left unchallenged, will become more sinister.

Every workplace needs an ongoing program that educates workers in understanding and accepting diversity. Language barriers can be overcome by teaching workers how to speak the non-English languages prevalent in the workplace. Much prejudice is perpetuated by language barriers and vanishes when workers understand each other's talk. Sexism can be counteracted by "group" discussions and open communication between the sexes.

Every manager of the future will have to be adept at raising cultural and gender awareness and seeking out opportunities to promote the understanding of differences. Sometimes workers' schedules will need to be flexible so that workers can attend English or language classes; pre-employment orientation meetings may be necessary in companies with large staff turnovers. Sometimes a worker may be required to attend a sensitivity group that examines sexist attitudes. One thing is certain: personal needs will dominate the workplace of the future and will demand greater attention than we give them now.

At a more subtle level, managers will also need to be adept at dealing with differences of perspective, such as sexual orientation and personality clashes. Not every worker "fits in" perfectly with the rest. And the more the workplace becomes composed of smaller units, with less hierarchy and greater teamwork expectations, the more a manager must help workers get along with each other.

I realize not everyone can be force-fitted to a particular workplace. A basic human chemistry we call "compatibility" is a fact of life. Some people will never be able to get along with everyone in the workplace. Competence and compatibility don't always match! So when a manager has an employee who is highly qualified for a job but doesn't cooperate with the team, that manager has a real challenge. How should such a problem be handled?

The truth is that no two people are fully compatible. Some degree of incompatibility is always present in every work setting. This is a given. The first responsibility of the manager is to foster the interpersonal growth necessary in both the problem worker and the team.

Sure, there are limits. A bad apple may have the potential to turn the whole barrel bad. It would be unfair to force others on the team to do all the adjusting to accommodate a bad fit. Under these circumstances the manager should obtain the help of a professional consultant.

Sharing power. A management paradox is that when one shares power one actually gains more power. It's like a car's hydraulic system that helps to power the steering or brakes. It's called "power assistance." How does it work? When you turn the steering wheel or press the brake pedal you release a little power to activate the larger power of the hydraulic system. The little power that you release is then used to control the larger power that steers or stops the car. It's a system of leverage, except it's all hydraulic. If you try to steer or stop the car without this assistance—for instance, when the engine cuts out—the amount of power you have to exert is enormous and almost beyond your ability. It's the same in management. Your little power should be used to activate the larger power of the workforce. But first you must allow workers to have this larger power.

How do you share power as a manager?

- by training your supervisors to take control and act autonomously within the boundaries you set
- by teaching them how to make their own decisions—and then let them make them, holding them accountable
- by minimizing bureaucracy, complex rules, procedures, red tape, and officialism
- by requiring workers to take responsibility for their work and actions
- by rewarding those who act responsibly and using their resources to the maximum benefit of the group
- by not treating workers as children; discouraging dependency, buck-passing, and blaming
- by ensuring good communication throughout the work system, so that everyone knows his or her boundaries
- by insisting that decisions be widely discussed, with contrary opinions expressed, before they are made final
- by facilitating the expression of feelings, especially frustration and anger, and owning up to your own contribution to these feelings when appropriate

Saying "no" effectively. Not being able to say "no" means that:

- You're a pushover and never reject a request or idea, no matter how ridiculous or farfetched.
- You give in to unnecessary demands on your time.
- You become overextended, overbudgeted, overspent and overstressed.
- You spend a lot of unnecessary time fantasizing how you should have said "no."

- You carry a lot of resentment and anger because you feel manipulated.

Why do so many of us have difficulty saying "no"? Often it's because we are afraid we won't be liked. It comes from our need for approval and fear of rejection. Sometimes it's because we've never learned to appreciate our own rights. We have been trained to subjugate our rights to the rights of others and cannot do what is right for ourselves. We sacrifice our rights, and sometimes the rights of our family, so as not to feel guilty. Sometimes it's because we haven't learned how to protect our boundaries. We let others overstep their boundaries and intrude where they shouldn't.

How can you strengthen your ability to say "no"? Strengthen your belief that you have a right to say it. That is your key to selectivity and to effective functioning. "No" prevents resentment and anger. "No" is the only way you can take a stand against impossible demands that will destroy you. Without "no" you are a slave to popularity and manipulation. You are without defense against the demands of others.

"No" is essential to creating a healthy workplace, just as it is to creating a healthy home. If parents never said no, chaos would reign in the home. A manager who can't say no creates chaos in the workplace. Remember that "no" also gives meaning to your "yes." When you selectively say "yes" fairness can prevail.

Sometimes past experiences, even from your childhood, have led to your difficulty with "no." Identifying these issues from the past is necessary, even though it can be painful. Identify the powerful people throughout your life. Did they punish you if you resisted? Was your privacy violated? Were your boundaries transgressed? Did you learn to accept these violations passively? Talking with a trusted friend or therapist may help to free you from the hidden binds that make it difficult for you to refuse another.

Once you have begun to understand why you have difficulty saying no, you can begin to change the pattern. Start with saying "no" in little things. If the idea of "baby steps" has any validity, it certainly does here. Begin by being assertive in small matters. Say "no" to the waiter who tries to push an expensive, post-dinner dessert on you. Say "no" to the neighbor who wants to borrow your portable TV to take to a football game. Say "no" to your kids who are asking for extra pocket money. Practice in saying no to little things helps to build courage to say no to big things.

Then move to the workplace. Say "no" to little requests at first. State your reasons calmly and clearly. Ignore your guilt feelings and fear of rejection. It's your responsibility to say "no" to unreasonable requests.

Slowly but systematically clean up your boundaries. In the beginning it may feel awkward, but with practice it gets easier.

If you are a supervisor, here are some principles you should follow in responding to requests:

First: Make sure you understand the request. More important, make sure that the requester knows that you understand the request. Nothing angers people who have been rejected more than the feeling they never had an opportunity to state their wants clearly. "She never even heard me. Before I was finished she'd already said no!" This makes enemies quickly. So make sure you take time to listen to and weigh the request. Ask clarifying questions. Explore alternatives.

Second: If you decide to refuse the request, give your reasons as clearly as possible. If you cannot articulate a reason but just "feel" it is wrong, then say so. Don't make up reasons that can't be defended. Remember, you are the boss and must carry the responsibility for your decision. Don't delay the decision. Don't chicken out by saying, "Let me think about it," unless it is something that truly needs more thinking. Decisiveness, in the long run, will earn you more respect than indecisiveness, even if your decisiveness tends toward "no."

Third: Don't apologize for your "no." Don't grovel, don't placate, don't plead for understanding. And don't give more than one reason for saying "no." This feeds your guilt-proneness. Besides, the recipient of your "no" will see through why you are giving a half-dozen reasons. If there is one main reason, stick with it.

MANAGEMENT AND LABOR: A TWO-WAY STREET

It is very easy to write about what companies need to do to make the workplace healthier and what bosses ought to do for workers. But what do employees owe their employers? As management becomes more humane, flexible, and sensitive to working conditions, employees need to deliver in return. What can you, as an employee, contribute to a healthier workplace?

- Show that you support the company and your team. Stop complaining; that causes friction and saps productivity. If you really dislike your job or your employer, move on to a new job.
- Develop self-motivation. Decide that you will give your work your best; participate wholeheartedly; show initiative.
- Don't gripe or put down other workers. Stop seeking blame for mistakes and adopt a problem-solving attitude.
- Foster cooperation; help those around you to pitch in, so that everyone wins.
- If you can save the company money or complete a task ahead of schedule, do so. You will benefit in the long run.
- Be positive. Everyone prefers to work with upbeat people, not downbeats. Listen to your conversations and read what you write, then edit out whatever sounds negative.
- Treat all tasks as if they are important. Small tasks can be irksome, but usually it is our attitude toward them that makes them so.
- Always be honest. If you goof, admit it. Tell the truth even when it feels uncomfortable or reflects badly on you. Stick to your word; keep your promises. This builds your character and fosters trust. Both will make you a prized worker.

Creating a healthy workplace, while an ongoing, endless process, is full of potential for deep personal satisfaction, both for managers and workers. The challenge pays rewards in lifelong friendships, self-respect, and happiness. Leaders who make a healthy workplace their priority inspire others to share the vision. They establish values about how employees, colleagues, and consumers ought to be treated.

Above all, leaders who help create a healthy workplace encourage the heart of every worker and thereby strengthen the spirit of every household represented in the workplace. A healthy workplace contributes to healthy families, communities, and lives.

Consequences of a Healthy Workplace

- high job satisfaction
- few complaints and grievances
- high morale, motivation, and loyalty
- lower absenteeism
- healthier workforce (physically and emotionally)
- fewer accidents
- low worker turnover
- high energy level
- creativity and flexibility
- superior communication
- career mobility
- lowered stress and burnout
- healthy interpersonal interactions
- healing atmosphere for even the most difficult of workers
- superior quality of work
- brightest and best workers retained
- self-managing, self-motivated workers

Are *You* Poisoning Your Workplace?

*Everything is being transformed up or down
—and this includes men and women especially.
It is not a question of whether you would be or
would not be transformed—you are being
transformed, for better or for worse. The life
forces which flow from you and through you
are transforming you into a pattern. You
stand in the midst of those life forces and you
decide the pattern. Even if you apparently do
not decide anything, but allow those life forces
free rein, yet in not deciding you decide not to
decide.* E. Stanley Jones
How to Be a Transformed Person

BEFORE WE GO TOO FAR in our examination of how a workplace can be dysfunctional, I think I should pause and suggest you ask yourself a very important question: "Am I dysfunctional?" I know that asking yourself this question is risky, but you could go from cover to cover of this book and not benefit one iota if you fail to own up to your own personal toxic contribution to your workplace.

Let's face it. No one is perfect. One must expect to find agreeable and disagreeable types whenever people assemble—as in large organizations. But what if you find yourself on the disagreeable side of the mix? Since each of us is somewhere on a continuum between emotional healthiness and dysfunction, between vitality and indifference, we may find ourselves on the functional side of the balance in one circumstance, but the dysfunctional in another. So even if we're creatively involved now, we could find ourselves malcontented and disruptive later.

Pete was such a person. When he graduated from the university and joined a company of surveyors he found it easy to shine. He was surrounded by malcontents, who were crippling the morale of a company. Now the point of my story is this: Pete was usually the cynical and sour one in any group. He had a reputation for being a sulker and wet blanket. But now a strange reversal had taken place. Pete found himself in an office where the atmosphere was downbeat. Several colleagues sought him out the first day to complain about the company, the boss, the pay, the working conditions. He was so overwhelmed that rather than do his usual thing of joining in with the complainers and even leading the pack, he did a reversal. He became the good guy!

"It can't be all that bad," he said to himself. "These unhappy, disagreeable people can't all be right. I'll make the best of it while I work here."

And he did. He changed his attitude as he saw what negativity looked like from the outside. Compared with the majority of his fellow workers, Pete behaved in an optimistic, positive way. He avoided their downbeat style and did extremely well.

Then a year later he moved to another company. The staff was high-spirited, functional and creative. Morale was high and a spirit of cooperation prevailed. But Pete felt outclassed and intimidated. His ego was threatened and his cynicism returned. He started complaining. Because everyone else was quite healthy he stood out like a sore thumb.

At this point, Pete realized that *he* was the problem and that on the continuum from functional to dysfunctional he was more on the dysfunctional side. If he was in a work situation where everyone else was toxic, he could shine as a reasonably healthy person. But when he was with healthy people, he stood out as dysfunctional.

Healthiness, therefore, is a relative thing. Very few employees are so dysfunctional as to disqualify themselves from work. But many need to move along the continuum to the healthier side so that no matter what work environment they find themselves in, they can be healthy and contributive. My goal is to help you move to the healthier side so that you are not part of making your workplace crazy.

ARE YOU A CANDIDATE FOR SELF-ASSESSMENT?

To evaluate your own propensity for dysfunctional attitudes and behaviors may be a lot more difficult than you imagine. The reason is quite simple: The more toxic you are, the more likely it is that you blame others for your problems. Dysfunction has self-blindness built into it—that's why it is dysfunctional. Alternatively, you may tend to take too much blame upon yourself and cannot remain objective when looking for insights about your problems. Neither denial nor too much self-blame helps you to become healthier.

So before we look at the components of a healthy self, let me ask you to review the following questions. If you tend to be too defensive or to blame yourself excessively, you may benefit from seeking an in-depth professional evaluation.

1. *Are you an internalizer?* Do you tend to take your painful or negative feelings and stuff them deep within yourself?
2. *Are you a personalizer?* Do you take everything personally, believing that you are always at fault and that you need to be punished for your shortcomings?
3. *Are you an excuser?* Do you excuse others for what they do to you, always minimizing their motives or finding reasons for them to remain the way they are?
4. *Are you self-pitying?* Do you feel pity for yourself, feeling that you don't deserve what you get?
5. *Are you a complainer?* Do you find yourself complaining a lot to your spouse or friends?
6. *Are you an accuser?* Do you blame others for what happens to you, always feeling that you are the victim of their mistakes?
7. *Are you a grudge keeper?* Do you hold on to memories of hurts or injustices done to you? Do you fantasize a lot about getting revenge or humiliating someone you dislike?
8. *Are you an escapist?* Do you run away from problems or escape into TV, drugs, alcohol, hobbies, sports, shopping or whatever, to avoid dealing with reality?

9. *Are you a pessimist?* Do you always expect the worst and tend to look on the dark side of life?
10. *Do you lack a sense of control over your life and destiny?* Do you lack confidence and feel incapable of taking control and changing your circumstances?

If you answer all of these questions with a "yes" you need more help than I can give you in this chapter. My guess, though, is that most of us would answer "yes" to at least some of these questions.

The perfectly healthy worker would answer "no" to all ten questions. This model healthy worker is also never late, rarely sick, always positive and productive, and willing to work for less than anyone else. Such a person is an employer's dream. And that's perhaps all he or she is! Such a person doesn't exist. All of us are less than perfect and what we must settle for is *as much healthiness as we can attain*. What issues, then, need your attention? What can you learn about yourself that can help you to change?

Issue #1: What is your capacity for self-evaluation? If you tend to internalize, personalize, or excuse, chances are that you lack sufficient objectivity to be able to stand back and evaluate yourself accurately. You will have a tendency to assume that you are the troublemaker in the office or that others are always right and you are always wrong. Your style of operating is likely to be depressive, self-accusatory and self-demeaning. Dysfunction goes to both extremes: You take the blame for everything, or you take no blame at all.

The tendency to excuse has a further handicap: it makes it difficult for you to forgive and forget. Many people confuse "excusing" with "forgiving." Let's suppose somebody goes behind my back and reports a mistake I have made to the boss, a mistake I've already corrected and for which there are no further consequences. I feel betrayed and unfairly treated. If I say to myself, "My coworker didn't mean to hurt me, she is just jealous that I so seldom make mistakes, I'll just forget it," am I forgiving my coworker? Absolutely not. I am "excusing" her—making up an excuse to explain her inexcusable behavior. When I excuse some action I am not forgiving it. It still festers and goes on hurting. Forgiveness' purpose is to stop the hurt—to help me get over it altogether. To excuse an action takes away the need for forgiveness so it aborts the process of healing. Obviously, if the excuse was absolutely legitimate, forgiveness would not be needed. You don't forgive a genuine mistake, you excuse it. No harm was meant so there is nothing to forgive. But when *harm is meant,* you cannot excuse it, you must forgive it. And if forgiveness is going to work *you must not excuse* a hurt before you have forgiven it. You must accept that the action *was intended* to hurt you, and then take steps to forgive it.

What then is forgiveness? Simply this: surrendering my right to hurt you back. When you hurt me deliberately, I have a right to hurt you back. My action of forgiveness, however, is my choosing not to act on this right—but to let it go. No excuses, no minimizing of the hurt. Just a willful act in which I choose to surrender my right to take revenge.

When I have chosen not to take revenge on the harm deliberately done to me, then, and only then, should I attempt to confront the person doing the harm. The reason I say this is that too often I have seen (and experienced myself) someone trying to confront a wrongdoing while remaining revengeful. The results are mostly harmful. The need to hurt the wrongdoer back is greater than the need to understand why the person who wronged you acted the way he or she did. And when you take revenge by trying to humiliate the wrongdoer, you only turn him into more of an enemy and start a war! And if the wrongdoer is your boss this can be disastrous, as I have seen so many times.

My advice, then, is never to confront until you have chosen to forgive the hurt done to you. This will go a long way toward minimizing the likelihood that you will step beyond trying to understand what is going on into taking revenge.

Issue #2: What is your capacity for self-confrontation? If you tend to feel a lot of self-pity, complain a lot or blame others for what happens to you, you may have a tendency to shift responsibility for your dysfunctional behaviors onto others. You always see yourself as the victim, never the victimizer. Consequently, you never confront yourself sufficiently to change anything. After all, if someone else is to blame why should you change?

Over the years I have dealt with many who feel they have been unfairly treated by an employer or fellow employee. Perhaps they were fired or demoted, perhaps someone was promoted over their heads. Work offers many opportunities for such apparent injustices. But what really amazes me is how few (one or two in my whole career) of these victims of apparent injustices have admitted their own contribution to the injustice. I have yet to hear someone say: "You know, I deserved that. I brought it on my own head because of what I did."

Doesn't this amaze you as well? Everyone is a victim. No one is ever a victimizer. Ask the typical child abuser; ask the worker who has just been fired; ask the graduate student who has just received a failing grade: "Who is to blame?" The answer is always *the other person.*

I would hate to be a judge. I think I would quickly lose faith in the human race! Seldom does someone own up to being guilty. Even when caught red-handed with the goods in the trunk of the car, they plead "not guilty." And when someone does own up it's not because the evidence is so overwhelming that they have no other choice. It's usually so that the punishment will be less harsh. And even then, they will blame their action on someone else. I suppose we must just chalk this up to human nature, but it does not help people to change or grow.

In normal human relationships, of course, we seldom deal with hard facts. Rarely is booty in the trunk. Seemingly harmless communications have hidden meanings. Motives are impossible to pin down. So crazy-making people are often a serious problem precisely because they won't own up to their toxicity. Until they are willing to admit their shortcomings there can be little hope for change.

Issue #3: What is your capacity for self-change? If you tend to harbor grudges, use something to excess so as to escape your responsibilities or avoid anxiety, believe that no matter what you do it will fail, and believe that you really have no power to change yourself or your circumstances, then you most certainly will have to work harder to become a healthier person. You are more apt to stay in your rut than pull yourself out. You probably don't feel happy about your life and have little prospect of improvement until you shake off your resentments and take responsibility for who and what you are.

Whom do you blame for your problems? Your parents? Forget it. I have yet to meet the perfect set of parents. They don't exist. Most parents do the best they can with the skills they have, so there is little point in blaming them. A time comes when you must pick up wherever they left off and take responsibility for the rest of your life. If you don't like what your parents have programmed into you, then start reprogramming yourself. You don't have to stay put—move on!

The first essential to being a healthy person is to recognize you have many options to choose from when you are confronted with a challenge. Based upon education, training and experience, each of us develops a unique, more or less characteristic set of traits, responses, and beliefs. These determine who we are. Some of us have wide-ranging interests, others have only a few. Some of us have a large repertoire of behaviors so we can respond in many different ways to challenge. Others with only a few responses tend to respond in stereotypic ways. If, for example, your learned response to criticism is angry counterattack, you suffer from a limited repertoire of responses. You need to learn some new behaviors. Whether your wife or boss is criticizing you, the larger your repertoire, the more you will feel in control because you have more options to choose from.

A second essential to being a healthy person follows from the first: you must be flexible enough *to adapt* to challenges by changing your behavior. Unless we can try out different responses, we get stuck using the same one over and over again. This keeps us as we are.

A third essential is to 'fess up to your dysfunctions—no denial, no rationalizing, and no blaming. Just own them. All successful adults take responsibility for every aspect of their well-being. They establish goals for their inner and outer selves, their work and their home life, and constantly seek to adapt to changing conditions. And you can only do this if you are honest about yourself.

My challenge then is this: Break out of your grudge-bearing, escapist, and helpless modes. Try to be a little more open to new ways of behaving. Learn by observing how others, healthier than yourself, respond to their challenges. Talk to successful people and glean what you can from them. Seek out a mentor who is functional and model your responses after him or her. Healthiness is catching, just like sickness!

EVALUATING YOUR PERSONALITY

Your personality defines who you are as a person. No self-evaluation would be complete that doesn't include an honest look at your personality. This may not be as easy as it sounds. Many people resist looking deeply at who they are for fear of what they might find. Such persons would be wise to see a therapist who can help them with self-exploration.

I need to begin by quickly reviewing the more serious personality problems. These are the most destructive, especially when such a person is placed in a position of power. People who suffer from them typically cut themselves off from help. Understanding them, however, can help in pinpointing where some crazy-making comes from.

Some personality disorders, when full-blown, can have alarming consequences. Prisons are full of people suffering from them. These people perceive, think about, and relate to the world in wide-ranging, toxic ways. Their disorders are well-entrenched by the time of adolescence, and are called "personality" disorders because the roots go deep into the cores of their being.

Whether you are a boss or a worker, you will find the following list of personality disorders helpful in understanding your workplace. If a colleague fits the category, you may find some relief in knowing you are not the one who is crazy. The boss may find it helpful just to understand how these disorders can be a problem.

- *Paranoid personality:* This person has a pervasive, unwarranted suspiciousness and mistrust of people. They make mountains out of molehills, exaggerate difficulties, and are excessively critical of others. They are prone to jealousy, have no sense of humor, are argumentative, and lack tender feelings. They frequently have job difficulties and cannot build or sustain friendships because they are so suspicious. When thwarted or fired they can be dangerously vengeful.

- *Schizoid personality:* These people have difficulty forming social relationships because they are cold and indifferent. They lack warm feelings, are indifferent to praise or criticism, and are typically "loners." They appear reserved, withdrawn, seclusive, and pursue solitary interests or hobbies. They prefer to be alone. This is more than shyness, however. Shyness is normal.

- *Schizotypal personality:* These people have a variety of behaviors and thoughts that are considered odd or eccentric. They engage in bizarre fantasies and don't feel embarrassed to share them. They use obscure or strange words (often invented by themselves), may overdress or dress bizarrely, and use makeup excessively. Their thinking is often "magical"—with a lot of belief in superstition, telepathy, clairvoyance, or a "sixth sense." They stand out as "oddballs" and do not make good workers—no matter what the work is.

- *Histrionic personality:* These persons tend to be overly dramatic, reactive and lively. They are prone to exaggeration, excitability, and have angry outbursts or tantrums. They crave novelty and stimulation and quickly become bored. While they are quick to form friendships, they are generally shallow, inconsiderate, and manipulative, often feigning illness or threatening suicide—just for the attention it gets. In the work setting they show a lot of dissatisfaction and can be very disruptive.

- *Narcissistic personality:* These persons have a grandiose sense of self-importance or uniqueness. They believe they are programmed for unlimited success and constantly seek attention and admiration. They are self-absorbed. They are the bane of any boss's life because they are above correction. Their self-esteem is so fragile they can tolerate no defeat. They have a strong sense of entitlement and expect special favors.

- *Antisocial personality:* Such persons have a history of antisocial behavior. They are likely to rip off the petty cash box or mutilate your family's photograph. They cannot sustain good job performance and are frequently fired. Check references carefully to avoid hiring such persons who lie, steal, fight, and resist authority. Basically they have no conscience, so nothing distresses them and they don't feel bad when they hurt you.

- *Borderline personality:* Of all these disorders this is the most difficult to identify and handle. Its main feature is instability—in mood, behavior, and self-image. These persons are your friend one minute, your enemy the next. They are impulsive and unpredictable (unlike the other disorders, where predictability is possible). They are also self-destructive, often threatening suicide. Often they spend excessively, get involved in inappropriate sexual activity, and shoplift. When caught, their anger lacks control. They throw and break things, so stay out of their way. In the workplace they are most destructive, often causing nervous breakdowns in those around them. They are difficult to deal with and quickly resort to legal action when thwarted. Keep them out of your workplace if you want a peaceful life!

What can be done to treat these disorders? Psychotherapy is essential. These problems are not amenable to self-help and the most competent friend or fellow worker can offer little. It takes a highly trained psychotherapist to know what is wrong and how not to get suckered into the manipulations that are characteristic of these disorders.

IRRITATING PERSONALITY TRAITS

Are we to be concerned only with the more serious personality disorders? Certainly not! Many less serious personality traits can be irritating in the workplace. These traits are easier to recognize in yourself and are more amenable to change. See how many you can identify in yourself.

- *The boor* tends to tell the same stories and jokes over and over again, causing boredom by tiresome repetitions. He or she can also be guilty of unwelcome attention or approaches. The boor is awkward and ill-mannered, often hiding rudeness behind clownish activity. Usually boors are untutored or unsophisticated, having learned their boorishness from a family member. They can use foul language and embarrass fellow workers.
- *The huckster* is out to sell him or herself. He or she aggressively pursues selfish interests, peddling whatever anyone will buy, including popularity, sex and friendship. You cannot trust such a person. He or she will turn on you the moment you no longer fulfill selfish ambitions.
- *The stickler* sticks to the rules. Oh boy, does he or she stick to the rules! Uncompromising to the point of being unreasonable. Permits no exceptions to the extent that the rigidity creates injustices. Such people make terrible bosses. They show no mercy. They want to see you squirm and squirt blood when they stomp on you.
- *The social climber* is overconcerned about social striving. He or she is very selective in picking friends and shuns anyone who is not the "right" kind. The primary goal is to gain unearned social status. Often such people are rejecting their background. They may put on airs, develop a unique accent and

try to "keep up with the Joneses." They become snobs when they finally "make it."

- *The squealer* tattles to the boss in order to win favors. Untrustworthy, squealers take delight in reporting others' failings. They complain to someone above you whenever you stand up to them. Every office or workshop has its squealer. Sometimes they are real crybabies. They are common in our culture mainly because parents tolerate or even encourage such behavior. When one child tattles on another, parents act on the squeal and clobber the accused culprit. This reinforces squealing as a way of taking revenge, even though it is a most undesirable trait.

- *The smart aleck* thinks he or she knows everything—butting in on every conversation, giving unwelcomed advice or opinions. Smart alecks try to show other people up. They lack sensitivity and overestimate their worth. When the chips are down they split, and you never see them around.

- *The slob* goes by different labels: wonk, slovenly Peter, pig, revolting, and grungy. All the names have one thing in common: they are gross. Slobs can be gross in their personal hygiene (dirty, smelly, unshaven), in their behavior (uncouth, foul-mouthed), or in their dress (dowdy, sloppy, bizarre).

- *The chiseler* is an aggressive bargainer or operator who tries to beat someone else down or out, by grabbing everything for him or herself. This person knows all the angles, can pull all the strings, and walks close to the edge of questionable operations. If you lose to such a person he or she looks down on you as a "sucker."

- *The snooper* goes to ridiculous lengths to spy on fellow workers. Anytime anything is going on, they must thrust themselves into it. They suspect "secrets" and feel ostracized. They also need to feel important and believe that if they know something about you that nobody else knows, you will be beholden to them.

These are some of the classic personality traits that make a coworker unpleasant to be around. Whenever you see these traits action should be taken to curtail the toxicity that accompanies them. The self-examination questions in chapter 1 can help you pinpoint your weak spots. When you recognize them in yourself, pull out all the stops and get help. No one has ever become healthier by ignoring personal weakness. Talking about your concerns will help you to be more honest and insightful and will point you to areas that need to be changed.

ARE YOU A HEALTHY THINKER?

In addition to examining your personality, you need to take a look at the way you think. Psychology teaches us that much anguish and bad behavior are rooted in the way we think. People feel what they think. In this sense the body is the servant of the mind. If you think hatred, you soon will feel that hatred. By the same token, if you think loving and kind thoughts, you soon will feel these thoughts.

Many unhappy people, therefore, can trace their unhappiness to the way they think. They misconstrue motives of others. They misperceive the actions of others. They misinterpret what people say, twisting it to suit their assumptions. Crooked thinking is what some have called it. Author Zig Ziegler calls it "stinkin' thinkin'," and he is right on target.

Every psychotherapist has to spend many hours trying to help patients straighten out their thinking patterns. These are basically habits that the mind has cultivated since childhood. Even the healthiest among us has some degree of dysfunctional thinking. The more you know about your "stinkin' thinkin'" the healthier you will become.

The influence of early exposure to bad thinking can easily be illustrated if you consider a child growing up with a father who is negative and pessimistic. The child receives a toy as a birthday present. Father says, "If I know you, you'll have that in pieces before the hour is up." The child cringes. "Am I as clumsy as he thinks?" "Do I break everything I touch?" Such thoughts stick like glue in the young child's mind.

"If you don't break the toy, you'll probably scratch the furniture with it before too long," father continues his haranguing. The child stores more negative programming to be recalled for years to come.

"Why don't you just pack the toy away? That way you won't break it and you won't scratch the furniture. It'll save you a lot of trouble."

All pessimism and negativity has one ultimate goal: to take away the capacity for fun. You must not allow yourself enjoyment. Pain is the only pleasure!

And so the little boy grows up with this pattern of thinking, modeled by a father who probably learned it from his father. What will this boy do when he becomes a father? He will say to his son, "If I were you I would...." Bad thinking is passed from generation to generation and is a major cause in many personal problems that take people to psychotherapists. In the workplace these "mental tics" can complicate how well we work with others.

Here are some of the "stinkin' thinkin'" patterns you need to be able to recognize and break away from at the earliest moment:

- *Overgeneralizing* is the tendency to interpret your failure in one area as indicative that you have failed in other areas as well.
- *Personalizing* means you take the blame for situations or events over which you really did not have any control.
- *Blaming* is when you believe someone else is always to blame for whatever happens—there are never any accidents. So you always look for someone to blame.
- *Obsessive thinking* means you dwell on one idea or detail to the point that you magnify its seriousness. You cannot eliminate the idea from your thinking.
- *Negative thinking* means you always see the pessimistic side of life. Consequently you are not able or willing to take risks.
- *Jumping to conclusions* results in forming negative interpretations with the barest of facts and making snap judgments without careful consideration.
- *Labeling* causes you to stereotype people in such a way that you do not see the real issue behind their actions. Labels perpetuate unhealthy ways of looking at others.
- *Irrational thinking* distorts the truth; it has no basis in reality and is illogical, absurd, and unreasonable.
- *Absolutistic thinking* allows for no exceptions. For instance, if you believe you must never make a mistake, this is an "absolute" way of thinking.
- *Prejudged thinking* bypasses logic and jumps to conclusions based on prejudice or bias.

The most effective way to recognize crooked thinking is to observe how you react in times of stress. When your female boss insists on your meeting a deadline do you tend to "label" her, jump to some conclusion about her competence because she's a blonde, and then engage in some irrational thinking about how much you hate your job because everything bad always happens to you? If you do, you have a definite case of "stinkin' thinkin'."

A difficult situation or crisis can bring out the worst in our thinking styles. We may assume the reason we feel resentment, guilt, sadness, anger, or jealousy is because of the crisis. We then fail to notice that *between* the crisis and our emotional reaction, a lot of unhealthy thoughts have intruded to disturb our peace of mind. The crisis in itself has not upset us, but the way we think when we are in crisis has caused our reaction. We react in a split second. What comes out as anger or depression is as much, if not more so, the consequence of our thinking patterns as it is the crisis. If we can catch our thinking and intervene with healthier thoughts, not only will we feel better but we will be more able to take positive, constructive steps to deal with the crisis.

EXPRESS YOUR EMOTIONS!

The degree of your personal toxicity is related to how freely your emotions are expressed. In other words, the degree to which you suppress and repress your emotions, especially your negative ones, the greater the likelihood that you are a toxic influence, not only at work but at home. Healthy people know how to express their emotions in open, nonthreatening ways.

Psychologists know less about emotions than they are willing to admit. Reason? Because emotions are very complex and no one has yet come up with a satisfactory theory or model of the emotions that can be widely accepted.

Emotions are difficult to study in the laboratory. For instance, to study anger we have to devise ingenious ways to make people angry. How do scientists do this? They frustrate them. They antagonize them. They confuse them. They even inject them with caffeine to create an anger-like arousal. But it's not real anger. Descartes, who lived from 1596 to 1650, might just as well have written his *Passions of the Soul* today, for in it he states that the sciences have been most defective in trying to help us understand the passions or emotions. Poets have done a better job than psychologists.

While emotions have been difficult to study, we still remain complex creatures who must struggle to master our emotional states. Even though we don't know a lot, one simple fact we do know: *Emotions are meant to be expressed.* Ignoring or denying them is never healthy, whether they are negative (like anger and guilt) or positive (like happiness and peacefulness). Emotions are meant to be experienced and shared.

We have known for a long time that the *repression* of emotions or memories (forcing them out of our awareness and into the unconscious) is bad for us. Freud said so. But many before him said this also. However, only in recent times have we begun to discover scientific evidence that repression is unhealthy, especially to our physical well-being. At the one-hundredth annual convention of the American Psychological Association in 1992, a panel of experts summarized present-day understanding of what repression can do by reporting its impact on three important health issues: heart disease, cancer, and asthma. They presented evidence that a "repressive coping style" can lead to serious health risks in all three areas. But there's a bright side to the picture as well: When people learn to express their negative emotions in a healthy, open way, their bodies respond positively.

For instance, research at Case Western Reserve University by Dr. Daniel A. Weinberger found that people who exercise a high degree of self-control over their emotions, especially anger, have higher levels of LDL (low density lipoproteins). These are the bad components in cholesterol.[1] This overcontrol of emotions is a form of repression. Such people are denying anger, rather than "owning it" and expressing it in a constructive way.

Similarly, studies have shown that a combination of a repressive style and extreme anger suppression fosters abnormal cell growth in cancer.[2] For instance, a study in 1975 showed that malignancy rates for breast tumors were 50 percent for women who rarely showed their anger, compared with 15 percent for women who can express what they feel. A PBS special by Bill Moyers, *Healing and the Mind* (KCET, February, 1993), covered fascinating research being conducted by a major medical school. Women with severe breast cancer were randomly assigned to two groups. Both groups received chemotherapy and other treatment. One, however, participated in group therapy, where they were encouraged to talk about their emotions, fear of dying, and anger at their disease. This group had double the life expectancy of the other. Having an opportunity to ventilate their feelings helped their bodies' immune systems immensely. Unfortunately for many, the only place they can do this is in the safety of group psychotherapy!

What is being advocated here as healthiness is *not* an unrestrained, "open warfare" expression of anger. It is simply the freedom to talk about one's anger. Many studies have emphasized that what is healthy is, *first*, to be able to recognize and accurately label what you are feeling, and, *second*, to have a safe place where you have the freedom to express your feelings in an acceptable way.

What is an acceptable way of expressing your feelings? Is group therapy, or any therapy, the only way? Certainly not. Here are some other ways:

- Write about your feelings, as in journaling. This helps to get them out of your system so you can reflect on them.
- Talk about them to someone else. You "externalize" and clarify your feelings as you discuss them.
- Address the one who is causing them. Many feelings are best handled by talking directly to their source.
- Arrive at some understanding of why you are feeling the way you are. To be angry is not enough. You must try to discover *why* you are angry.
- Develop an acceptable course of action in order to deal with the cause of the feeling.

Let's suppose a fellow worker has offended you. He is the classic "squealer" described earlier. You are a salesman for an electric supply company and, due to a misunderstanding, a company buyer threatens to cancel an order and buy from another company. You call up the client and apologize for the misunderstanding. You misquoted a price. It was your fault, you say. It won't happen again, you reassure her. She accepts the apology and agrees to stick with your company.

However, Squealer Joe has been listening to your side of the telephone conversation. He doesn't hear it all because before you are even finished he has sneaked out of the office and headed for the boss to squeal. "Jim lost us a contract," he announces to your boss, who's not in a good mood anyway because sales are down. The boss gets mad. He calls you in and you explain what has happened. The boss is satisfied, but you leave his office boiling. Once again Squealer Joe has done you harm. What can you do about it? If you repress your anger and minimize or excuse Joe's behavior, or if you deny that you are angry, you will do great harm to yourself. Physically your anger raises your blood pressure and cholesterol. Your doctor has told you this a trillion times. Your high adrenaline is going to send you to an early grave.

But is it healthy to blow up at the squealer? Is losing your temper at him directly good for you? Probably not. The problem is that your anger can start a war. We also know that just the expression of rage itself doesn't prevent heart disease. People who scream and shout often drop dead from stress. Many angry personalities out there are dropping like flies from heart attacks. Acting out your anger doesn't deplete it, it only rehearses it and keeps it alive so you get angrier.

You need to take a few minutes to calm down. Count to one hundred. One thousand! A million if necessary, but simmer down. Review the cause for your anger and ask yourself how best you can deal with the squealer. Should you complain to the boss? Perhaps. Depends on whether you have a toxic boss or not. Some bosses are hopeless at resolving conflict. Let's try direct action. Ask the squealer to meet you in a private room. Don't humiliate him in public. Explain to him that the boss has just bawled you out because he, the squealer, had given him misinformation.

"I want to ask you not to do that again. You don't know the whole story. And even if you do, it is my responsibility to report the problem to the boss. I don't want to have bad feelings between us, and the best way to assure this is for me to talk to you directly about it. So, please, don't do this again."

You are frank and honest, not accusatory. You show your willingness to forgive. This is a healthy response. Try it. You will find that your anger will dissipate more quickly than if you had lost your temper. If squealer cannot receive your direct communication, it is his problem. You've done the healthy thing *for yourself.* The next time, complain to your boss and demand action. If your boss doesn't handle it satisfactorily, go over his or her head. But first try to talk out your feelings in a calm, rational way.

What ways are *not* acceptable for expressing your feelings?

- To have a temper tantrum, shout, scream, or throw things
- To stuff your anger and not confront it

- To blame others for your anger
- To hold on to your resentment after you have confronted your antagonist
- To overcontrol your feelings so that they never get your attention

To move a more functional coping style into the workplace, we have to cultivate greater openness to the expression of feelings. Workers need help in recognizing the causes of frustrations and anger. While many unpleasant feelings can be exaggerated through faulty thinking, the freedom to feel emotions can relieve stress and make everyone easier to work with.

Are You Healthy?

We often overlook how important it is for us to be physically healthy if we are going to be effective in the workplace. A healthy body maximizes our ability to deal with problem people, unreasonable deadlines, and troublesome bosses. Your mind will think more clearly if your body is healthy. So strive for physical health as a prerequisite to mental well-being.

Here is a brief test of whether or not you are attending to your body's needs. Answer the statements with a 0 for *never*, 1 for *sometimes* and a 2 for *often*.

SCORE

_____ 1. Do you get enough sleep so that you wake up feeling rested and full of energy?

_____ 2. Do you know what your blood pressure is?

_____ 3. Do you take regular vacations?

_____ 4. When you are upset can you express your feelings?

_____ 5. Can you do without caffeine to pep you up or energize yourself?

_____ 6. Do you eat a balanced diet, high in fiber, low in fats and cholesterol?

_____ 7. Do you exercise regularly?

_____ 8. Do you have regular physical check-ups?

_____ 9. Can you laugh at your own mistakes?

_____ 10. Is your smoking and drinking under control, or do you avoid them altogether?

_____ TOTAL

If your score is above 15, you are probably in excellent physical health and know how to take care of yourself. If your score is between 10 and 15 you are reasonably healthy and self-caring, but could do with some improvement. Look at the questions you answered 0 or 1, and make some changes in your life. Below 10 spells trouble. The lower your score, the greater is your risk of developing health problems. You are definitely sacrificing your health for your career. A score below 5 means *get urgent attention* and make some dramatic and immediate changes in your health habits.

Are You Emotionally Healthy?

Emotional healthiness is not easy to define, let alone measure. However, several qualities are consistently found in healthy people. Rate yourself on the following checklist, giving yourself a score of 0 if you *never* feel that way, a 1 if you *sometimes* feel that way, and a 2 if you *often* feel that way.

SCORE

_____ 1. Do you know how to handle the losses of life that inevitably come your way?

_____ 2. When you are criticized, do you keep a balanced outlook and avoid punishing or rejecting yourself?

_____ 3. When you feel angry, can you readily admit your feelings to yourself or others?

_____ 4. When you are angry, do you avoid becoming depressed and down on yourself?

_____ 5. Can you resist blaming yourself for mistakes?

_____ 6. When something happens that threatens your self-esteem, can you bounce back and reverse the damage?

_____ 7. When you genuinely do something wrong or harmful, can you own it and ask for forgiveness?

_____ 8. When someone forgives you can you let it go and stop feeling guilty?

_____ 9. Can you celebrate the accomplishments of others without feeling unusually envious?

_____ 10. Can you behave in a loving way toward people you don't like or who reject you?

_____ TOTAL

If your score is above 15 (the higher the better) you are a remarkably healthy person, assuming, of course that you have met the one remaining qualification for healthiness: *honesty!*

A score between 10 and 15 shows reasonable healthiness, but below 10, you are showing signs that you are not so healthy. The lower your score, the greater is the urgency with which you need to address your emotional well-being.

5 | Toxic Bosses

Leaders don't inflict pain—they bear pain.

The first responsibility of a leader is to define reality. The last is to say thank you.

Max De Pree, former chairman and CEO,
Herman Miller, Inc.
Leadership Is an Art

"HE'S THE BOSS FROM HELL." Cynthia's eyes filled with fear as she said it. "Attila the Hun is a teddy bear compared with my boss."

Cynthia has a good job in movie production and knows many TV and Hollywood celebrities. She gets a generous salary, nice perks, and her work is exciting, all reasons why she doesn't want to change jobs. The only problem is her boss's behavior. He is a classic tyrant: temperamental and erratic. He excuses himself by saying, "That's just what we artistic types are like." Yes, he is creative. Yes, he is a genius in his work. The movie business is not for thickheads or left-brain, unimaginative types. But Cynthia's boss uses his creativity as an excuse to behave as he wishes. He is disorganized, makes unreasonable demands on her, and then withdraws for hours or even days so that she has no one to guide her through the zillion decisions that have to be made. Most upsetting for Cynthia is that while her boss expects her to make these decisions, he is never satisfied with the results. "I have yet to hear him say, 'You did the right thing.' Every decision I make is criticized. He flies off the handle, even screams at me, and then expects me to just forget it and excuse him because 'it's my style!'" Cynthia can't go over his head because the top brass is afraid of her boss. His Caligula-style terror works upward as well as downward. So Cynthia just takes it.

But it is beginning to take its toll on her. Because of the constant tension she is beginning to make real mistakes. She checks everything twice and this is slowing her down. She's letting deadlines slip by with serious consequences. Now her boss is beginning to have real cause to blame her. The stress is taking its toll on her body.

Cynthia is not alone when it comes to suffering at the hands of a "boss from hell." Surviving your job will often depend on your skill at knowing how to handle a problem boss. And since one typically does not learn how to do this in college, I thought it would be helpful for me to provide some guidance here. This chapter, then, will focus on helping you understand what makes a boss toxic, how such a boss is different from a healthy boss, the effect that a problem boss can have on you, and then give some practical suggestions on how you can handle a problem boss and change your working relationship for the better. A tall order? Not really. Just a little understanding can often go a long way to creating a happier workplace for yourself.

WHEN YOUR BOSS DOESN'T LIKE YOU

Toxic bosses don't have to be alcoholic, incompetent, or tyrannical to be problems. They can appear to be quite normal on the outside. Sometimes the toxicity arises out of the chemistry of your relationship. Something in you does something in her or him that starts something going between the two of you. It can happen insidiously. Your boss treats you well at first. Then things change. While others are treated well, you seem to be the one with the problem. No one else is complaining about bad-boss behavior— just you. So you begin to think you are the problem.

Sharon often comes home from work feeling frustrated these days. Tonight is no exception. She flops onto her bed exhausted and tells her family, "Fix your own dinner. I've had it!" Dad and the kids are puzzled—again. What's going on?

For two years she has been a researcher for a large manufacturing company. After analyzing how the company can take advantage of a change in the tax law, she has come up with some creative ideas. Two weeks ago she sent a memo to her boss describing her findings and making recommendations that could save the company many thousands of dollars. "I haven't had time to read it yet," was the response when Sharon asked her boss whether she could implement her recommendations.

"Another brush-off," Sharon said to herself. "What do I do now?" She wished she had the courage to complain to the branch manager. She knew that top management would jump at her ideas. Why doesn't her boss? Her boss has never acknowledged her creativity. "Some other time," is all she gets from her when she tries to talk about her ideas. So her memos have gotten longer and longer. Sharon suspects that the problem may be related to her boss's jealousy. She has also noticed that her boss has begun to assign her more humdrum chores. Even the professional journals that circulate through the office have been removed so that Sharon doesn't have access to the latest developments in her field. Sharon spotted this and spoke up, but it didn't help the relationship with her boss.

What Sharon couldn't figure out was "why me?" No one else in the office got her treatment. She had never had problems with a boss before. She knew that she was a hard worker. She had never been disrespectful and certainly never inappropriate in her dealings with her boss.

I had judged Sharon to be a fairly healthy person, not defensive or unpleasant. She did seem a little overzealous about her work, but why would a boss resent that?

As we explored her situation I became convinced that the problem was not hers, but her boss's. Previous bosses had liked Sharon. There had to be a straightforward explanation for why this job had turned sour. And there was.

Her boss felt threatened by Sharon. The boss had had a brilliant career. She was considered to be extremely intelligent, creative, and on the ball. Still only in her thirties, she had never run up against any competition. She had been so brilliant that she never had to worry about being eclipsed—until Sharon showed up. Suddenly, this normally calm, tolerant, understanding supervisor found herself challenged. The younger Sharon matched her in wits and wisdom. The boss didn't know how to respond so her natural mind did the natural thing: it became jealous. And in fairness to this supervisor, she did not know how to deal with this intrusive emotion because she had never experienced it before.

The jealousy accounted for the differences in treatment between

Sharon and the other researchers. The jealousy accounted for why Sharon's creativity was ignored, why her memos never got a response, why the journals were surreptitiously removed, and why her boss avoided her.

"How can I get her to like me?" Sharon asked pleadingly.

"Wrong question," I replied. "Liking has nothing to do with it. What we have to work on is finding a way to get your boss to respect you without feeling threatened. We have to help her overcome her jealousy. It's just possible that you are feeding it unwittingly."

Sharon and I began to strategize a new way of relating to her very competent boss. Rather than trying to be self-reliant and never approaching her boss until she had worked out a whole strategy, we talked about how Sharon could approach her boss for guidance *before* she ran off with an idea. This, I told her, would communicate her respect for the boss's expertise and superior experience. Sharon was honest to admit that she had tried to be self-reliant. She was part of a team and she needed to behave like a team member.

"If you want respect, give respect." I suggested. "Don't expect to be pals with your boss. Role differences make this impossible. Build an alliance. Become a team player with your boss. Instead of saying, 'Here is my conclusion and recommendation,' say, 'Can I run my conclusion and recommendations by you so that I can check out whether or not I'm on the right track?'" Such an approach is not dishonest. It recognizes that wisdom often comes from experience, not intellect, and that one knows more as a boss than when one is not. It is presumptuous to think that you know everything when you are not privy to important information or company policy. Sharon had neglected to respect her boss's role and was slowly turning her into a toxic boss.

The strategy paid off. Respect given brought respect reciprocated. The boss's jealousy turned to support and admiration. An enemy had become an ally.

WHAT MAKES A BOSS TOXIC?

A boss can be dysfunctional for many reasons. Many bosses are tyrants because they have had damaging or traumatic experiences.

These have shaped their personality and turned them into bitter or resentful people. Pain can leave a residue of dysfunctional tendencies. Others are jellyfishes and have no backbone. They've been shaped this way by genes or bad parenting. Some are perfectionists and drive you crazy with their pickiness.

Every boss is based in a home or personal situation. A painful home life can cause a boss to be unreasonable at work. We all have a tendency to transfer behaviors from our personal lives to our work lives. The more unpleasant one's personal life, the more difficult it is to keep those problems out of the workplace. When one is going through a divorce, for instance, or when a teenage child is having drug problems, one's role as a boss is bound to be affected.

Since being humans means being imperfect, all of us have some degree of emotional pathology. This pathology can affect our work. Bosses with psychological hang-ups such as anger, jealousy, suspiciousness, addictions, and depression can be less effective.

Not every boss deserves to be a boss. Sometimes a competent employee is promoted above her or his level of ability. Authors Lawrence Peters and Raymond Hall state in their book, *The Peter Principle*, "In a hierarchy every employee tends to rise to his level of incompetence."[1] If you keep getting promoted sooner or later you hit the ceiling of your abilities. If you go higher than your ceiling your incompetence becomes obvious. Many bosses rise above their level of competence. Since demoting is difficult for most organizations, these bosses can stay in their positions for many years.

Some bosses are attracted to bureaucracy. They worship company policies. They are sticklers for protocol and resist change. They love detail and paperwork. They are rigid and supercautious. They work "by the book" and drive others crazy.

Bosses are not superhuman. They are ordinary people who have the same needs as anyone else. They need respect and wish to be effective. It's not easy to be a boss today. Competition is intense and the rewards are not always that great. And many of their workers are not exactly pussycats either.

WHAT MAKES A GOOD BOSS?

In chapter 3, I discussed management styles; here I want to pinpoint specific qualities that characterize first-rate managers. *There are many good bosses* who are healthy, functional, and a joy to work with. They draw out your good side and make you feel energized, hopeful, competent, and happy. When they ask you to go the extra mile you gladly go two. In fact, this is a good test of how good a boss you've got: Are you willing to overextend yourself when asked?

In their book *Problem Bosses*, Drs. Mandy Grothe and Peter Wylie write, "Good bosses are all alike; every problem boss is a problem in her or his own way."[2] Since good bosses are easier to describe, let's begin with them.

What are the characteristics of good bosses?

- They are decisive, but democratic.
- They are strong, but respect the strength of others.
- They are organized, but flexible.
- They are sensitive, but objective.
- They show they care, but control their sympathies.
- They are hardworking, but know how to relax.
- They are ambitious, but their ambition extends to everyone on the team.
- They are principled, but know when to bend.
- They can be humorous when appropriate and serious when appropriate.
- They are fair while holding others accountable.

What, by contrast, characterizes toxic bosses?

- They are autocratic and tyrannical—the bullies of the workplace.
- They avoid conflict and tough decisions.
- They overreact, and blow off at slight provocation.
- They blame others and don't own up to their own mistakes.
- They are highly prejudiced, racist, or sexist.
- They are compulsive and demanding.
- They overcontrol and tend to be rigid.
- They cannot delegate, yet blame others for their failures.
- They can be super-moralistic and judgmental.

If your boss doesn't seem to have any of these characteristics, one very effective test can be used to determine whether he or she is toxic: If you are made to feel afraid, insecure, belittled, or demeaned, or if you are humiliated, or have to put up with unpleasant insinuations or unwanted advances, you have a toxic boss. Furthermore, if you are left to struggle alone in your job with little support or guidance, or if you get little help in coping with such problems, you have a toxic boss.

A TOXIC BOSS CAN LEAD YOU TO AN EARLY GRAVE

A lousy boss can kill your happiness, destroy your self-esteem, suffocate your individuality, poison your mind, threaten your sanity, and dead-end your ambitions. Bad-boss behavior seems to be on the rise. In a recent study of seventy-three managers conducted by the University of Southern California, nearly 75 percent of the participants reported having had difficulty with a supervisor.[3] Increasing pressure on managers due to restructuring and cutbacks is bringing out the worst in them and they are taking out their frustrations on workers as never before.

With bad-boss behavior on the rise, we are also seeing a rise in the work-related stress disorders. If you're stressed out at work, your problem may be a lousy boss. Poor supervisors are a chief source of workplace stress, according to a survey by the St. Paul Fire and Marine Insurance Company, one of the nation's largest medical liability insurers. In its study of 215 companies, friction with supervisors was found to lower productivity, diminish quality and increase absenteeism.[4] Furthermore, of the employees who claimed to have a bad supervisor, 76 percent said coworkers talk about leaving the company, 68 percent said they are tired during the workday, and 65 percent indicated their productivity could be improved. A bad boss can bankrupt a good company!

A toxic boss triggers excessive work stress through failing to supervise workers. This increased stress can cause many pain syndromes (headaches, backaches), gastrointestinal disturbances (diarrhea, chronic stomach problems), and heart disease (elevated blood pressure and cholesterol), and loss of sleep. Also, job stress is often believed to weaken the body's immune system, so that serious diseases like cancer can accelerate.

But stress disease does not take its toll only on the body. As I will show in chapter 11, friction with your boss can cause disharmony and misery for your family and other relationships. Contrary to popular belief, studies have shown that problems at work are more likely than personal problems to have a negative effect *both at work and at home*.[5] People take their job problems home with them. In some cases they drive them to drug or alcohol abuse or other harmful habits. They can lead to the break-up of the family.

THE DOWNWARD SPIRAL

How boss-induced job stress can have a downward spiraling effect is alarming.

In her early thirties, Anna has held several jobs since graduating and has always been complimented for her thoroughness and accuracy as an accountant. This quality got her a job in a large manufacturing company.

She was recruited by the personnel department and did not meet her boss until the day she started working. But from the moment she saw him she realized she had made a mistake.

All went well for the first week. Then her boss asked to see her work. He went over it with a fine-toothed comb. He didn't find mistakes, but the manner in which he scrutinized her work unnerved her.

Anna went away feeling a little unsure of herself. She began to check everything twice and to hesitate before taking routine steps which she had performed for years. Result? Her work slowed down. Her boss noticed and took the opportunity to comment about it. Upset, Anna tried to work faster again but in rushing made more errors. Her boss caught them immediately. This was what he was waiting for. He drew them to her attention and said he would have to place a report in her file.

By now, Anna's head was reeling. She began to feel dizzy at work and could feel her stomach knot. She doubted her competence and her confidence eroded. Her performance dropped below her ability and she lay awake nights worrying, making matters worse. "If I blow this job it will go on my record. I may never be able to get a good job again." A downward spiral had begun and was out of control. Her toxic boss was trying to destroy another worker. Turns out he had made a habit of this!

Well, he didn't quite succeed with Anna. The personnel department intervened just in time. They had observed this destructive pattern several times in her supervisor and had become convinced he was a serious problem for the company. He was fired.

But it took Anna a long time to recover her confidence. Just a few weeks of toxic treatment by a dysfunctional boss undid eight years of confident skill-building. Such can be the power of a destruction-minded boss.

What could Anna have done? What if the personnel department had not been on the ball and she had been left to fight her own battle?

STRATEGIES FOR DEALING WITH A TOXIC BOSS

Every work situation is different. Toxic bosses differ also. The strategies about to be outlined may not perfectly fit your situation but can serve as guidelines. You may want to talk to a counselor before attempting to develop your strategy. This will help you to keep your goals realistic and to confront your own contribution to the toxic relationship.

Confront your helplessness. Among the debilitating effects of a bad-boss relationship are that it shuts down your mind, stifles your creativity, and causes you to believe that you can do nothing to change it. Most employees with a problem boss, therefore, *do nothing*. They become helpless. They settle down and passively accept whatever is dealt them. Even the thought of doing something makes them nervous.

But doing nothing *is* doing something. Usually it is the wrong thing. You complain to your friends. You try to get sympathy from your family. You slack off and this makes for more trouble. You internalize your stress and pay for it in headaches and insomnia.

Now there may be reasons for delaying taking action. Your boss may be retiring in a month or two, so why rock the boat! You may already have another job so you can grin and bear it. But what if you see no alternative? Timing is all-important. Staying in a state of helplessness invariably creates feelings of hopelessness and depression and will not help you to change a bad situation.

So own up to your helplessness. That is a start. It will give you the determination you need to deal with your situation.

Consult a counselor or competent friend. If there is one absolutely essential step, this is it. Before you take any action against your boss, consult an independent outsider, preferably a counselor. That person must be objective and honest with you. Why? So you don't make mistakes. So you own up to your own contribution to the problem. So that you have an unbiased observer's opinion. So that you have someone to support you through the tough times ahead.

Will a spouse do? Not really. Obviously, keep your spouse fully informed, but a spouse is not an impartial third party. She or he will be biased and may even feel threatened by the conflict you are having at work.

Why is a counselor preferred? Because a counselor is trained to recognize pathology and to resolve conflicts. When you are caught in the cross fire of conflict with a toxic boss, you do not have enough distance to understand what is really going on. A trained counselor can help you get in touch with your emotions and confront your anger, so that pain or frustration doesn't sabotage your actions. You can save yourself a lot of misery if you have someone like this to talk to.

Identify the issues. With the help of your counselor, put in writing, as succinctly as you can, the problems you are having with your boss. Boil them down to the essential issues. It's not enough to say "I don't like my boss. Her hair style drives me crazy," or "I am unhappy because this boss isn't as understanding as my previous boss." If you are going to confront a boss, *you must have cause.* You have to be specific. If your problems are due to personal likes and dislikes, or if the clash is due to your personality or lifestyle differences, you really cannot expect your boss to pay attention, let alone change. You may have to change your expectations and learn to accept that your boss is different from you. There is nothing wrong with being different.

Take Patsy for example. She was promoted and moved to another department in her company. Everything went well the first month. Her supervisor seemed competent. He never did anything to offend her. But then she found out that his personal life was a mess. Divorced, he spent most evenings drinking in a local pub and living it up at parties. Patsy despised that sort of lifestyle. Straight-laced and somewhat rigid, she found it difficult to respect her boss. And as she saw more of her boss's lifestyle and heard of escapades through the office rumor mill, she became increasingly dissatisfied and unhappy.

Does Patsy have cause to complain about her boss? Not really. She should try to separate her personal lifestyle preferences and learn to accept her boss for what he is. She doesn't have to condone his private lifestyle, but on the other hand, she should focus on the facts as she experiences them—namely, that her boss is doing his work satisfactorily and what he does in his private life does not affect her directly. Patsy has no complaint.

Our concern here is with the toxic boss whose work is not satisfactory, not the boss who lives a life different from yours. So try to identify the legitimate issues that trouble you. Also try to define clearly a goal you would like to achieve. For instance, one of the following:

- Have my boss stop certain behaviors.
- Create a more harmonious working relationship.
- Transfer to another unit so I can start afresh.
- Have my boss accept me for who I am.
- Force the company or organization to see how toxic my boss is.
- Move my boss from his job to another where he can't harm anyone.
- Remove my boss from his job altogether.
- File a formal grievance against my boss for harassment. Stating a clear goal will determine the specific action you should take.

Planning a course of action. You now have a statement of the problem and a goal you would like to achieve. These will point to several actions that you can take. My purpose here is not to prescribe a course of action but to lay out alternatives. What might they be? You can talk to your boss yourself, talk to your boss with a fellow worker or group present, go over your boss's head and complain, file a formal grievance against your boss, or bypass all of these and ask for a transfer so that you change your boss. What are the advantages and disadvantages of each?

Talking to your boss alone. For some bosses, this is the most straightforward way to deal with your problem. You state your complaint and ask for his or her cooperation in helping you achieve your goal. The problem is that this strategy only works with healthy bosses, and by definition toxic bosses *are not healthy*. They become defensive. They don't like criticism, especially the "constructive kind." They don't problem-solve very well; they can be dishonest and later misrepresent what you say; they can be vindictive and make you pay for your forthrightness during your working life. But if you are convinced that your boss will listen and respect your concerns, try this approach. If your boss is a real tyrant, don't give this strategy another thought.

Talking to your boss with a fellow worker present. This feels a little better. At least you have a witness present who can verify what you say. There is safety in numbers, so, if several of you go to the boss with the same complaint you will get an even better hearing.

There is a snag, however. The boss may feel ganged-up on, so this strategy works only if you make it clear your goal is to create a more harmonious relationship. Also, you must have confidence that your boss is capable of changing. Many are.

Sometimes this option can be a "first step" in a series of strategies. Give your boss a chance to face up to your complaints. Your boss will be miffed, however, no matter how polite you are, so some preparation is necessary to ensure a satisfactory meeting. How can you do this? Have a meeting with your fellow worker or workers to ensure that all of you are in agreement on the issues and goals. This may not be easy, so give it time. Explain to the group what you have in mind and be willing to let others contribute ideas. If you go into a meeting with no consensus, the whole purpose for the meeting could backfire.

In setting up the conference, keep one rule in mind: *Create no surprises.* A letter to your boss requesting the meeting is probably the best way to start. State clearly what your purpose is and what you hope to achieve. This will prepare your boss for what is to come. Catching him or her off guard will not help your cause.

Throughout the meeting, the rule is: *Don't attack your boss's character.* By all means complain about his or her behavior, but don't attack character, integrity, or motive. You cannot possibly know why your boss does what he or she does. State the facts plainly and simply, such as:

- You criticize too much.
- You don't affirm us.

- You make us feel incompetent.
- You get angry too quickly.
- You don't tell us what you expect from us.
- You communicate indirectly.
- We never see enough of you.
- We need more of your respect.

Try to end on a constructive note. Don't threaten anything. State what it is you would like to see happen. *Then listen.* Ask your boss for feedback and be willing to receive it. It may not be pleasant or what you want to hear, but you cannot ask your boss to change if you're not willing to change also.

As you close, ask for a follow-up meeting. You need a way to keep the momentum for change going.

If and when improvement does take place, affirm your boss immediately. Your appreciation is a powerful reinforcer for your boss to change. Be generous with it whenever you can.

Going over your boss's head. This is more risky, but if your boss is really toxic, taking the whole office in to confront him may only get you fired. The greater the toxicity, the greater the risk you must take to deal with the problem. Either that—or quit your job.

Whether or not you can go over your boss's head depends on whether there is anyone over his head. If he is married to the company owner, your options are limited. If your boss is the owner, get another job.

Your boss's supervisor may also be toxic. That won't help either. Sometimes toxic bosses clone toxic subordinates as middle level managers. If you complain to your boss's boss about your immediate supervisor you are likely to end up with two enemies.

So if you're going to go over your boss's head you need to pick the right upper level manager to go to, and this position differs from company to company. If you have a personnel department, talk to its manager. Perhaps there's a hierarchy. Your supervisor has a middle level manager who is bossed by a division manager who in turn comes under a vice-president. So do a careful review of all the bosses above you. Ask questions. Find out who is the healthiest and has a reputation for listening. Someone higher up may give you a better hearing and call for more prompt and equitable action than someone lower down.

Again let me state a rule: *Don't complain to anyone you know will not listen.* Choose someone with a reputation for fairness and who has the power to effect change.

When you've chosen the boss to whom you want to express your complaint, prepare your case as thoroughly as possible. No one is more of a turn-off than a waffler. Make notes so you will stick to your point. Keep your presentation short. State your complaint and goal succinctly. Then let your boss ask clarifying questions. Wherever possible, set down your issues in writing. Compile a folder of supporting documents (memos, evaluations, notes) that clarify your concerns. Don't make it bulky. Remember that managers are busy and don't want to use time to read lengthy reports. They like information in "digest" form because it can be assimilated quickly.

Here again share your feelings about your job and your toxic boss, but *do not attack* anyone's integrity or motives. Don't get angry. Focus on behavior.

Finally, be prepared for the worst. If you succeed, count your blessings, but confrontations can backfire. Unless you are willing to accept that your complaint may be rejected and you will then have to work in an even more unpleasant environment, consider some other action, including finding another job. If you believe that your complaint is legitimate and that someone in upper management is fair and open to receiving information that will improve the organization—go for broke!

Filing a formal grievance. Most companies or organizations have procedures for filing a formal grievance against bosses, as well as fellow workers. Such procedures are usually set out in your company's personnel policy handbook. If no such policies exist where you work, then pushing for their creation is perhaps your first step.

(In some cases of toxic treatment, such as racial or sexual harassment, legal action is possible through the courts or government agencies. This course of action is dealt with in chapter 9.)

In their book *Problem Bosses*, Drs. Mandy Grothe and Peter Wylie make suggestions about when you should take a formal, or even legal, stand against your boss:[6] Refining some of their suggestions, I advocate filing a formal grievance when:

- You have been unjustly treated and neither your boss nor anyone above has been willing to take action.
- Your boss is engaging in illegal, immoral, or unethical activity.

- Filing a formal grievance is the last course open to you.
- Upper level management fails to act on information you have provided that something dangerous or illegal is going on.

The label "whistle blower" has a derogatory connotation, almost as if the label itself has been created to discourage traitors to a company's illegal practices. But "whistle blowers" serve an important function in an often evil world. Some bad-boss behaviors may need to be exposed because they have the potential to harm. While some may blow the whistle only when they are aggrieved and want revenge, many, if not most, do so out of concern for honesty and safety. These courageous workers deserve medals. And bosses who cheat or put people's lives at risk deserve the consequences that follow. So don't be afraid of the label "whistle blower."

The bottom line is to ensure that you survive the grievance procedure. Otherwise, what is the point? It is never an easy process. Companies differ widely in their commitment to justice through these procedures. Healthy companies provide fair hearings with guarantees of no reprisals. Truly unhealthy ones can be downright abusive.

In any case, don't become over-involved with "winning." One seldom "wins" in the sense of being totally satisfied with a grievance outcome. Since some disappointment is inevitable, don't allow your ego to become too invested in winning.

Also, beware the danger of becoming too invested in revenge. You've been hurt so it's natural that you want to hurt back. But watch your motive in filing a grievance. Focus on the need for change, not your desire for revenge. Getting revenge never helps you to become a healthier person; it only teaches you to seek gratification through revenge.

And be prepared to be overwhelmed. You may be fighting a whole department, not just your boss. Since you may feel very intimidated, build a support group you can talk to often about how you are doing.

Be prepared for your grievance to backfire. You may have to face counter-grievance charges or answer unpleasant questions. Don't be surprised if your integrity or performance is challenged. If you've done your homework well, you must have some justification for your grievance.

Be prepared to fight for your rights. The more toxic the company, the more it will see your grievance as a threat. But then again, the more toxic the company the more likely you should consider moving on anyway.

Be prepared to lose. Don't wrap your self-esteem in your grievance. Leave it outside the room when you go into a hearing and don't let the counterattacks or the outcome erode your self-image. This is hard. When we don't get our way, our egos take it as personal rejection. Let it go. You've tried your best, but didn't get through. It's not a race where only one side wins. If you "lose," then the whole company has lost, too. It has lost out on integrity and destroyed some of the goodwill of other employees. They will some day reap what they have sown.

If you do decide to stay, go back to your job and do the best you can. Your conscience is clear!

Ask for a transfer. Finally, a course of action open to you is to bypass all complaint or grievance procedures, and ask for a transfer to another unit, department, division or company. Obviously, this option isn't available to you in a very small company. But for many, especially in government work, it is a viable option.

You should consider it when you cannot afford to take any risks. You may be a single parent who struggled to get a job that gives you flexible time, and now you find that your boss is a tyrant. If you lose this job you could be out of work for a long time.

You should also consider it when you are uncertain whether the problem is your boss's or your own. You may be caught in a classic "personality conflict." Your boss could resemble a parent and you find that you cannot stop projecting parent-type feelings on your boss.

Another provocation could be when you are troubled by your boss's lifestyle. His or her lifestyle may not affect his work, but if you cannot stop being obsessed over it, maybe you should move on. Your respect for your boss is being eroded. It would be better for you to transfer.

Finally, consider a transfer when you've had a personal relationship with your boss that has deteriorated. For example, you may have dated your boss for a while, believing you would marry and leave your job. Now the engagement is off. Can you go back to your old relationship? Not easily. Perhaps it would be better if one of you transferred.

These are just some examples of why you could want to move to a different job and boss. You may have long service and good prospects in your company, so why would you want to throw those assets away? Consider, instead, a transfer.

If you decide to make a fresh start within your company, study your options. Ask yourself, "What kind of boss do I want? What unit appeals to me? What sort of work do I really want to do?"

Consider taking a temporary demotion to effect an improvement. If you are initiating a change, you are more likely not to repeat a mistake by stepping back and taking time to process what has happened. If all goes well, you will regain your status in your new situation. The retreat should be only temporary.

Talk to the personnel manager or whomever can authorize the change. In requesting the transfer, don't run down your present boss. Don't reveal details of your conflict unless necessary. Merely make your request and see what options are available. Too much information about your dissatisfaction may work against you. Everyone is entitled to a change or greater challenge. Present your request in those terms.

Finally, don't be in a hurry. If another job is becoming vacant, but not for a while, be prepared to wait to get what you want. Don't jump at the first opportunity. Don't believe "a bird in the hand is worth two in the bush." Be sure the job you take is what you want.

DEALING WITH A YOUNGER BOSS

One special type of worker-boss relationship deserves special attention here, because it is becoming increasingly a problem. The problem is not boss toxicity; it is a relationship problem. In other words, neither you nor your boss may be toxic but the relationship is. The problem? Your boss is younger than you are!

The longer you work and the older you get, the more likely you will end up with a boss younger than you. Piece of cake? No way. Younger-than-you bosses can be a real problem. When you are young and still inexperienced, it is easy to become insecure and threatened by older workers. Daniel Defoe said, "All men would be tyrants if they could," but I think this applies especially to young bosses who are threatened by experienced workers. They may respond by becoming "bosses from hell." They throw their weight around. They insist on compliance to their every instruction. They are unnerved by criticism, and woe betide anyone who questions their lack of experience! The truth is that they *are* short on experience and long on defensiveness, so their management style can readily deteriorate into heavy-handedness.

But there's another side to this story. Older workers can be a real problem for young bosses. True, young bosses don't have the experience but there is usually a good reason why they are now in charge. Special qualities or qualifications have indicated to someone higher up that they are the persons for the job. So why don't older workers just accept this and get on with the job? Rhetorical, of course. They resent younger bosses because they are younger. Youth is valued over experience in many fields. They develop a deep-seated resentment at taking orders from someone who is just a "pip-squeak." They feel like their son or daughter is bossing them around. And there is always jealousy! "Why was I never given the opportunity?"

So it is natural for older workers to have problems, at least initially, when a younger boss takes over. If the young boss is worth his or her salt, he or she will understand this reaction and allow for a period of adjustment. Of course, if your boss is not only young but dysfunctional, then you must deal with him or her as you would any bad boss.

The problem is more likely to lie in the way you interact with your new boss, so let's focus on how you can deal with a youthful boss you don't respect. Let's look at the sober reality of your own aging and at the "chemistry" of such a work situation.

There has to be a reason why this person is now the boss. With rapidly changing technologies, younger and more recently trained workers, especially in the professions, have the information edge. They are now up-to-date. Furthermore, an organization has to look to the future. Youth must have its turn. With the "graying" of America, we have to make room for younger workers in leadership positions or else a whole generation could pass through the workforce and never have a turn at bat! Their leadership potential would be lost.

Try to understand why you feel resentful, why your behavior is so resistive. Unconscious feelings can get you fired! Are you angry because you were passed over for promotion? Are you jealous because someone else is making better progress than you? Do you feel envious and wish you could also get a break? Get these feelings into the open. It will speed up your adjustment to your new boss.

Avoid saying, "We used to do it another way," or "When so-and-so was here, we did it better." Comparing the old with the new is a sure symptom that *you* are getting old. The sooner you "get on board" with the new reality of your job life, the sooner you will recover your equanimity.

As we get older we can develop fears of aging and therefore develop prejudices against youth. We don't like what we see in the mirror, and take it out on upstarts who couldn't possibly know more than we do. As older persons, we don't like being stereotyped so let's not stereotype youth. We were young once and the world survived our leadership, and I am sure that the boomers will do as well.

By communicating that you understand how difficult it is for a young boss to take over an operation filled with older workers you can go a long way to preventing a toxic situation from developing.

Return your focus to your responsibilities and stop being obsessed about the youthfulness of your new boss. Doing your job well will keep your esteem up. So even if your new baby-boss turns out to be a brat, you can still take pride in a job well done.

To sum up, bosses are not unlike the bossed. Both managers and those they manage are human and therefore fallible; both can be functional and dysfunctional. Some bosses seem heaven-sent—others, hell-sent. Whether you are a manager or one of the managed, your challenge is to strive for working relationships that rise above the potential for toxicity that exists in every human being.

The Seven Deadly Sins of Toxic Bosses

1. Failing to keep in touch with the grass-roots workers in the organization.

2. Using fear to motivate workers to greater productivity, rather than respect and affirmation.

3. Not understanding that their primary responsibility is to guarantee that their workers succeed, not just themselves.

4. Being blind to the unique gifts of those who work for them, and not affirming the value of diversity.

5. Not giving priority to the growth of their employees so that they stagnate and lose motivation.

6. Failing to foster the free expression of feelings so as to create an open and safe workplace.

7. Failing to say "thank you" for a job well done.

CHAPTER

6

Dealing with the Crazy-Makers

Deep in every healthy person's heart simmers a longing to be a good person. A pretty good person, at least. Lewis B. Smedes
A Pretty Good Person

All men would be tyrants if they could.
Daniel Defoe

WHETHER YOU ARE a manager or a worker, sooner or later you will be confronted with this question: "How do I deal with this problem person?"

Such people are all around us. Companies revolve around personalities, not routines, and given the law of averages, every mix of people will have its share of difficult workers. Stand back and observe, wherever you are employed. They are there, above you, beside you, and below you. They breathe the same air you do, share your office, and get paid with the same money. If you want to stay sane you must not only be able to recognize toxic people, you need some basic skills in how to deal with them. This chapter is about developing those skills.

Some years ago, when I was still an engineer, I had a hellish time with a colleague. Engineers are not exactly the world's most sensitive and affectionate of God's creatures. This particular engineer was bullheaded and obstinate, and I'm being polite! You couldn't get through to him with ordinary words. He would just push past you and ignore your instructions. He was nevertheless a brilliant engineer, so we put up with his peculiarities, suspiciousness, and anger.

I lay awake at night wondering how to get through to him. And then one morning, without premeditation on my part, I lost my cool and lit into him verbally. Like the knockdown, drag-out fights of the old westerns, I blasted him with words. He blasted back. He nearly hit me several times, but fortunately, restrained himself. I told him exactly what I thought of him. No mincing of words, no holding back on my emotions, we went one-on-one. I didn't back off an inch. Slowly he began to settle down and became quiet.

When the verbal dust had settled I felt we had really communicated. He had tested my limits and knew how far he could go. From that day on I felt respect and support from him. Never again did he resist me. We slowly became friends despite his eccentricities.

Intense emotional exchanges like this are often quicker and more effective in breaking down toxic barriers. The problem is you can't orchestrate them. When you do they are artificial and ineffective. You can learn an awful lot about someone in just a few minutes when you are totally honest. With some toxic people it's the only way you can get through.

Let me hasten to add that I do not advocate a knockdown, drag-out verbal fight to resolve all problems. It worked in my case because it was spontaneous. If I had carefully premeditated and planned the encounter, it would have blown up in my face. Fortunately there are other less drastic strategies that are amenable to forethought.

THE PROBLEM IS PEOPLE

It's true, dysfunctional people are capable of unsettling even the most confident among us. But all people present challenges, even the most ordinary. The workplace is not only about work, it's about people. It's a life all by itself, lived out in close proximity with others.

We are not born with an inbuilt set of instructions on how to relate to one another. We have no gene for connectedness or affinity. Everything we need to know about relationships and getting on with one another we have to learn. And those who teach us, our immediate family, don't always do a good job. Work organizations do not have training programs for new employees in how to overcome dislikes and awkwardnesses. Companies have volumes of manuals on the do's and don'ts of making a sale, signing a contract, or negotiating a settlement, but nothing about how to subdue a jackal of a person who is on your tail merely because he's taken a dislike to you. You're on your own! That's why psychotherapists like myself are able to make a living—being on your own isn't always enough.

One prominent author, Don Capp, once wrote about management that after years of surviving the company trenches he crawled out with one overriding conclusion: "You may start your white collar career as a vital, healthy, and optimistic human being, but you'd be well advised to armor-plate your insides if you hope to stay that way!"[1]

Rather pessimistic, but it reflects the reality of work life: getting along with toxic people isn't easy. This chapter is about how to develop an armor plate. And you need it not only for dealing with the seriously disturbed persons you will have to cross swords with every day but for run-of-the-mill folks as well. Why? For the simple reason that people are flawed and unpredictable. They have learned their relationship skills from flawed and unpredictable parents. A workplace can be crazy-making not only because a boss is a problem or because it is full of dysfunctional people, but because ordinary people don't know how to get on with each other.

Excluding the very disturbed boss or dysfunctional company, the average worker experiences more stress from relatively average people than from anything else. The machine that breaks down doesn't cause a headache; the way people respond to the breakdown does. Sartre said it: "Hell is other people!"

Now I don't want to sound like someone who is really down on humanity, because I'm not. People are also the source of life's joys. The unhappiest among us are the lonely and isolated. My point is simply to hold up the mirror of reality and to make sure you see the workplace for what it is: a place where you don't get to choose who you spend your life with, unlike marriage, where you do get to choose a mate. At work, "mates" are chosen for you. At least in a family you have genes in common with those you live with. When you're not related, it is difficult to put up with someone who is obnoxious. And in the workplace you may be required to put up with these folks for a very long time.

WHEN DOES THE MINOR BECOME MAJOR?

Perhaps this is the most difficult question of all, and one that you need to resolve as quickly as possible: At what point does a minor aggravation become serious enough to warrant special attention? Is it enough that you don't "like" someone? Does someone have to be really destructive before the label "problem" is appropriate?

Our local newspaper reported two interesting work incidents recently. In the first, a teenager was fired because his car failed an "image" test.[2] He had refused to stop parking his 1977 Olds-mobile near the main building of a prestigious engraving company. Customers typically came in Lincolns and Mercedes, so his car was considered an eyesore. When asked why he had refused to park his car at the rear of the building, the seventeen-year-old said he was just doing what he had been taught: To stand up for what he believed in. He believed that company "image" was not a good enough reason to park behind the building. Is this youth a "problem" worker?

In the second, a police officer was suspended for writing his number sevens European-style, with a line through the down stroke.[3] His superiors were so upset by his refusal to omit the stroke that they ordered him to undergo a psychiatric evaluation. Apparently the typists couldn't get used to them and their complaint was at the bottom of it all. Is this police officer a "problem" worker?

I am sure that in both cases there is more than meets the eye— or the newspaper's report. But I can't help wondering: were these really problem employees or were there personality conflicts at work? I think it is important to make such distinctions. Keep personal likes and dislikes, which have nothing to do with job effectiveness, out of conflicts.

Setting aside personality clashes, early in our understanding of human relationships, experts recognized that some individuals are "different" or "nonconformist" to the extent that it can be predicted they will have difficulties in the workplace.[4]

What differences can interfere with work effectiveness and damage relationships with fellow employees or the company? The following were considered predictors of problems between workers:

Differences in level of cooperation. Typically a workplace requires a high degree of cooperation between workers. Teamwork is always important. Take an assembly-line production unit, for instance. The productivity of a given worker depends on the level of cooperation of the preceding workers, and this affects every step that follows. But the same is true for an office, hospital ward, or engineering project. A worker who refuses to cooperate or indulges occasional impulses to do things differently does not belong on the team.

Differences in intellect or skill. A worker who doesn't match up to the competencies of the rest of the team will also be a problem. A group of writers in a public relations company, for instance, has a right to expect that all members of the team measure up to a consensual standard. If one is less than competent, it affects all of them. The same can be said of a fire-fighting team, a surgical team, an airline crew, or any team.

Resistance to change or growth. Since all humans are flawed, one expectation of a work group is that members change and grow with the group. Everyone is trapped in a web of habit. We are most comfortable doing things the way we have always done them. It's natural to resist change. But when our reluctance to give up old ways impedes the effectiveness of the group, we become a problem.

Lack of respect for the feelings of others. We must never forget that the workplace is populated by people, not machines or robots. A well-known science-fiction movie, *Blade Runner*, portrays the future as including a group of genetically engineered people called "replicates." They look just like humans and work like humans but they differ in one very significant way: they can feel only what they are programmed to feel. Since no love was programmed into their artificial brains, they are cold and calculating. They never feel bad when they hurt someone. In fact, they all go crooked eventually. This is science fiction, but the truth is that many humans have deficient awareness of feelings also.

Real people, unlike the replicates, have complex, unlimited feelings. And every job performed by a human is done out of the depth of all sorts of good and bad emotions. Feelings are always present and cannot be disregarded if you want to create a healthy workplace. Any worker who lacks respect for feelings prevents others from being fully human in the workplace. Our emotions help us cope with our environment. Emotions push us to do something to change our environment. They must never be discounted or disrespected.

These, then, are just a few examples of when being "different" is a problem. When deviating from the norm interferes with work progress, alienates or emotionally abuses coworkers, and damages the effectiveness of a company, this deviation is cause for concern.

Imagine working day in and day out with someone who is depressed, overly anxious, or extremely insecure. This person makes going to work a nightmare for you. You have no idea what is going to happen. Will your colleague burst out crying at the slightest criticism or will he or she refuse to do something or go somewhere because of anxiety? Every day, in factories and offices across the country, scores of workers have to put up with the emotional troubles of fellow human beings.

Now don't misunderstand me. As a psychologist I have often thanked God for those coworkers of my troubled clients who have exercised great patience and tolerance for turmoil in their coworker. I believe that they found it easier to "hang in there" because they knew their colleague was getting help. A coworker, or even an employer, has no obligation to hang in there and patiently tolerate the emotional turmoil of a worker if that employee refuses to get help. Surely this is reasonable!

Of course some behaviors should not be borne. Sexual harassment, prolonged or intense displays of anger, persistent criticism, and life-threatening behaviors have no place at work. You have a right to expect your employer to intercept such abusive behavior. My assumption here, however, is that mostly you are having to deal with reasonably normal, or at least not abusive, behavior. Fits of crying, a brief angry outburst or temporary social withdrawal, should be accepted with some patience if the storm is within normal limits or is justified.

DEALING WITH PROBLEM PEOPLE

Chances are that you are not trained in psychology, so don't play psychologist with a fellow worker. Your aim is not to "cure" anyone. This is especially true if you have had some exposure to psychology. Playing psychologist, when you are not trained for the game, usually means you get too emotionally involved in trying to help a problem person; you get in the way of those who are required to deal with the problem person; you become a compulsive advice giver and don't know when to quit, and you will have it all backfire on you.

This last point is especially important. When you try to help someone with a problem you don't understand *you* will end up with the stress of the encounter. We call this "triangulation," and it is a well-known fact that when you interfere in the life of a troubled person and get drawn into their pathology, you end up with the tension of their problem.

You *can* be very helpful to a problem person, but your effectiveness will depend more on your ability to remain objective and listen, than on your advice-giving interference.

A great risk you take when you give advice is that your involvement can escalate. If your advice fails, you will feel duty-bound to give more advice to offset the failure. Early in my practice as a clinical psychologist, when I was still very green and overly enthusiastic, I gave advice to a patient that cured me of this tendency. I had been seeing an older woman who was depressed. In the middle of a therapy session one day she complained that she had a toothache.

"How long have you had the toothache?" I asked innocently, not realizing I was being triangulated.

"A long time."

"Why don't you go see a dentist?"

"Oh, doctor," she whined, "I don't know a good dentist. Can you recommend one?"

Seemed innocent. Why shouldn't I help her—that was what I was there for!

I gave her the name of a dentist I knew. Mistake! I should have given her the name of a referral agency, or at least several names. I should have told her to ask her friends or just open the yellow pages and grab the first dentist that took her fancy. I didn't. I gave her a name.

Two weeks later, back in my office, she said to me: "That dentist you recommended botched the job. He was terrible. I now have half a tooth. What am I going to do? It hurts worse than before. I can't go back to him because I told him off. What must I do now? You got me into real trouble." The last sentence was said in such a way as to imply that her broken tooth was now *my* problem.

This is what advice-giving tends to do. It sets up the problem as your problem. If your advice fails, *you* are now the problem and if you give further advice, this can fail also. There is no end—better emigrate to a far-off country!

If your advice is successful it won't end either. "I have a brother and he has eye problems. Can you suggest a...." You become Mr. or Ms. Fix-It-All.

Another pitfall to avoid is playing parent to a problem employee. Perhaps you are the manager. You see yourself as a person of power. It feels good to be wanted and it's all too easy to adopt a benign "I'll take-care-of-you" attitude. It strokes the ego like nothing else I know. Overprotection or overdependence has never helped a child, and it certainly won't help a problem employee.

If you have strong codependency traits (which means that you are compelled to "rescue" others at every opportunity) you may also find yourself doing more harm than good. Especially in religious circles, codependency can be rationalized as "love," but it lacks toughness and merely relieves the helper's guilt feelings.

At all times, remind yourself that the person's problems remain his or hers. Try to be understanding, provide a good listening ear, but restrict your advice to pointing the problem person in the direction of getting professional, or at least competent, help.

Let's now turn our attention to some specific problems from which people in the workplace can suffer:

Alcohol. Alcohol has wrecked many brilliant and promising careers. And even when an alcoholic is in recovery, work-related problems may continue.

Alcoholism is one of the "toxic escapes" that some people use when life is not fulfilling. But is work always the cause of the alcoholism? For many years it was believed that work stress promoted problematic alcohol consumption, especially among vulnerable individuals. "Vulnerable individuals" are those who possess few personal and social resources for responding adaptively to work-related stress. Research conducted by the State University of New York Center for the Study of Behavioral and Social Aspects of Health seriously questions this belief. It tested 574 employed adults from age sixteen to sixty-nine years and found no support for the idea that workers drink alcohol to reduce tension or to deal with work stress.[5] It's much more complicated than that. Problem drinking can occur even when there is no stress in a person's life. I am sure that this doesn't imply that alcohol is never used as a tranquilizer or escape. *Other* factors also play a role in alcohol addiction, including biological ones.

But how does one deal with an alcoholic in the workplace? In many respects drug addictions are handled in the same way. You need to work at understanding the problem of addictions. An addiction is not a simple matter of connecting the substance with the brain or any other part of the body. Many "hidden" mechanisms are involved. (See my book *Healing Life's Hidden Addictions*, Servant Publications, 1990.)

Alcoholics Anonymous as well as the U.S. Department of Health have excellent resources available that can help you understand addictive tendencies.

As far as alcoholism is concerned, it is important to understand that there is a difference between the heavy drinker and the alcoholic. The heavy drinker does not let alcohol (or drugs) disturb his or her life pattern or work. Drinking is confined to weekends and is kept under reasonable control.

Once someone crosses the "invisible border" between social and addictive drinking, he or she can never drink normally again. There is no going back, once the addictive process has kicked in. Alcoholism can be arrested by abstinence, but it can never really be "cured."

These are signs of addiction to alcohol:

- The individual drinks more than others at social occasions.
- The individual makes excuses to drink more often ("Boy, am I thirsty. Must have eaten something salty.")
- The individual tries to "cover up" the drinking. *Denial* is very common. A secretiveness develops as one becomes captive to the bottle.
- The addict begins to conceal the alcohol nearby and makes frequent trips to a private place (toilet, etc.) to consume it. You can't always smell it because an addict is very good at covering up with cough drops, breath mints, and so forth.
- At a later stage, alcoholics may have "blackouts." They may pass out, be merely confused, or fail to recall events from the previous day.

- As alcoholism progresses, alcoholics gulp rather than drink. They do not enjoy the process of drinking; they want to get the booze into their system as quickly as possible.
- Most alcoholics show remorse when sober, but strike out when starting to consume. Mood changes, therefore, can be common as the workday progresses and as the alcoholic starts to fill up, often secretly or during lunch.
- When usage is far-advanced, the worker may no longer try to hide the activity. At this stage definite action must be taken before others begin to think that such behavior is tolerated.

The strategy you adopt may be different if you are a coworker rather than a manager. As a coworker, always consult your manager *before* you take any action. However, you may be able to do something before your boss can, simply because a boss may have to wait until there is work interference before acting. Remember, however, that interference with *your* work is sufficient grounds to complain to a boss and to expect that some action be taken.

For yourself, separate out heavy drinking off-the-job from on-the-job consumption. It may be that drinking at home at night might interfere with work the next day but perhaps it doesn't. Your boss is the best judge of this. But no matter how much your colleague drinks recreationally, it is out of bounds for you to interfere.

Also, make a nonthreatening approach to your coworker if you suspect a problem at work. Try to couch it in terms such as "I really am concerned about you. How can I help?" Don't judge. Don't accuse. Don't condemn. You may be able to suggest that he or she see a professional for help.

Finally, keep your ego out of the way. Don't become invested in healing your coworker. Also, you may be rebuffed, so don't let this bother you. If you are right about what you see happening at work, others will see it also. Persuade someone else to join you in making a nonthreatening approach.

If all else fails, inform your superior or personnel office. They ought to know what to do.

Depression. Depression is very common. While many psychological reasons can cause depression (getting fired, death of a loved one, friend moving away, discovering your spouse is having an affair, etc.) biological causes also underlie much depression. The general diagnostic rule is: if no obvious psychological reason exists, depression is most likely due to biological factors. Much depression also results from stress, whether from tension, deadlines, overwork, or conflict.

How can you help? Depressed persons usually are helped by being able to talk about their sadness, so make yourself available to listen. Many lay helpers have difficulty accepting this depression talk. They try to reassure the depressed person or distract him or her from the sadness. *This does not help!* Depression is like an infected wound; it needs to be drained, not covered over. So it takes a special kind of listening to be helpful.

If your coworker suffers from one of the several biological forms of depression, there is hope. Very effective antidepressants are available to treat these depressions. And before you say, "Oh no, not another drug," let me hasten to add that for some depressions, medication is essential. If the depression is psychological, the medication will have no effect—nor will it do any harm.

Also, antidepressant medications are not addicting. Quite the reverse. Sufferers often stop taking the medication too quickly. They don't feel that it does anything—and they are right. These are not tranquilizers that can make you "feel high" in half an hour. Antidepressants take two to four weeks, or even longer, to take effect.

Your role in helping a depressed coworker, therefore, can be summarized as follows:

- Encourage the sufferer to get professional help, then ensure that he or she continues to follow through on this help. A supportive presence is essential even if the treatment is with antidepressants.
- If medication is prescribed, encourage that it be taken and keep reminding the sufferer that it will take several weeks before improvement occurs.
- If after three or four weeks there is no improvement, suggest that the treatment be reviewed.
- Don't patronize the sufferer. The condition is dramatically reversible, so don't treat him or her like a chronically ill person.
- Don't let the depression get to you. You need to maintain a strong, positive, and nonanxious presence. This will reassure your coworker of hope.

- Be on the lookout for suicidal behavior. Talk openly about whether thoughts of death are occurring. Most depressed people think about death as a way out of misery. This is normal. But make sure a friend or spouse is alerted if there is some risk. It is better to be safe than sorry, so don't keep any suspicions to yourself. Alert your boss or call the sufferer's spouse or family if you don't know what to do.

Anxiety problems. Like depression, there are many forms of anxiety as well. Some are psychological (worry, obsessive thoughts, fear of separation, phobias) but many also have biological roots. One of the most rapidly growing problems is clearly a biological disorder. It is called "panic anxiety disorder" and it is considered the fastest-growing disorder today by the National Institute of Mental Health. It is the most common mental health disorder in women; for men, it is second to substance abuse. Stress triggers this disorder, though some people are more susceptible than others.

Panic attacks mimic heart attacks. The person can't breathe, feels a tight band around the chest, and is overcome by fear that something terrible is going to happen. Victims often pass out.

While most of the symptoms are psychological, the problem is a biological one, brought on by too much stress for too long. The brain stops producing its natural tranquilizers and whamo—one day the person starts having panic attacks.

What can you do to help?

Give a lot of understanding. Anxiety sufferers are not weak people. Panic anxiety most commonly hits the strong and competent, but overactive, among us. If you are a hard-driving go-getter, you could be the next victim in your workplace.

Insist that the sufferer get help. Panic anxiety attacks, if left untreated, turn into agoraphobias where the sufferer is imprisoned in his or her home and is unable to leave for fear of the anxiety. Untreated panic disorders can lead to serious incapacitation.

Support the treatment. Almost always a combination of medication and stress management is prescribed. Highly intelligent and formerly high-functioning sufferers of panic anxiety may feel like their treatment is simplistic—but it's not. Very simple biological mechanisms must be restored and the brain's natural tranquilizers rejuvenated. Sufferers need all the encouragement they can get to see treatment through to success.

Don't fight the problem. The sufferer may become quick-tempered, irritable, and fearful. Don't take it personally. Stand your ground, be firm, but don't overreact. Improvement will come sooner or later.

Anger. Anger can be most upsetting. Though anger has its place, it also can grow out of proportion or be unjustified. We all have an obligation to keep our anger within reason and under control, no matter what its cause.

When you are confronted by an angry coworker, face the individual firmly and assert your right not to be treated this way. Often, just standing up to an angry person can bring matters under control. Also, a lot of anger is designed to be manipulative. The display is designed to intimidate you—so don't let it. If you stand up to it you resist the manipulation.

Also, be assertive, but don't get angry yourself. Countering anger with anger only leads to an increased conflict. Often anger in others makes us afraid, and our fear causes us to get angry in return (a primitive defensive response).

Insist, too, that the person go with you to a private room or quiet corner where you can talk. Don't have it out in public. Ask the reason for the anger. Don't be defensive. Just hear what the person has to say. Let him or her ventilate feelings. Examine the explanation. If you are guilty of causing the anger, apologize and close the matter there and then. If you are not guilty, say so and attempt to get understanding of your response.

If you cannot get agreement, suggest that you each try to see the situation differently and leave it there. Suggest that you talk about it again later, when you've both had time to simmer down.

DEALING WITH GARDEN VARIETY DIFFICULTIES

Work can bring out the worst in people. The reason is that we probably spend even more time with coworkers than we do with our families, so our colleagues have much opportunity to see the worst in us.

Difficult people are not necessarily pathological. They may

merely be having a bad experience or they may have some disruptive habits. They may be difficult in one situation but not another, and with some people but not others. Sick or not, they can still cause a lot of crazy-making on the job.

Argumentative people. For example, I am convinced that argumentative people suffer from an addiction. They get a "fix" (probably an adrenaline rush) from picking arguments. Often they like to start an argument, then walk away. I'm not talking about the person who genuinely wants to debate an issue. Argumentative people want more than a debate—they want to fight with words. They bait you. They set you up for a disagreement. They have developed their skill of argumentation and have elevated it to an art form. It is a game as sophisticated as chess. An opening gambit, a simple incident such as dropping a word at the coffee dispenser—and you're hooked. There is a middle game with the arguer trying to pin you down, then the checkmate (in their thinking, that is).

They pick up on the tail end of conversations and say something provocative. They disagree on anything just to get an argument going. The end result is always the same: You get angry, and they walk away smug in their accomplishment.

Most arguers are negative and pessimistic by nature. They have to be, else they would not have much to argue about. This distorts their thinking and fuels their mind with issues to challenge. Many suffer from poor self-images and derive a sense of power by being contentious.

How do you deal with argumentative people? Don't get hooked. Walk away from the argument. Don't reinforce bad behavior. Don't take the bait. When the rope is handed to you, drop it. If you catch yourself defending some belief or issue, stop right there and leave. Just a simple "excuse me" is all that is needed. You don't have to explain anything—your explanation could become the basis of further argument.

Religion is a favorite target for arguers. Enthusiastic evangelists for particular beliefs are often trapped into arguments, believing that since they have the truth they will win. No one wins such an argument. It's a game—and it has no rules. Don't waste your time and breath with an argumentative person.

Jealous people. Jealousy is about being resentfully envious. You want what someone else has got and you resent that you do not have it. It is also about not wanting someone else to have what you don't have. Because there is a fair degree of competitiveness in every work situation (some companies thrive on it) workers can easily become jealous of each other. To be the target of jealousy you just have to be a little bit better than someone else or have your boss give you more attention.

Revenge taking, sulking, and wallowing in self-pity are all "dividend paying" for the jealous person. In some strange way humans derive satisfaction from expressions of bad feelings. The person who is jealous may actually enjoy the experience at your expense.

Most destructive jealousy usually stems from a deep insecurity and a history of damaged self-esteem. Often the jealous person has had a series of unsatisfactory or broken relationships. Loss is difficult. Jealousy for such people can be a way of protecting one's life from further loss.

How do you deal with a jealous coworker? The first strategy is to get closer to the one who is envious. Jealousy subsides when you get closer to someone, because trust grows stronger. Try to understand the underlying insecurity or lack of love in the person's life, and communicate this understanding through loving behavior. A client of mine, who was the recipient of jealousy at work, brought a bunch of flowers occasionally to the office for her coworker. Just a small gesture of friendship and loving concern but the jealousy quickly vanished. It's hard to be resentful toward someone who is treating you lovingly and respectfully.

If this doesn't work, the second strategy is to confront the jealousy head on. This is more hazardous, but what else can you do? Call it for what it is. Bring it into the open every time it occurs. "You're being jealous again. I've done nothing to deserve your envy. Please stop doing this to me." Either the person will knuckle down and be more cooperative, or over time will decide to leave. Just don't feel guilty if the person quits. It was her or his problem, not yours.

Liars. People who tell lies in the workplace can be a serious problem. They get you into trouble and never take responsibility for their own mistakes. You can't trust them, so how can you work with them?

Lying is an interesting phenomenon. People lie regularly. They don't mean to lie, but they do. Even deeply religious and otherwise honest people tell lies occasionally, especially to avoid trouble. How come? Because the mind is unreliable. If you say something often enough to yourself, you come to believe it. When you tell it, then, it doesn't feel like a lie. It feels like the truth. Also, memory distorts things. You think you're telling the truth, only your brain mixed up all the facts. What you think you said was what he said, only he said it after you thought it, so you think you said it. Confusing!

But even if we have convinced ourselves that our version of the story is correct, nature has equipped us with our own built-in lie detector. We call it guilt. Look into the eyes of the child caught with his hand in the cookie jar. What you see is guilt. Not just children, but most adults give themselves away when they lie. All, that is, except the sociopath who has practiced lying all his or her life. Most are inexperienced at lying, however, so their body language gives them away. They squirm. They lack eye contact. They fidget. Somehow they betray their lies.

But accomplished liars, who are real problem people in the workplace, don't have this built-in lie detector. Either they missed out when this equipment was being handed out at birth, or something has gone wrong with the subsequent development of their conscience. Also, with lots of practice, most people can learn to lie— without showing it. Actors can certainly learn to be consummate liars. What about the proverbial used car salesman? (What a terrible stereotype!) But the truth is that if *any* salesperson told you the absolute, honest, nothing-to-hide, but the whole truth, so help them God, about any product, they'd make fewer sales. It is very easy to convince yourself you are telling the truth when you are not.

But what do you do with a coworker who looks you straight in the eye while telling a whopper? No flinching. No touching of the head or face. No twitch in mouth, nose, ear, or cheek to act as a tell-tale sign. And furthermore, the consequences are serious. The lie, if ignored, might get you into trouble.

Your response must depend on whether or not you are absolutely sure about the truth. If you have the evidence that he or she is lying, reveal it there and then and demand an explanation. Problem liars need to be confronted right away. If you give them a little time they can wiggle out of any lie.

When confronting a lie, don't humiliate the person by calling him or her a liar. You may have to demand that they make restitution right away. For instance, if they have lied about you to your boss, insist that you both go immediately to correct the lie.

Courageous assertiveness at the moment of discovery is the best way to respond.

What if you don't know absolutely that it is a lie? Move cautiously since you may be wrong. So ask for proof. Request that you both go and verify the truth. "Can we both go to the boss and check out his instructions again? Please don't be offended. I could be mistaken." Ask for the person's permission, where appropriate, to verify a statement. Or if it is OK, check it out by yourself. When you have absolute proof that the person is lying, then confront it directly.

Selfish people. Some people are so selfish, self-indulgent, self-absorbed and self-seeking, they can be a real problem to even the most unselfish person in an office or workshop. They think only about Number One. Their selfishness runs the gambit from wanting to be the center of attention to demanding that they get preferential treatment. They want the best seat, best desk, best view, best work, best tools, best instruments, and the best rewards. They are a pain because if they get the best once, they want it always.

While selfishness eventually reaps its own cost in unpopularity and rejection, those who must work alongside the selfish person suffer meanwhile. What can you do? *Use diplomacy.* Check out first how others in the workplace feel. If you are the only one who sees the problem as selfishness, then let it be. The problem may be more of a personality conflict. If others agree with you, then try to get the group to agree on a course of action.

The next time the "selfish one" tries to demand preferential treatment, suggest that you have a group or team meeting to discuss the demand. Allow everyone who objects to have a say. Put the matter to a vote. Let consensus decide who gets what.

At a personal level, *learn to be more assertive*. Force yourself to say "no" when the selfish one asks you to do a favor or complete some unpleasant chore. Don't agree to a change of anything, *unless you want it*. If the selfish one says, "You don't mind, do you, if I change places on the roster with you for next week?" (a real set-up often used by selfish people). Respond with, "Yes, I do. I don't want to change, thank you." *You do not owe any explanation for a "no."* Explanations can be challenged. A simple "no" says it all and ends the conversation.

Don't be afraid to offend selfish people. They derive their power from intimidation. Fight back. You will never stop selfishness if you don't offend it sometimes. People who always get their way will, unfortunately, always get upset when thwarted. That is their way of getting their way! Be willing to become bad friends with someone who is selfish. It's a part of being tough with your friendship. Sooner or later they learn that if they want your love, they must be less selfish.

Gossips. Gossips are also members of that not-so-elite group we call "difficult people." Sure, there is harmless gossip—a way of venting frustration. Slanderous gossip, though, can destroy careers and reputations.

Gossip can make nervous wrecks of innocent people. I once was the victim of a gossip who spread an ugly rumor with absolutely no truth to it. Once it was out it could not be stopped. I became paranoid and kept wondering how many people had heard it. Should I risk speaking up to defend myself? If they hadn't heard it, then I could do more damage than if I kept quiet. Trying to deal with malicious and untrue rumors can drive you crazy.

Gossips feed off the mowing down of the reputations of others. They ignore facts and the truth. It's been said that "Superior people talk about ideas. Average people talk about things. Little people talk about other people."

Other people's problems embellished with innuendos are the stuff of gossip. The motive is always to demean someone else or to gloat over someone else's misfortune. What can you do to discourage gossips? Ignore the information being imparted. Suggest that it is only a rumor and that you will go and check it out. Such a threat usually stops a rumor in its tracks.

Frankly and politely, tell the gossiper that you would prefer not to receive the gossip. The gossiper might be offended, but are you not being offended by the gossip? The gossip begins, "Have you heard about Bill?" You reply, "No, but let me tell you about an experience I had last summer."

It may seem cruel to inform the one being gossiped about, but it's better in the long run. The best person to subdue a rumor is the victim of that rumor. He or she can address the gossip directly and demand an apology or restitution. If the gossip fails to respond, legal action always can be taken.

Teasers. As with gossip, teasing has an innocent form as well as malicious. All teasing, though, becomes malicious when taken too far. Ridicule and sarcasm, no matter how playfully applied, are always malicious.

Sometimes a person being teased may be grateful for the attention. It can be a sign of affection. It's nice to be noticed. But if the content and method of the banter is belittling, it becomes harmful and destructive.

Teasing can be an indirect way of attacking another person's character. Comments intended to compliment someone could have more than one meaning. Often it has the effect of ridiculing the other person and is a muted expression of anger. The only judge of whether a jest is hurtful or not is the person being teased. He or she must decide whether to allow this behavior. If you don't like it because it hurts, then put a stop to it.

If you tease other people a lot, then don't expect a lot of sympathy if you ask them not to tease you. Stop your toxic behavior, before you ask others to stop theirs. Also, try to avoid reacting angrily to the malicious teaser. This only reinforces the person's motive. The jab is designed to unsettle you, so don't give the teaser what he or she is looking for. If the teaser is not intending to hurt you in any way, then getting upset may spoil your relationship. The teaser will pull away and not want to relate to you anymore. So respond calmly to all teasing.

Since teasing can be a sign of affection (or at least a sign that the teaser trusts you), receive it from a non-malicious teaser for what it really is. Respond by acknowledging the compliment or affection, even if you tease back. Teasing as an indirect expression of affection is quite appropriate, provided there is also a direct expression. In other words, we should always try to say what we feel directly, not indirectly.

For instance, I might tease one of my daughters who is off on a special outing about a dress because she is looking glamorous and dressed to kill. But is this enough? I try always to say what I mean directly, so at the end of our teasing banter I say it straight: "Honey, you are really looking beautiful tonight. That dress suits you to a T!"

As a responder to affectionate teasing you can help others to be more direct in their expressions by telling them how much you appreciate the affection reflected in their tease.

When the tease is malicious (usually in the form of sarcasm or ridicule), the same rules apply as with affectionate teases: receive it with grace but respond by calling for a direct communication. To the affectionate tease we say, in effect, "You are showing me your affection, now tell it to me directly." To the malicious tease, we say in effect, "You are showing me your anger, now tell it to me directly."

Sarcasm and ridicule, as muted expressions of anger, are always toxic. Feeling angry is not evil. Anger is an important signal that should be heeded. How we express it, however, has great potential for evil. When it comes out in revenge and a desire to humiliate, it is dysfunctional.

So call it what it is. Tell the teaser that you don't appreciate the put-down, implied criticism, or insult. Invite the teaser to say what he or she would really like to say, then take it from there.

Most malicious teasers will just retreat, hurling verbal rocks at you, but you will have made your point, namely, that you are open to discussing any feeling someone might have toward you, but only if it's addressed to you directly. You cannot deal in a healthy way with indirect anger expressed through sarcasm and ridicule.

Difficult people can be disruptive at all levels of the workplace. While a good manager or supervisor can go a long way toward minimizing the crazy-making consequences of a few, every healthy workplace has to learn how to tolerate some degree of dysfunction. A competent manager will try to limit the damage caused by human imperfection.

But there is another important reason why I say this. Some difficult people are only *temporarily* crazy-making. Their emotions may be disturbed by home circumstances, illness, or other ups and downs. And since all humans react emotionally, every one of us, sooner or later, has a turn to bat at the emotionally troubled plate.

If you are functioning well, cooperate with your manager or supervisor in helping those who are temporarily upset. The healing of problems brought on by prolonged stress is dependent upon having an understanding workplace and cooperative fellow workers. Show respect for those who are suffering a transitory emotional upheaval.

Who knows? You may be next!

CHAPTER 7

Your Job, the Pressure Cooker, and Occupational Stress

Pity the workhorse, do not hate him please, for workaholism is a disease. Charles Osgood

The mind is where heart disease begins.
Dean Ornish, heart specialist

TALKING ABOUT STRESS has become fashionable. Everyone likes to complain that they have too much of it, but they don't do very much to get rid of it. You can sell books if you write about it, but people want the good news about it more than they want the bad.

Books on the topic like *The Joy of Stress, Stress for Success, Making Stress Work for You* are popular because they emphasize the positive side of stress. Their message is: "Stress doesn't kill you if you use it right," or "Unless you have a fair amount of stress working for you, you will be worse off than if you have no stress at all." This is what the average person wants to hear. But is it true? Or is someone stretching the truth a little?

Books that put stress in a positive light overlook the seriousness of the problem. They mislead people into believing that simply because they are "enjoying" their work it can't be bad. Whatever stress they have must be good for them. These authors overlook the essential ingredient in all stress disease, namely over-arousal of the adrenal system. Too much adrenaline for too long is bad for you, whether it's caused by exciting challenges *or* tension, fun *or* frustration, amusement *or* anxiety. Your good stress will kill you as

139

surely as bad stress if it continues for too long. My message here is quite simple: *the only stress that is good for you is the stress that is short-lived!*

The distinction between healthy and unhealthy stress is a complicated one. You can't determine which type of stress you are experiencing simply by the degree to which you enjoy or don't enjoy what you are doing. Every person I know who has died young of a heart attack was "enjoying" life right up to the last minute. That crushing sensation in their chest was their first serious warning signal—but it came too late.

The stress that kills us is not always unpleasant. Often it masquerades as stimulating challenges, passionate preoccupations, or thrilling life games. It hides behind our need for adventure, novelty and excitement. Boredom is the antidote for stress, but we have lost our respect for, and tolerance for, anything relaxing. We want excitement, not dullsville. Most of us are addicted to high-octane living. So set aside the books on the positive value of stress and heed the message of this chapter. It could save your life. I know, it saved mine!

WHERE ARE WE HEADED?

Both on the job and in the home, stress is causing trouble. Exhaustion, depression, insomnia, migraines, tension headaches, ulcers, colitis, high blood pressure, asthma, allergies, alcoholism, heart disease, and divorce have been linked to stress. Chronic stress depletes the brain's natural tranquilizers, so anxiety increases and can reach panic proportions, as more and more sufferers are discovering. Stress depletes the brain's natural pain killers, so pain increases in all parts of the body. Stress depletes the body's immune system so we become susceptible to infections and disease. Consequently, we consume tranquilizers, painkillers and antibiotics to replace what the body can no longer provide because it is being forced to cope with the challenges of life in the modern world.

"Stress is running like wildfire through the American workplace and the recession is adding to it," says Peggy Lawless, project director for a new study on workplace stress and burnout conducted by the Northwestern National Life Insurance Company. "American companies have become pressure cookers, with over-stressed employees who are less able to perform their jobs and more afraid to leave them."[1]

The workplace is toxic to the degree that it causes stress disease in workers. Show me workers who have a high incidence of headaches, exhaustion, depression, demoralization, high blood pressure and anger, and I will show you a toxic workplace.

Occupational stress is one of the hottest topics in business and industry today, but until recently the reasons for this were seldom clearly articulated. Companies and organizations lose billions of dollars a year in lowered productivity, absenteeism, and disabilities. Some put the national estimate at over 150 billion dollars.[2] On any given day an average of one million workers are absent from their jobs, primarily because of stress disorders.

And while the direct cost to companies and organizations in terms of absenteeism and turnover is staggering, it pales in comparison with the indirect costs of stress, especially to the worker. Low morale, poor motivation, and dissatisfaction are only a few of the indirect costs that lead to reduced performance.

The assumptions behind the granting of these claims is a legitimate one: The influence of a stressful work environment goes with the worker even after he or she has left the job. Conflict that causes stress doesn't stop its damage when you're away from the office.

While stress-claims can be abused, I don't want that possibility to detract from my primary purpose, which is to address the ways in which a dysfunctional work environment can cause stress disease.

UNDERSTANDING STRESS AND BURNOUT

Most books on stress use the words burnout and stress interchangeably or at least see them as inextricably connected. I don't. Stress and burnout, while sometimes related, are different phenomena. Burnout will be examined in the next chapter.

The roads of stress and burnout are much traveled. But they are separate roads. The road you travel will depend on your personality, the nature of your job, and how the two interact.

In engineering, stress refers to the force exerted upon an object. The opposing force is called "strain." In psychology we use the word "stress" to describe any demand (or force) placed upon the body and mind. The "demand" can be the need to hurry as we run to catch the bus, the irritation caused by a teenager's ghetto blaster, or the anxiety of facing a tax audit. Stress is anything, good or bad, that forces the body to change what it is doing or to go into "emergency mode" to cope with an imposed demand. The body mobilizes itself for action by secreting a variety of hormones.

The external force that causes the stress is called the "stressor." Noise, crowded freeways, deadlines, angry spouses, recalcitrant teenagers, toxic bosses, harassing coworkers, and even Christmas-time are *stressors*. These external forces are not themselves the stress, they cause the stress. How the body and mind reacts to and copes with these stressors determines the stress response. You have the ability to control only your stressors (external forces). Stress (the physical reaction) is the body doing what it is designed to do.

When the demands placed upon the body exceed our limits for coping (and this differs from person to person), stress becomes "distress." The body and mind begin to break. Headaches, ulcers, high blood pressure, anxiety, and depression emerge as signs that stress has become distress.

When distress becomes chronic or permanent, distress becomes stress disease. Cardiovascular disease often is a form of stress disease, the physical consequence of too much stress for too long.

Underlying the body's response to stress is a system that arouses the body. Stressors induce feelings of excitement by releasing adrenaline and other hormones to help us cope with the stress. This "arousal" stirs us to *fight* or *flee*. Normally the arousal subsides after the stressor or demand has passed and we return to a lower state of arousal with lowered adrenaline and a more relaxed mind and body. The adrenal glands play a vital role in this arousal response and are the key to understanding all stress. (See my book: *The Hidden Link Between Adrenalin and Stress*.[3])

If the arousal does not subside, even after the stressor has gone away, a state of *adaptation* follows. As the word suggests, the body "adapts" to the higher state of arousal. It has equipped us to function at this higher level of excitement. When attending a football game, at first the noise and excitement are noticeable. After a while the body gets used to it, shuts down hearing, and "adapts" to the excitement so you no longer notice it, even though your body is in high gear. Adaptation like this keeps the blood pressure high and the adrenaline pumping, long after the need for this arousal has passed. In this way the body moves up the ladder to a new "resting" level. Stress, therefore, slowly moves us to higher and higher levels of resting arousal.

The most important protection that the body and mind can have over stressors is the feeling of being in control. When we lack control, we magnify our stress, which accelerates the onset of distress and stress disease. A sense of control is essential for a low stress life.

BASIC ASSUMPTIONS ABOUT THE STRESS RESPONSE

Research on stress has arrived at four assumptions.[4] If you can grasp them you have all you need to know about how stress works and when it becomes dangerous. These assumptions also point to the strategies needed for coping with stress.

First, our level of stress is directly proportional to the level of our physiological arousal. To put it simply: the greater your body pumps adrenaline, the greater your level of stress.

Second, adaptation or performance under stress diminishes as arousal increases. In other words, contrary to popular opinion, the higher your stress level the less efficient and less effective you become, whether your work is mental or physical. This is why athletes are now being taught how to relax. High arousal is helpful in emergencies, but when sustained, doesn't make you a better performer.

Third, the relationship between stressors and stress affects the entire body and mind. The body is like a long chain of elastic bands joined together, each band representing a part of the body. If you pull on the outside *they all stretch*. If one band represents the brain, another the stomach, and so on, and you become stressed, then *all* of you is stressed.

Fourth, the body and mind respond to stress as a unit. Because people differ in the ways they react to stress, each of us has a "weak link" in our bodily chain. Some of us may suffer headaches, others ulcers. Some may become depressed, while others may have heart attacks. We each need to know what our particular vulnerability is.

Every worker should strive to maintain a sense of control. This doesn't mean you should resist your boss or refuse to do unpleasant work. It means you should avoid feeling helpless. You can do this by increasing your coping skills, whether for your job, your relationships with coworkers, or your boss, along the lines that I will be describing later. You should learn to be honest and speak up when necessary, and refuse to be manipulated. It also helps to be tolerant of imperfections.

WORKAHOLISM AND STRESS

The Japanese have a word for it. They call it "karoshi." They have to have a word for it because it happens so often. In a culture that breeds work addiction at every age and where children go to school six days a week and clean their own classrooms, and where workers have the longest work week in the industrialized world, karoshi has become a dreaded syndrome. It means "death from overwork." You get it stamped on your death certificate if your widow can prove you worked continuously just before you died. She gets a small pension as a reward.

Workaholism is our equivalent of karoshi. It may not directly kill us, but it certainly does indirectly, because workaholics are among the most highly stressed in any company. Because karoshi has become such a serious problem in Japan, top business leaders have begun to urge workers to take time off and try to relax. Good luck! True workaholics don't easily give up their "fix."

But what has workaholism got to do with the toxic or dysfunctional workplace? Surely it is a worker problem and not an employer one. I'm not so sure. While it is true that workaholics are the product of their own inner dynamics, the workplace both creates and reinforces the addiction to work. Any workplace that has more than its share of workaholics is bound to be a toxic place. Its values are skewed in such a way that they imbalance the personal lives of those in its clutches.

As I have already hinted, workaholism is an addiction. Work provides a "fix" not unlike cocaine. Adrenaline stimulation probably underlies this fix, but I suspect other hidden mechanisms are at work as well.

Not everyone who works hard is a workaholic, however. A "work enthusiast" is different in that work isn't used to anesthetize emotions. Work enthusiasts can take time to goof off and have no problems relaxing. Their identity is not defined by their work. Management would do well to reward this type of service over that of the workaholic.

WHAT CAUSES WORK STRESS?

Occupational stress is the hottest topic in the business world today. The reason is clear: about 14 percent of worker's compensation illness claims appear to be stress-related. Insurance benefits paid out for job stress average twice the amount paid for physical injury.[5] Nationally, an average of one million workers on any given day are absent from their jobs because of some stress disorder. Most of this stress is due to mismanagement of the workplace. In other words, it could have been prevented.

When those in charge don't gather sufficient information to inform their decision-making, stress levels are bound to be higher. The same is true where managers fail to make appropriate decisions in a timely way. Work flow is thwarted, errors are multiplied, and morale eroded.

All organizations suffer to some degree from insufficient communication. Workers can never know enough. But some things cannot be known to everyone. One must be content to know just enough to do one's work effectively. And here comes the rub: How does one achieve this balance? How can management know if workers have the information they need to do their work and are not wasting time learning more than they need?

A manager needs to ensure that effective feedback mechanisms are in place to monitor whether the right information is getting to the right person at the right time. The larger the organization and the more complex the problem, the greater the need to monitor the effectiveness of communication.

Whenever a message is communicated to someone else, there are at least six different messages involved: What you meant to say, what you actually said, what the other person heard you say, what the other person thinks he heard you say, what the other person says he heard you say, and what you think the other person says he heard you say.

Good communication often means you have to err on the side of being repetitive. Say it in more than one way. Then the real message may get through without distortion.

Quite understandably, relationships between workers have a greater influence on stress than, say, relations between workers and machines. A machinist may become frustrated when a computer-driven lathe goes faulty. But this anger is nothing compared to that he could feel toward a person. Machines are not malicious, people sometimes are. Humans can cause us more pain because they can hurt us "with malice aforethought." We attribute motives to people, not to machines.

Perhaps surprisingly, stress is caused not only by tension, but by insufficient challenge. For years, business and industry intentionally created highly specialized jobs. The belief was that repetition made workers more efficient, so business could become more profitable. Slowly everyone came to believe that earning a living was usually boring and a chore, but one had to grin and bear it. Then boredom began to take its toll in stress disease. Workers became dissatisfied. The lack of variety caused irritability. Workers lacked social contact and found work meaningless. As the body resists being restrained, stress levels go up. Lengthy sitting or standing and lack of mobility contribute to this sense of boredom. Headaches and ulcers develop when workers have time to brood.

Today researchers are telling us that humans need variety in order to be their best. They also need social contact and challenge. Confining someone to a narrow work task is bad for the worker. Progressive managers try to design variety into jobs by including movement, partnership in decision-making, and opportunities to be creative.

EVALUATING YOUR LEVEL OF STRESS

Stress is not new. Our ancestors no doubt felt it as they sought to club a bison or fight a saber-toothed tiger.

All workers need to be able to gauge their stress levels and evaluate their reaction to it. Managers, too, should know how to read the signs of stress in workers.

Everyone can learn to detect the signs of stress in the work environment, in the home environment, and in one's personal well-being.

Let's examine each of these.

Stress signs in the workplace. Look for these changes:
- You arrive late or leave early.
- You always seem to be scrambling to handle a backlog.
- You feel frantic about what work to tackle next.
- You seek diversions to escape work, such as taking walks, wan-

dering around the building, or reading magazines or the newspaper.
- You take long lunch breaks, or persistently never take a break.
- You overreact to slight frustration.
- You blow-off at little provocations.
- You are making more mistakes; you have become accident-prone.
- You cannot meet reasonable deadlines.
- You are obsessed about minor details and cannot grasp the bigger picture.
- You increase your complaining; you have become dissatisfied at work.
- You overreact when given an additional assignment, even if it is minor and replaces another.

I must emphasize that one needs to look for changes in the above areas. If a worker is always a certain way, the problem is not stress, but the individual. When someone who is normally calm, competent, and able to roll with the punches becomes edgy, resistant, and overreactive, that person is sending a message loud and clear: "I AM UNDER TOO MUCH STRESS."

Stress signs in the home. Here again, change is the key signal:
- You come home from work in a bad mood.
- You give the "silent treatment." You are unresponsive to conversation or will not talk about problems at work.
- Alternatively, you grumble more about work problems.
- You become irritable and short-tempered with your family members and intolerant of the slightest infractions of home rules.
- You escape into TV or isolated activities.
- You have difficulty falling asleep or wake too early.
- You use alcohol or other substances excessively.
- You neglect chores or activities like gardening or hobbies that normally give you pleasure.

In the final analysis you have to take responsibility for your life and for monitoring your stress levels. The signs are always there. All you have to do is pay attention to them. Everyone has limits. If you are under too much stress you will discover this limit when it strikes with vengeance. Better to heed the "lesser" signals.

The list at the end of this chapter, titled "Signs that You Are Over-Stressed," spells out the major symptoms of over-stress. As you review them, keep in mind a few very important points. The first is this: The symptoms of overstress often occur *after* the stressors are passed. After weeks or even months of overwork, unremitting demands, coworker conflict, or living in the shadow of "a boss from hell," the body will throw in the towel and send out distress signals. But not all stress is chronic. Most of us have to live with acute stress, the stress that comes from deadlines and crises. It may only last a few days or a few weeks, then the unpleasant experience passes. *During* the acute stress, the body can work wonders. It draws on its reserves to see us through. It even overdraws at the bank of our immune system to give us extra protection against getting sick. But when the crisis is over, you pay for the consequences of being overdrawn: you get sick. You will certainly feel exhausted. That's when you will get the headaches or suffer from diarrhea or stomach cramps.

The body is telling you that you have gone too far and now you need time for healing. While you were in crisis it gave you what you needed and protected you so that you could fulfill the demands placed on you.

This is why one should quit before getting to the point of exhaustion or before getting the headache. Once distress has set in, it's too late. You may say to yourself during a period of high stress, "But I must be OK; I feel no discomfort." But the body may just be waiting for you to quit before cashing in on your overdrawn account. So, quit *before* you hurt, or you may hurt more than is good for you.

The key, then, to managing your stress lies in learning to quiet and subdue your adrenaline over-responsiveness. There are many ways to do this, as we will see in the next section.

TAMING YOUR ADRENALINE

"Stress management" is a large topic. Fortunately much helpful literature is available. Since I believe the stress response lies in the overuse of our adrenal systems (most of us are adrenaline addicts), this is where I will focus my suggestions. My bottom-line message is quite simple: Whatever technique you use to manage your stress, it will not be effective unless it lowers your general arousal level. If you jog to soothe your stress but your jogging gets your competitive juices flowing, chances are that you have more adrenaline pumping at the end of your jog than you had when you left the house. Your jogging is causing you stress, not lowering it. The same can be said about golf, fishing, or any other recreational activity. Whatever you do will only relieve stress *if it lowers adrenaline.*

Now here comes the rub: Most people feel more uncomfortable, even miserable, as they lower their adrenaline than when they elevate it. This is understandable. Adrenaline makes you feel better. It's designed to do this—but it stabs you in the back if you try to live on it. So, effective stress management does not make you feel better at first. If anything, it makes you feel worse. Did you get that? If you are effective in lowering your stress you may feel worse to begin with. And this is how you can tell if you are doing it right: if you feel edgy, restless, irritable, and uncomfortable, chances are your adrenaline is subsiding. The reason? You have to go through the withdrawal symptoms of your adrenaline addiction. Adrenaline is a drug as powerful as any I know. It elevates arousal, so it is a stimulant. Take it away and you go through classic stimulant-withdrawal systems. Face it courageously. There is no other way but to go "cold turkey." If you are successful you will begin to feel better eventually.

Now let's get down to some specifics. You need to master four skill areas if you are going to control your stress and avoid its destructiveness.

1. The first skill is cognitive. Most stress enters the body through the mind. Not all stress, of course, but most of it. Physical stress comes from sitting or standing too long, exposure to cigarette smoke, poor ventilation, bad lighting, and so forth. Physical causes create stress without your thinking about them. They bypass your mind and go straight to the body.

My emphasis here, however, is on the nonphysical causes of stress, such as worker-boss conflicts and excessive personal expectations. These stressors are channeled via the mind where they are filtered by beliefs, values, and attitudes. If you are a male with a chauvinistic bent, you are not going to feel good about having a woman for a boss. Your beliefs and attitudes will cause your stress, not your female boss. Every time she asks you to do something you will bristle, your blood pressure will rise, and some calcium will be deposited in your arteries. Where does this stress come from? Your *mind*, of course. It arises from your chauvinistic beliefs about male superiority. Until you change this belief, you won't be free of stress.

My point is this: We attach meaning to everything that happens to us. This meaning causes us stress, not what happens. To reduce stress we have to block or modify unhealthy meanings. You can "block" them by improving your understanding of your prejudices and biases. The more you understand these, the easier it is to "pull them out" of your thinking when you need to.

Learn to reason more clearly. Much stress is caused by faulty reasoning. You will never be able to teach yourself how to reason more clearly unless you talk about what's going on in your mind with someone else who, preferably, won't always agree with you. A good psychotherapist can work wonders here, but so can an honest friend.

Learn to "filter" what you see or hear. Reject anything that does not seem truthful. A good "filter" system is able to detect exaggerations on the part of others ("you *always* make mistakes") or even recognize when someone is trying to "put the monkey on your back." Whatever it is, a good filter system cuts off stress at its source.

Learn to engage in healthy "self-talk." "Healthy" means honest and reality based. Lies never bring healing. If someone blames you for making a mistake, it is not healthy to say to yourself, "That's not my problem," when in fact it *is* your problem. This is denial, not healthy or honest self-talk. Take responsibility for your own problems. Force yourself to substitute healthy self-statements in those lengthy conversations you have with yourself.

When filter skills fail, you have a second line of defense: You can increase those behaviors that help you interact more positively with your environment. Often stress arises because your behavior skills are deficient. So let's discuss important behaviors that can help minimize stress.

2. Good communication skills are essential. They calm your adrenaline system. Miscommunication causes a panic reaction and shoots up the adrenaline. Highly stressed people seem to have three types of communication problems.

The first is the "decibel" or "yelling" style. This style believes that the best way to get a message across is to say it loud and often. Parents use this method with their kids, and so do some supervisors. Does it work? Judge for yourself. Yelling shuts off listening. You become scared when someone shouts and your brain rushes to block out the threats.

The second is the "selling" style. This style assumes that the listener is a passive receiver. "I speak, you listen," is its message. It is a one-way transfer of information. Does it work? Not really. Passive listening sends the brain to sleep. Surely you've observed this in church or synagogue, especially when the message is about something dull. I think we could revolutionize preaching if we allowed more interaction.

The third is equally useless: the "minimal-information" or "ignoring" style assumes you don't really want to know anything, so why bother! "All you need to know is where this fits in the machine, so that's all I am going to tell you. This way you don't have to bother with details." What a message! The supervisor doesn't bother to communicate. Unfortunately, that person is ignoring most recent findings that workers work better, harder, and with less stress if they have the "broad picture." Companies are increasingly going out of their way to communicate more than just the bare essentials to their workers, which helps them feel a part of the operation. It also helps them bear the stress of deadlines because they have a greater understanding of the broad picture.

Here are a few suggestions to improve your communication style.

- Speed is greater when communication is one-way, but accuracy is better when it is two-way. So make a point of getting involved *actively* in the communication.
- Give feedback on what you are hearing and ask for feedback to test whether you are hearing what is actually being said.
- Be aware that language differences can be a barrier. Ours is a pluralistic society, and many workers have home languages other than English. Be sensitive to this and test your definitions of words periodically.
- If you are confused, speak up. Be assertive, your job may

depend on it. Don't guess, and don't try to mind-read. A healthy boss will never resent your eagerness to make sure you know what is being communicated. A bad boss may resent your questions, but if he or she is bad, it is even more imperative that you ask.

- Pay attention to emotions in communication, not just the facts or words. Try to understand the feelings behind the words being spoken.
- Work at being a good listener. Stop thinking about your response or other things, when you should be listening. Pay attention.
- Beware the bad communicator, who abounds. Some people are notorious for distorting messages. It's bad enough when what you say isn't what you intended to say, but when the receiver hears selectively, you can be in real trouble. When possible, put everything important in writing, or confirm everything you say in a memo.

3. Learn to prioritize and manage your time. Like it or not, time is becoming a scarce commodity. Racing against time, especially when you haven't managed it well, is a major cause of adrenaline overproduction. Take your pulse rate next time you are in a rush. You might be alarmed at how fast your heart is pumping in response to the adrenaline aggravation.

Knowing one's priorities is the third of Stephen Covey's seven habits of highly effective people.[6] He quotes Goethe: *"Things which matter most must never be at the mercy of things which matter least."*

Effective time management, which is more a matter of self-management, can lower your stress substantially. Here's how self-management can be achieved:

- *Regularly review the demands placed upon you* and categorize them into "important," "not so important," and "unimportant." First take care of the important tasks. If you have time, you can attempt the less important.
- *Plan ahead.* Keep a calendar of obligations you must complete over the next few weeks or months and keep it at hand for regular review. I try to keep the year before me in a notebook that I review frequently. In this way I know when to do the necessary preparations for upcoming events.

- *Eliminate nonessentials.* No one who is successful is controlled by nonessentials. Force yourself to be focused. Don't try to do everything. Refuse to take on more than you can finish. Carrying a list of unfinished tasks in your mind can unstring you.
- *Clarify your roles, goals and values.* Periodically write down where you are and where you are headed. Ask yourself: What drives me? What do I need to do to make me happy? Why? This helps establish your priorities and weeds out the non-essentials.
- *Get organized.* Sometimes we have the time, but we waste it because we can't find that paper we need to accomplish the task at hand. File things. Organize them so you don't waste time searching. Tidy up after you've finished a task and *before* you begin the next.
- *Delegate.* If you don't need to do it, don't. Let someone else do it. Ability to delegate is the hallmark of successful people. They realize that time is limited and that they can only do a few things well. They concentrate on doing what only they can do, and delegate the rest to others.
- *Learn to say "no."* Assertiveness is not a bad word. It is healthy, provided you can do it without anger. You have a right to say "no." It is your "noes" that give meaning to your "yeses." You owe it to commitments you have already made, not to be unduly burdened by additional commitments.

4. Body skills are the last, but perhaps the most important, stress-reducing skills. Their development will help you implement your cognitive and behavior skills more effectively.

Your focus here is on preventing stress from damaging your body and mind. A healthy body handles stress more efficiently than a neglected one. It's like fighting a war. Strong and rested soldiers can fight better than weak and tired ones. Your body is like a battalion, waging constant battle against outside invaders.

- Exercise regularly. An unfit body tires easily and becomes more stressed when fatigued.
- Maintain awareness of what is going on in your body. Listen to your pains and discomforts; they are telling you a lot.
- Watch what you eat. Consult a nutritionist if necessary, but

bad eating habits can cause a lot of internal stress.

- Develop skill at relaxing (see relaxation techniques at the end of the chapter). Relaxation is a powerful antidote for stress because it lowers adrenaline.
- Watch your aggression and anger. Improve your conflict management skills so as to cool your anger as quickly as possible. Anger is a boomerang—it hurts the one who gets angry.

Since some people tend to have more trouble with the last two points than others, let me add some specific advice to them. This high-risk group is known as the "Type-A" personalities. They suffer from "hurry sickness." They are impatient, easily angered, not tolerant of delays, believe the world can't function without them, and have a highly developed sense of justice. "Type Bs" are the opposite, and I will have more to say about them in the next chapter.

How can you make a break with Type-A destructiveness? Here's how:

- *Master a relaxation technique* and use it at least twice a day to lower your adrenaline arousal. Around midday and just before you go to bed are the best times.
- *Sleep more.* Your body burns up energy faster, so you need more time for it to rejuvenate. Add a half-hour or one hour to your sleep and see how much better you feel.
- *Develop distracting habits and hobbies.* Music can be a great soother; hobbies can get your mind off problems.
- *Retrain your reactions.* Your adrenal system is super-reactive, so don't let it just go. When you realize you are becoming aroused, use your relaxation technique to calm yourself. *You* must control your body, not vice versa.
- *Take control of your life.* Demand regular breaks. Limit telephone interruptions. Schedule your appointments realistically, and build in adequate time for recovery.
- *Don't rush.* Learn to slow down. Take more time for meals. Take walks. Smell the roses. Listen to the birds.
- *Focus on essentials.* Type-A personalities try to do too many things at the same time. Try to do only one at a time.
- *Listen more.* Try to talk less. Focus on listening. This will reduce your rushed feeling and lower your arousal.
- *Don't work until you drop.* Stop before you become distressed.

If you stop only after you've got a headache, you've gone beyond your limits. We don't drive motor cars until they stop. We try to prevent them from breaking down by preventive measures (changing oil, replacing fan belts, hoses, etc.). At least give your body as good treatment as you give your car!

HOW A MANAGER CAN HELP CREATE A STRESS-FREE WORKPLACE

Much of what I have written about stress prevention can be applied by managers. Let me list a few suggestions to managers:

- If your business is driven by "seasonal" demands (e.g., holidays or tax-time) start early by communicating with your staff. Emphasize the need for focus, set aside unnecessary chores, and remind employees it is only for a season.
- Offer incentives for productivity and a reward for the additional stress. This helps keep anger at bay.
- Set up forums for employees to talk about their pressures. This provides relief and shares responsibility.
- Provide a sounding board to address problems.
- Reassign staff to pick up heavy work loads in one section when others have a lighter load. Workers feel less stressed when justice prevails.
- Celebrate the completion of significant goals. This helps workers feel appreciated and provides symbolic milestones.
- And when a job is well done, don't forget to say "thank you."

Signs that You Are Over-Stressed

The signs of too much stress are not difficult to identify. They fall into three categories: health signs, emotional signs and personal signs.

1. *Health Signs:*
   High blood pressure
   Cold hands
   Headaches
   Constant fatigue
   Ulcers and other gastro-intestinal problems
   Sleep problems
   Aggravation of other health problems (diabetes, asthma, colitis)
   Racing heart or skipped beats
   Increased problems with PMS
   Muscle tension and general muscle aching
   Increased susceptibility to disease and sickness
   Diarrhea or constipation

2. *Emotional Signs:*
   Increased tension and anxiety
   Restlessness and irritability
   Sexual problems; lack of responsiveness
   Distrust of coworkers
   Panic feelings; fears of "going crazy"
   Feelings of helplessness; detachment from work
   Increased daydreaming, fantasizing
   Scapegoating; anger
   Periodic depression

3. *Personal Signs:*
   Avoidance of friends and family
   Dislike of certain coworkers without cause
   Conflict in marriage or with children
   Use of substances (alcohol, drugs) to escape problems
   Overuse of distractions (hobbies, TV, books) to avoid facing up
       to issues
   Overall unhappiness; feelings of misery

A Relaxation Technique Worth Mastering

Sit in a comfortable chair, or better still, lie on a comfortable bed. Set a timer for thirty minutes or more.

Make yourself comfortable. Close your eyes and shut out the world. Don't cross your arms or legs. Remove shoes and glasses. Clear your mind of worries or resentments.

Exercise 1: Stretching. Raise your hands above your head and rest them at the back, but don't grasp onto anything. Take a deep breath. Hold your breath for a few seconds. Relax and breathe out.

Now stretch your hands up as far as they will go. Stretch them further. Hold them there. Now push your feet down as far as they will go. Further! Hold your arms and feet stretched out as far apart from each other as possible. Count slowly to ten.

Relax and let your hands and feet return to their original position. Repeat the stretching exercise once more. Now relax. Take another deep breath. Hold it for a few seconds. Relax and let it go.

Exercise 2: Tensing. Return your arms to your side. Starting at your feet, begin methodically to first tense and relax each muscle group in your body. First, tense the muscles of your feet and toes (without tensing any other muscles). Count slowly to five. Relax the muscles of feet and toes.

Now move to your lower legs and knees. Tense the muscles (making sure the feet are kept relaxed). Count to five. Relax and let go.

Next the thighs. Tense them. Count to five. Relax and let go.

Now the lower-waist region. Tense all the muscles. Count to five. Relax and let go.

Repeat for the upper torso, hands, arms, and shoulders. Tense each of the muscles. Count to five. Relax and let go.

Finally, the neck and face. Tense all the facial muscles. Count to five. Relax and let go.

Now remain absolutely still. Try not to move any muscle. Become aware of your entire body. Do you feel tenseness anywhere? If you do, tense that muscle, count to five, then relax and let go. If your whole body feels tense, repeat the entire exercise from the start.

Remain as still as you can. Slowly your muscles will lower their tension. Resist the urge to scratch or move (it gets easier after the fifth try at relaxation). Breathe in and out rhythmically, keeping your mind on your body and away from your problems.

When the timer rings, get up slowly and go about your business. Try to remain in a state of low arousal. Mastering this technique will enhance your life and your sanity!

8 Burnout on the Job

Not every personality is susceptible to Burn-Out. It would be virtually impossible for the underachiever to get into that state. Or the happy-go-lucky individual with fairly modest aspirations. Burn-Out is pretty much limited to dynamic, charismatic, goal-oriented men and women or to determined idealists.

Herbert J. Freudenberger, Ph.D.
Burn-Out

BURNOUT IS NOT THE SAME as stress. Yes, I know that many see burnout as one of the "aftereffects" of stress, but I don't.[1] Stress and burnout are two significantly different experiences. To understand the difference can determine what you do to prevent and recover from them.

Burnout! What does this term mean to you? What fears does it evoke? What visual images does it create? This syndrome afflicts all "people helpers." A common penalty for those who must "care too much" as a part of their job can be burnout.

WHAT IS BURNOUT?

Burnout can be defined as a syndrome of emotional exhaustion, in response to the chronic strain of dealing with the pain of others. If one feels great helplessness in trying to assist these troubled humans, burnout can be particularly rapid.

No amount of theorizing will help to appreciate how depleting the care of others can be. See the social worker who once patiently dealt with housing project tenants, now a depressed recluse who cannot get out of bed in the morning, and you'll glimpse the reality of burnout. See the nurse, who has spent several years in the oncology ward where most of the patients die, go into a deep depression and become unable to express any sympathy toward the dying person. Or see the personnel officer of a large manufacturing company decide he would rather be a laborer working with his hands than deal with complaining people. Such burnout is as real as a heart attack.

THE ESSENCE OF BURNOUT

Helpers are particularly prone to burnout because:

1. They usually have not been taught to care for others in the right way.
2. They care too much out of guilt.
3. They feel inadequate in providing solutions.
4. They allow their caring to dominate their thinking.
5. They do not sufficiently love themselves; they do not take adequate steps to care for their own feelings or to facilitate their own self-recovery.

Helpers tend to overextend themselves and then feel overwhelmed by the emotional demands that follow. And the more people they "feel responsible for," the greater their opportunity for burnout.

Burnout has also been called "compassion fatigue." The muscle of a loving heart has grown weak, unable to pump care to the needy. At first its beat is erratic and irregular. Short bursts of compassion can be mustered in times of emergency but surprisingly cease at inopportune times. Finally it becomes silent, or "burned out."

UNDERSTANDING BURNOUT/STRESS DIFFERENCES

Some similarities exist between burnout and stress. There are also many differences. Why should we differentiate between the two? Because the *causes* of burnout are quite different from those of stress; the *cure* for burnout is significantly different, and the *prevention* of burnout is significantly different.

Understanding the difference also has important implications for supervisors of those at high risk for burnout. It can certainly guide those who are not suited to "people helping" away from jobs that take their toll in burnout. Toxic workplaces neglect to protect those at risk for burnout because they don't really understand the phenomenon of burnout. While all people can become emotionally burned out, some are at greater risk than others.

Not only is it common to confuse stress problems with those of burnout, but it is common to confuse depression with burnout. This complicates the depression unnecessarily, since blame is being placed in the wrong place. Many who should be seeking treatment for a major depression think their job is the problem when it may not be. If the problem is really depression, the cure lies in seeking treatment for the depression, not in blaming or changing the job. Burnout may in fact require a job change; depression may not.

To develop understanding of the differences between burnout, stress and depression, let me describe the essential features of each. Hans Selye, the father of stress research, has defined stress as "the *nonspecific* response of the body to *any* demand." He emphasized that the body can respond in the same manner to many types of pressure—both good and bad. The excitement of installing a new computer or watching your home football team play a winning game can be as stress-producing as meeting a publisher's deadline or facing an angry staff member.

While we cannot eliminate stress completely (you are only stress-free when you are dead), every leader needs to know how to recognize "over-stress": that is, when your physiology is unable to recover quickly from over-arousal.

While prolonged distress can lead to emotional burnout, stress is essentially different from burnout in that symptoms of stress are the *consequence of overuse of the body*. These symptoms are often seen by the victim as obstacles to success. Seldom does the disease of over-stress in and of itself slow the victim down—not until a severe physical manifestation occurs.

Burnout is qualitatively different. It is much more *protective* than destructive. It may intervene when you are on the road to stressful destruction and take you out of the stressful environment. When it does it is often a blessing. It instantly slows you down, by producing a state of lethargy and disengagement. In this sense it may even be functional. The system gives out before it blows up. Burnout is a kind of "shut down" that can save you from self-destruction.

Depression always accompanies burnout. Depression may also be present in some stress disorders. In such cases, it is a symptom of the disorder and not necessarily a problem in and of itself.

The depression of stress is always the consequence of "adrenal exhaustion." The depression which results from overuse of your adrenaline produces a low mood, disinterest in regular activities, and physical fatigue. It is designed to pull the victim out of the rat race and force the body into a recovery mode. The lethargy, for instance, forces the body to rest and recover from the over-stress.

Sometimes stress will bring out an underlying endogenous depression. This type of depression is produced by complex disturbances within the body's chemistry in a way not yet clearly understood. Much depression seen in high-pressured, overworked and ambitious people may be of this sort. It may be a precursor to burnout.

Extreme burnout will comprise most, if not all, of the following:

- *demoralization*—a belief that you are no longer effective.
- *depersonalization*—you treat yourself and others in an impersonal way.
- *detachment*—you withdraw from responsibilities and refuse to fulfill obligations.
- *distancing*—you avoid social and interpersonal contacts.
- *defeatism*—you feel "beaten" and give up hope of succeeding.

But is all this talk about burnout for real? Could it be that our Western minds have such a propensity for the faddish that we may be creating a malady simply by giving it a name? Will we not rush to excuse laziness or incompetence as symptoms of burnout? Will the cry "burnout" not become a smoke screen for "cop-out?" In writing on the topic of burnout, one pastor claims he is becoming "bombed out" by all the talk of "burnout," and suggests that the present preoccupation with burnout creates the danger of being "sold out." Burnout becomes an excuse to leave your ministry, abandon a marriage or give up on any activity that demands persistent, unrelenting dedication.

This skepticism has even reached *The New York Times:* "We have stumbled upon a worthy and thoroughly modern concept with which to label our discontent.... The word *burnout* covers our personal failures much better than ordinary forms of irresponsibility to ourselves and others. It gives us, as I see it, the perfect out."[2]

This warning should be heeded. But I have seen too many cases of burnout not to believe that it is a real phenomenon. I can only appeal to the readers not to label every low feeling as burnout and make it an excuse to run away from responsibility.

BURNOUT AND THE WORKPLACE

How does the workplace contribute to burnout? In several ways:

- *Failure to protect* workers who are at high risk. For example, those with a lot of "people contact" need more emotional support than those with computer or machine contact.
- *Failure to limit the amount of change* in a worker's job assignments. Too much change, too quickly, can increase the risk and speed of burnout.
- *Failure to provide adequate support* for someone who has responsibility for the care of others. Support—meaning encouragement and opportunity to talk about problems—is essential in preventing burnout.
- *Failure to carefully screen out* those whose personalities don't fit well with people-helping or who, because of their proneness to sympathy, are at high risk for emotional involvement with hurting people.
- *Failure to provide adequate resources* for those helping others. For instance, the manager of a social agency's food kitchen for homeless people would rapidly burn out if hungry people had to be turned away because of insufficient food. And if no one would be available to listen to complaints about it, the harm would be aggravated.
- *Failure to keep expectations realistic.* Idealists burn out more rapidly than realists. They build up insurmountable expectations, often encouraged by supervisors because this makes for a stronger work commitment, and their dreams are dashed when reality strikes. This creates disillusionment and burnout.

Now from this list it is easy to see why burnout has been linked to the helping professions (physicians, nurses, counselors, teachers, social workers, police, etc.), but people in every work situation are at risk for burnout. Supervisors and middle level managers are good examples. They have to interface both upward and downward. They get the complaints, they see the deficiencies, they have to defend the lack of adequate resources for the job. These roles are fraught with frustration.

Every worker who is responsible for others in the workplace must guard against burnout. The daily interaction between worker and organization cannot be overlooked.

BURNOUT IN ORGANIZATIONAL SYSTEMS

A very helpful book by William White has explored the connection between burnout and organization. He sees burnout not just as a problem inside the individual worker or as a problem in the work environment, but "as a breakdown in the *relationship* between the individual and the organization."[3]

In this approach the organizational group is likened to that of a family. Supervisors function like parents. Interactions between workers are like actions between siblings or other family members. Some of the phenomena observed in families has been applied to the workplace and has provided explanations for how people operate in social systems, whether that system is a closely-knit organizational family or a large, extended, organizational family, and whether the organization is paid or unpaid.[4]

How does systems behavior produce burnout? Three difficulties that I frequently encounter in social systems are easy to overlook.

Triangulation. A triangle is formed whenever two people are in conflict over an issue *or* a third person. The triangle is an "emotional triangle," in which large amounts of feeling are released.

Here's how a triangle works in a family. Husband has a drinking problem; wife is most disturbed by this, so one day, while husband is at work, she impulsively pours his booze down the drain. He comes home, finds his alcohol missing, and rages at his wife. She becomes upset and is now triangled between his booze and her relationship with him. Of course, it can also be an issue over gambling, his chronic unemployment, and even over disciplining the kids. Any conflict that can cause intense emotions can create triangles.

What is the result? If you are triangled, you always end up carrying the stress of the problem. In the example above, the wife gets it in the neck from her husband for interfering with his booze.

The general consequence of being triangled, then, is that you get clobbered! You pay for your interference with stress or burnout or both.

The innocent person, then, who allows him or herself to be triangled by a conflict will always be the person who suffers the most. To illustrate how this works, allow me to give an example of another common family-type triangulation (or "strangulation" as one of my patients once erroneously but very descriptively called it!). Suppose a father is having a conflict with his teenage son. Father and son are so much alike that they can't get along with each other. They bicker all the time. One day, mother decides to "help" their relationship. She asks her husband to sit down because she wants to talk to him about his relationship with his son. This, in and of itself, is not a triangulation. But when she starts to blame him for the conflict by saying something like, "You know, you've never liked the boy. He's so much like you that you don't like what you see... ," she has crossed the line and created a conflict. Father gets angry. He storms out, searches for his son and rages at him for being a "crybaby" and hiding behind his mother's skirt. Son gets mad also, not at his father but at his mother. Now mother has alienated both husband and son, who are both angry. They are angry at her for trying to "fix" their relationship. She now carries the stress of the conflict, gets a headache, pumps more acid into her stomach than it needs and soon develops an ulcer. Happens every time! If you interfere, you pay for it in stress or burnout.

How does triangulation operate in the workplace? Suzannah comes to you and tells you that Mary Beth, who works two doors down, is out to get you. She says that she overheard Mary Beth bad-mouthing you in the department, but you mustn't worry because she is behind you and will defend you to the hilt! If you run off to attack Mary Beth, you've been triangled.

What do you do? Triangulation always starts with some "baiting." A juicy, fat worm of a temptation, say, to get revenge. Do you bite? If you do, you're triangled.

Any position of responsibility is fraught with risks for triangulation. Someone complains about someone else. A lazy worker asks you to do something for him that then goes wrong and you get blamed. If you are a "rescuer," triangles can often trap you. If you try to make someone's job easier, try to help someone give up a bad habit, urge someone to change an opinion, or help two people "make up," you run the risk of being triangled. Your intentions can backfire and those you are trying to help can turn on you.

Whatever the reason for "getting in the middle," you should "de-triangle" the moment you realize you're caught. In the case of Suzannah saying Mary Beth is out to get you, you should respond to Suzannah by informing her that you will first check out the accuracy of her report with Mary Beth. In other words, it is believing the report that triangles you. Your response is also an effective way of warning Suzannah that she should tell the truth.

The wife who discarded her husband's alcohol can detriangle herself by telling him she will no longer put up with his behavior and that she is going to get counseling. He can join her if he wishes. Never interfere with the "other side" of a triangle, namely the booze itself. In an emotional triangle it is generally not possible to bring change to the relationship of the other two parts by trying to change their relationship directly. You can only deal with your relationship. This is true for the wife of the alcoholic, the mother who is concerned about a father-son relationship, or any other triangle.

Since you can bring change only to a relationship of which you are directly a part, the way to help change the other two (husband-booze, father-son, etc.) is to strengthen your relationship with each. Avoid taking responsibility for the relationship between the others. For the father and son, this is straightforward. But how does this work for the wife of the alcoholic? How does one develop a relationship with alcohol? By getting all the literature you can about alcoholism. Join a recovery group. Learn about the problem. You will be better informed and make fewer mistakes. Then apply all your energy to dealing with your husband and what is going on in your relationship. Say to him, "You may choose not to deal with your drinking if you want. But I will not continue to expose myself and the children to the abuse it causes us. Make up your mind and choose. Do you want us or the alcohol?"

It is preferable, of course, to avoid being triangled in the first place. If someone wants you to team up in opposing a decision of your boss, encourage the person to deal with the boss independently. Don't get involved unless you want to be involved. If someone says to you, "I want to tell you something bad I've heard about the new plant manager they've hired but I don't want you to tell anyone," gently decline the offer. "Secrets" often form triangles and get you involved when you don't want to be. They can backfire later when someone challenges you, "You knew about it but you didn't say anything." Furthermore you can never test the truthfulness of a secret. If you could, it would no longer be a secret.

Enmeshment. This is another helpful "family systems" concept that is applicable to the workplace. In dysfunctional families parents are often enmeshed with children. Obviously there is a high degree of enmeshment with babies. But as the child grows into adolescence, he or she needs to be "let go." Enmeshment ensues when grown children continue to be caught in the family net. They remain entangled in the affairs of and dependent on the parents. They can make no decisions without parental approval.

While enmeshed systems offer a high degree of mutual support, it is at the expense of independence and autonomy. Sure, enmeshed parents are loving and considerate; they spend a lot of time with their kids and do a lot for them. But enmeshed children never really grow up. They rely too much on their parents and tend to be too dependent, emotionally and materially. They may even have trouble relating outside the family or letting anyone else, spouse included, become a part of that inner group.

An enmeshed organizational family has the same characteristics. Managers function as "parents" and workers assume the role of "children." Workers become dependent on their bosses, making excessive demands for time and emotional support. Problems at home are discussed with supervisors, who then get involved in domestic disputes. Slowly, too much overlap develops between personal matters and matters of work. Supervision becomes difficult because the role of the supervisor conflicts with the role of parent. "Am I a parent or a boss?" Parents love and forgive. Bosses have a responsibility to supervise and give direction. Too much overlapping of these roles can burn out a supervisor and harm a worker.

Sometimes an enmeshed workplace breeds control systems that are tyrannical, authoritarian, and manipulative, because a certain style of parenting develops. All the dysfunctions of a family system follow: members not speaking to each other, imprecise communication ("read my mind"), and emotional separation. Family members may feel that they own each other because of the blood bond, but in the workplace no one owns anybody.

Organizations where the nature of the work demands isolation, such as prisons, security, hospitals, and especially psychiatric hospitals, are especially vulnerable to enmeshment. The closeness and isolation inherent in such places causes workers to be more dependent on one another than is healthy. Every effort should be made to "open up" such organizations by creating outside involvement and interaction because, in the long run, enmeshment breeds dysfunction, and isolation is a major cause of burnout. There isn't enough social ventilation to refresh the system.

Incest. A normal family balances social intimacy and sexual distance between family members. In contrast, the incestuous family is overconnected, and inappropriately so.

Incest, whether in the family or workplace, is a very sick condition. Organizational incest exists when workers increasingly meet their personal, social, and sexual needs inside the organization. The behavior doesn't have to include sexual intercourse for it to be incestuous. Often it is just emotional incest, but this can be as damaging.

Why is a high degree of intimacy inappropriate in the workplace? Because it creates too many conflicting roles. You cannot be somebody's lover one moment and his boss the next. You cannot be an intimate friend and objective supervisor at one and the same time. If you try to exercise your supervisory responsibilities, you violate the expectations of intimacy. The roles conflict, setting up emotional strain on one or both of the parties. You cannot be the close friend of a supervisor who may, in the course of responsibilities, have to demote you.

Incestuous behavior can also affect the quality and quantity of work done by others. Some will always be "left out." The dynamics present in an incestuous system (whether sexual or not) create burnout casualties because someone is always getting hurt. Furthermore, such a system breeds an atmosphere for sexual harassment and uses intimacy of various sorts to manipulate and control others. It *always* becomes an abuse of power. A conspiracy of silence then develops that shuts off open and honest communication.

Such a system slowly becomes "closed" with decreased access to the outside. Those who do not "fit" or accept the incestuous nature of the workplace are rejected and a high level of internal paranoia develops out of fear of discovery and disclosure. The system also becomes consumed by problems surrounding relationship difficulties—accusations, jealousies, and conflicts over not getting one's personal needs met.

What can one do to change such a workplace? Unless you are the owner or president, not much. You can try complaining to the top brass, but don't be surprised if you get dumped. My advice generally to someone caught up in such a closed system is to get out. You need extraordinary courage to stand up to the type of people who thrive on incestuous social and sexual intimacies.

Boundary problems. Any confusion of responsibility and ownership in our lives is a problem of *boundaries.*[5] Homeowners set up boundaries to their physical property by establishing fences, hedges, or just imaginary lines. Each person must also set up mental, physical, and emotional boundaries to help distinguish what is his or her responsibility from what isn't. Boundaries are important in all areas of our lives, but especially on the job.

For instance, if it is my job assignment to be the sales representative for Northeast Los Angeles, and I keep going into the Southwest to find extra business, I am violating someone's territory. This is a physical boundary. But let us suppose that while sitting at my desk I overhear Janice tell someone else that she thinks her husband is having an affair with his secretary and she is trying to figure out a way to confront him, and I get a bee in my bonnet, go to the nearest telephone, call Janice's husband, and say to him: "What are you doing to Janice? She's worried that you are getting too friendly with your secretary...."

I am overstepping my boundary of responsibility. Janice has not asked me to help her. Overstepping one's boundaries always hurts someone else. The damage can be permanent.

In dysfunctional families, boundaries are violated all the time. Mother reads letters intended only between daughters and friends. Fathers scratch through drawers to see whether dirty books are being concealed by sons, or barge into the bathroom to "catch" naughty behavior. Later, parents interfere with children's marriages, give unsolicited advice, or take over celebrations without permission. These are boundary problems.

It's bad enough when family members cannot respect each other's boundaries, but what about the workplace? Percy sneaks around and interferes in everyone's business. One day he looks up from his worktable and sees Mike packing away his drawing instruments. "You can't leave now. It's forty-five minutes to quitting time."

Mike always bristles at Percy's interference. He'd like to go over and punch him in the nose. Instead he uses a verbal punch. "What I'm doing is none of your business," he tells Percy.

But Percy is stubborn. "I'll lodge a complaint. You can't quit before the rest of us."

Mike ignores him, takes his briefcase, and leaves. Percy runs into the manager's office to complain, only to be rebuked. Mike had asked permission to go home a little earlier. His wife had had a tooth extracted and wasn't feeling well. Percy had overstepped his boundary. He didn't have all the facts. Most people who persistently violate boundaries don't bother to get facts. They just like crossing boundaries.

Boundaries set limits on our responsibilities and help us maintain sufficient autonomy to secure our internal safety.

OVERCOMING BURNOUT

The cost of burnout can be high, both for the victim and the job. Recovery is not without its price. All those involved in the life of the one who suffers will be affected by it.

Many turn to drug or alcohol abuse (often secretively), or become depressed. Even more unfortunately, many will not acknowledge they have a problem. Their need to appear strong means they will deny they are needy, refuse to accept help, and even blame others or circumstances for their "temporary" discomfort.

You may not be able to change a workplace to make it less prone to burnout. But you can do a lot for yourself—both to heal whatever burnout already exists, and to prevent it from getting worse. Here are some commonly-asked questions by those suffering burnout:

- *Is burnout a sign of failure?* Not at all. It may be a sign of too much success. Since most burnout situations are more the product of bad circumstances than of bad people, you must reassure yourself that your burnout is not necessarily a sign of personal failure. Unfortunately, our sensitive guilt mechanisms make most of us more likely to attribute burnout to personal defects than to work circumstances. This can lead to a sense of personal loss and depression, which interferes with healing.

- *Should you seek professional help?* Mild cases of burnout are amenable to self-help. Severe cases—where the victim is emotionally torn, extremely fatigued, negative, depressed, and withdrawn—should be treated by a professional. Burnout can be intertwined with so many other problems that a self-help approach in severe cases may only aggravate it.

For most, though, burnout is a less serious problem. Since no two burnout situations are identical, coping needs to be tailor-made. Attention must be given not only to personal aspects of the burnout, but also to social and institutional aspects as well.

- *How quickly should I deal with my burnout?* It is important to realize that burnout begins slowly. This is good news and bad news. The good news is that you have plenty of time to take preventive steps. The bad news is that it can creep up so slowly you won't recognize it and it can be well established before you realize it. The sooner you catch it, the quicker and easier it will be to fix it.

The key to preventing and healing burnout lies in developing effective coping strategies for the work that tends to produce it.

"Coping" means any effort you make to master the conditions causing your burnout. Coping, in itself, does not mean that you must be successful—just that you make the effort. What always surprises me is how just some small step toward changing circumstances can dramatically restore a sense of control and hope. Helplessness is the real enemy that causes burnout, so anything you do to restore a sense of control will prevent burnout.

Richard Lazarus, a prominent stress researcher, has suggested two types of coping which I believe can be applied to burnout: Direct action and indirect action.

In direct action, the person actively confronts the source of the problem and finds positive solutions. When the source of the problem is ignored, the likelihood of burnout is increased.

In indirect action, the person tries to understand the source of the problem by talking about it, making adjustments toward the source, and diverting attention from it by getting involved in other activities.

Both of these coping strategies are necessary for successful prevention or recovery from burnout.

Three important coping skills have to do with personal functioning: becoming more assertive, reducing role conflicts, and avoiding the pitfalls of sympathy.

Much stress and burnout, especially in people-helpers, can be caused by inadequate assertiveness. Misunderstandings and miscommunication multiply in a nonassertive environment. Consequently, there is great difficulty in dealing with interpersonal conflicts, manipulative people, bossy superiors, and powerful authority figures. Under-assertive workers cannot say "no" to demands made of them. They often feel abused, hounded, ridiculed, criticized, and humiliated, but do not know how to handle their feelings or the abusive situation. Suppressed anger and passive-aggressive behaviors then emerge; these predispose the worker to burnout.

The antidote is clear: Learn how to be assertive in a manner consistent with your personality. Don't confuse assertiveness with aggression. Assertiveness always heals. Aggression always hurts. Check around your community for an assertiveness training workshop or see a counselor for help. The bookshelves of most bookstores or libraries have dozens of very helpful resources.

In many jobs, the roles one plays are many and diverse. Teachers, for example, can be trapped into playing parent as well as teacher, roles that are often in conflict. Pastoring is unique in this respect. The pastor is expected to be a good preacher, teacher, counselor, administrator, business manager, and friend to many. The multitude of expectations can cause stress because they are in opposition.

Research in industrial settings has demonstrated that role conflicts, as well as role overload, lead to stress and burnout. When, for instance, the expectations of your job are unclear or overly demanding, or if you are expected to do one thing and it is in conflict with another, you can quickly burn out. You lose a clear sense of purpose and goals.

The following steps can be helpful in preventing role conflict and role overload:

1. Know what your goals are for your job. Clarify your internal expectations by talking them over with a confidant or your boss.

2. Clarify the expectations others have of you and decide which

you believe are consistent with your job description. Be assertive and ask: "What do you expect of me?" Then be assertive in accepting or rejecting these expectations. Negotiate changes in these expectations when that seems warranted.

3. Focus your roles. Scattered goals produce scattered people. Identify your strengths and talents and then concentrate on these. Don't take a job that doesn't draw out your best.

Much burnout in "people-helpers" is due to their inability to keep their emotions sufficiently detached to avoid over-involvement in the pain of others. Stated bluntly, the question is: How much can a helper take of the pain of others before it starts to burn him or her out?

While not becoming indifferent to the pain of others, it is necessary for people-helpers to develop an appropriate degree of self-protection so that they do not become emotionally impaired.

People-helpers may use their "weeping" over the pain of others as a way of alleviating their own guilt feelings. Or they may be satisfying some deep personal need (conscious or unconscious). They also may need to "rescue" because it provides recognition or appreciation. In some strange way the vicarious sharing of pain helps to alleviate many personal needs and may even be a boost to self-esteem.

Many in the people-helping professions have not been taught how to differentiate sympathy from empathy. They erroneously believe that they are required to feel "sympathy" for all who hurt. Psychologists prefer the concept of "empathy," which is a restricted form of sympathy that does not cause burnout. Empathy is a way of relating to another that shows care and love but does not result in reciprocal pain. Special training is needed to cultivate empathy over sympathy.

To better understand the difference, consider the following: Sympathy, as it is most commonly experienced, is a way of comforting others by showing that you also feel their pain. It too easily becomes patronizing. It robs others of the right to feel their own pain because you diminish its importance by claiming the same pain. The vicarious suffering with another in sympathy can easily become selfish and self-satisfying. Sympathy in effect says: "I know how you feel because I feel that way also." Empathy, however, says, "I can never know what you feel because your pain is unique. But I do want to understand how you feel. Please share it with me."

Clinical research has shown that empathy is much more comforting and healing than sympathy. Hurting people only hurt more if they see that their hurt causes others to hurt also. Hurting people are healed by understanding, not by a helper becoming emotionally affected by their hurt.

IMPLICATIONS FOR THE WORKPLACE

Much of what I have written concerns ways in which a workplace can be modified to reduce the likelihood of burnout. But what can you personally do to resist the burnout? Here are some recommendations:

Build an effective support system. People burn out more easily and quickly when they lack a support system. You can build this support either inside or outside the workplace, depending on your circumstances. If you cannot rely on anyone where you work, then look for support in a friend or small group outside the job.

Ideally, a support group should provide:

- *Affirmation:* Problems at work can undermine your confidence. An understanding support group can restore your confidence and affirm you for who you are.
- *Encouragement:* Some work is by its nature emotionally draining. It's very easy for your emotions to get you down when all you see every day is people suffering or needs that cannot be met. A support group helps with encouragement.
- *A place to talk:* When you keep problems and feelings bottled up you accelerate the demoralization that leads to burnout. To be able to "externalize" these feelings is essential. A good support group is made up of a few good listeners.
- *Realistic and honest feedback:* You are not always right. Sometimes *you* are the problem. You sometimes have to be, because you are only human. An effective group will not always side with you nor agree with you. Honest and realistic feedback, if you can use it to change, will help you make fewer mistakes.
- *Perspective:* You need to pull back occasionally and see the

larger picture. This is very important in jobs that have a high degree of helplessness built into them. The sailor who must work in the engine room of a battleship won't last long under the pressure of war, if all that person sees is the machinery that runs the ship. Burnout comes quickly when you can't see how what you do fits into the larger scheme of things. You need others to help you get perspective. We can seldom get it for ourselves.

It stands to reason that if you expect one or a few others to be a support for you, you need to reciprocate and be there for them. Try to agree together on how often you will meet and the "rules" for the group. Confidentiality is essential. No group can be effective if members can't trust each other.

What about a spouse as a support? It is a great blessing to have an understanding mate who listens, affirms, encourages, and gives perspective. But don't expect your spouse to serve this way all the time. Dependence on the family as the sole source of support can be hazardous to the family. I know several marriages that have landed on the rocks because of too much "dumping" of problems at home. Try to build an independent support group when you can, but then make sure your spouse is "in the loop."

Build a balanced life. The natural cycles of life must be respected if one is to prevent burnout. High arousal needs low arousal to counterbalance it. High activity needs rest and refreshment. The human body and mind have limited resources, and like all machines, need time to cool off and replenish energy.

One of the first things I notice about my friends who have survived heart attacks is how quickly they change their lives so they are more balanced. Suddenly their families become important. They take walks, listen to the birds, watch sunsets, go back to church or synagogue, and take time for recreation. Why does it take a heart attack to bring this change? Because most of us don't face up to how unbalanced our lives are until we are faced with the realization that life is brief and our days are numbered.

Included in the well-rounded and balanced life must be exercise and good nutrition. A healthy body not only wards off stress disease, but it counteracts demoralization and helplessness, the main causes of emotional burnout.

Watch your personality. In my discussion on stress in the last chapter, I referred to the "Type A" personality which has been linked to the more serious stress disorders, such as early heart disease. Is there a personality type more prone to burnout? I believe there is.

Type A people are pragmatic, highly-driven, anger-disposed, and intolerant of being out of control. Type B people are more easygoing, less frustrated and less driven. However, Type B personalities are also more feeling-oriented, tend to be more idealistic, and also tend not to use support systems very effectively. As a result, they carry more emotional burdens and internalize them. This makes Type B's more burnout-prone, in my opinion. They experience more reactive depression. They just feel hurt more intensely and become demoralized more easily.

If you tend toward being a Type B personality and feel things more deeply, you may need to be more determined to set up and use a support group. Otherwise, get into therapy so you can learn how to stay less involved.

Although burnout can be a traumatic and even life-threatening experience, it can also be a turning point and the beginning of true maturity. It can be the start of greater self-understanding and increased awareness of your need for growth.

Such leaps in personal growth seldom occur to those who live sheltered lives or for whom everything seems to go right. The man or woman who has weathered and mastered burnout is wiser, stronger, and more insightful. While I would never wish burnout on anyone, I do know that it can revolutionize one's existence and bring life-enhancing changes to those who respond to it with determination and courage.

Test Yourself: Burnout Checklist

Review the past twelve months of all aspects of your life—work, social situations, family and recreation. Reflect on each of the following questions and rate the amount of *change* that has occurred during this period. Place more emphasis on change that has occurred during the past six months.

Use the following scale and assign a number in the rating column that reflects the degree of change you have experienced. BE HONEST; the value of this self-assessment is negligible if you aren't!

1. No or little change
2. Just noticeable change
3. Noticeable change

4. Fair degree of change
5. Great degree of change

SCORE

_____ 1. Do you become more fatigued, tired or "worn out" by the end of the day?

_____ 2. Have you lost interest in your work?

_____ 3. Have you lost ambition in your career?

_____ 4. Do you find yourself becoming easily bored (spending long hours with nothing significant to do)?

_____ 5. Have you become more pessimistic, critical, or cynical of yourself or others?

_____ 6. Do you forget appointments, deadlines, or activities and don't feel very concerned about it?

_____ 7. Do you spend more time alone, withdrawn from friends, family and work acquaintances?

_____ 8. Has any increase occurred in your general level of irritability, hostility, or aggressiveness?

_____ 9. Has your sense of humor become less obvious to yourself or others?

_____ 10. Do you become sick more easily (flu, colds, pain)?

_____ 11. Do you experience headaches more than usual?

_____ 12. Do you suffer from gastrointestinal problems (stomach pains, chronic diarrhea, or colitis)?

_____ 13. Do you wake up feeling extremely tired most mornings?

_____ 14. Do you deliberately try to avoid people you previously did not mind being around?

_____ 15. Has your sex drive lessened?

_____ 16. Do you now tend to treat people as "impersonal objects" or with a fair degree of callousness?

_____ 17. In your work, do you feel you are not accomplishing anything worthwhile, and that you are ineffective in making any changes?

_____ 18. In your personal life, do you feel you are not accomplishing anything worthwhile or that you have lost spontaneity in your activities?

_____ 19. Do you spend much time each day thinking or worrying about your job, people, future, or past?

_____ 20. Do you feel that you are at the "end of your tether"—that you are at the point of "breaking down" or "cracking up"?

_____ TOTAL

INTERPRETATION

20-30 You have no burnout. You may be taking your life or work too casually.

31-45 This is a normal score for anyone who works hard and seriously. Make sure you relax periodically.

46-60 You are experiencing some mild burnout and could benefit from careful review of your lifestyle.

61-75 You are burning out. You should seek help, reevaluate your life and make changes.

Over 90 You are dangerously burned out and need immediate relief. Your burnout is threatening your physical and mental well-being.

Differences between Burnout and Stress

- Burnout is a defense characterized by disengagement.
- Stress is characterized by overengagement.

- In burnout, the emotions become blunted.
- In stress, the emotions become overreactive.

- In burnout, the emotional damage is primary.
- In stress, the physical damage is primary.

- The exhaustion of burnout affects motivation and drive.
- The exhaustion of stress affects physical energy.

- Burnout produces demoralization.
- Stress produces disintegration.

- Burnout can best be understood as a loss of ideals and hope.
- Stress can best be understood as a loss of fuel and energy.

- The depression of burnout is caused by the grief engendered by the loss of ideals and hope.
- The depression of stress is produced by the body's need to protect itself and conserve energy.

- Burnout produces a sense of helplessness and hopelessness.
- Stress produces a sense of urgency and hyperactivity.

- Burnout produces paranoia, depersonalization, and detachment.
- Stress produces panic, phobias, and anxiety disorders.

- Burnout may never kill you but your long life may not seem worth living.
- Stress may kill you prematurely, and you may not have enough time to finish what you started.

9 | Women at Risk

Because women are culturally the providers of nurturance and caretaking, they far more than men suffer the particular strains of what psychologists call stress contagion. *Ever ready to listen and be understanding, many women feel their friends', husbands', boyfriends', children's, coworkers', or bosses' stress rubs off on them.* Harriet Braiker, Ph.D.
The Type E Woman

A WORKPLACE MAY BE perfectly normal and functional for men but completely dysfunctional for women. That's a fact! And, sadly, very often the toxicity present in such a workplace is created by men, so this chapter is not just for women.

Women are an increasing force in today's business and industrial world. Various reports have indicated that the percentage of women in managerial positions, for instance, has increased 150 percent during the last two decades and that by 1995, one out of every two new businesses will, in fact, have been started by a woman.

Yet the business world, especially at the managerial level, is still male-oriented, and in some cases, male-dominated.[1] While some change is now taking place even in the staunchest male bastions, workplaces remain chauvinistic and uncomfortable with this change. From problems that surround sexuality, to how males bond with each other and use sports analogies as illustrations in business meetings, masculine ways of working dominate every place of employment. And even where there has been some change, the truth is that this change hasn't necessarily made it safer for women in the workplace. In many places the atmosphere on the job has become meaner. Some companies are reporting a decline in the mutual respect and caring between the sexes because of increased job insecurity and competition. Others are finding difficulty in helping workers adjust to the different "styles" of work between males and females. And when women achieve positions of authority and power, many men still flip out. The need to control women is so strongly built into the male psyche in our culture, that having a female boss is an anathema. The male ego is taught to be dominant, not subservient. Significant changes in attitude are therefore required in most men if they are going to serve side by side with, or under, women.

This is why a workplace can be functional for a man but not for a woman. A new truth, however, is emerging: If a workplace is toxic for women, in the long run it will not be healthy for men either. If we cannot treat all persons with equal respect, then we are less than fully human, and all will suffer from this prejudice. Disrespect for one group can only lead to disrespect for all groups. All forms of prejudice and discrimination are pathological because sooner or later everyone suffers, including the prejudiced group.

Much of what I am going to say in this chapter can equally be said about racism. Many workplaces are toxic to those who do not match the race of the dominant group in the workforce. And racism is not only a problem of whites acting against people of color, but also of other ethnic minority groups acting against each other. The abuse of power, whether through racism or sexism, is reprehensible and needs to be confronted and eradicated at every opportunity.

ARE WOMEN THAT DIFFERENT FROM MEN?

The best, and most honest answer I can come up with is "no and yes." No, they are not all that different when you look at fundamental human motivation. Yes, they are very different when you look at how success and achievement have different meanings or connotations for women than for men.

Let's take fundamental human motivation first. What motivates all humans—both men and women? I believe it is *the need for power*. But I use "power" in its healthiest sense. I don't mean just the need to control others and have authority. I mean the need to have some influence, to make a difference and to be productive. *All* humans have a need for this sort of power. We want to count. We want to be remembered for something good, even heroic, that we have done. We also want security. We want the power that will ensure our security, that will guarantee we can pay our mortgage and put food on our table. We want the power that can help us to be self-reliant and self-efficacious. (I love the concept of "self-efficacy." It's better than self-esteem because it is less subjective and describes what I believe I am able to do with my life, not just how I feel about myself.) Above all, we want the power to survive. Survival is a fundamental human instinct, and we all need to feel that we have the ability to live a durable life.

Women, as bearers of the young, have traditionally sought security through their mates and children. Men, as providers, have sought security through status and authority. At a fundamental motivational level, however, both sexes have a need to achieve the power that will provide this security.

While the women's movement may be impacting both men's and women's dependency on traditional roles, it has not, nor will it ever change the fundamental human motivation to achieve security. We will merely adjust our roles in order to find our security in different ways.

So while there are differences in the ways each sex plays the game, the game remains the same. We need a greater appreciation of how we can cooperate with each other to achieve those needs that are so fundamentally the same.

On the matter of how women view success and achievement differently from men I will have more to say in due course.

THE MALE ADVANTAGE

For a long time, men have had the upper hand in the workplace. Women have had to take a back seat and be content with less responsibility and less pay. They have also had to put up with put-downs and demeaning jokes. This was, and still is in many places, the way men try to maintain superiority. Again and again women (at home as well as at work) have had to put up with dumb-blonde and mother-in-law jokes, all reflective of male prejudice. As women are coming into their own they are taking their revenge on male insensitivity and unjustified claims to superiority. The "in" thing in the workplace these days is jokes about dumb and insensitive men. Want a sample? "Do you know how to get a man to do sit-ups? Put the remote control between his toes."

Ouch! What about: "Why did the man cross the road? Who knows why they do anything!"

Or have you seen the greeting card with the picture of tiny men climbing in a hamster (or rat) cage? The card explains, "Oh sure, they're fun for a while, but you get tired of cleaning up after them!"

On office faxes and at cocktail parties, women are lambasting their insensitive boyfriends, husbands, or fellow workers. Especially white, middle-class, macho-type men.

I rather enjoy hearing women make fun of traditional male values and take aim at the male ego. It feels sort of appropriate, like it's now the guys' turn to get dumped on. I do have a concern, though. Where will it all end? Poking a little fun may ease the tensions a little, but doesn't it set up another pattern of stereotyping?

Some say it's a form of personal protest, a form of female bonding. After all, men have found it necessary to bond in the workplace, why not women? Most of the jokes aren't vicious and they help to give expression to the frustrations most women feel about trying to understand and work with men. But for a few, it is revenge, not just good fun. It may backfire and set back progress in developing an egalitarian workplace.

Let me emphasize that a lot of antifeminine prejudice still operates even in well-educated, non-macho, clean-cut, otherwise sensitive males. Have we really made all that much progress? Women started entering the workforce in great numbers after the "sexual revolution" era. You'd think that by now we would have developed a more tolerant view of working women, but we haven't. A survey by the magazine *Working Woman* took the wraps off what contemporary, enlightened male executives really think about women in the workplace.[2] Five men from five big companies were invited to speak out about what was on their minds. They had all learned the correct political language and understood the struggles many women have had to overcome, but they admitted that underneath, they felt a lot of resentment and hostility. Here's my summary of how these top men saw women in the workplace. It captures the most common male prejudices still encountered.

On how women approach their work:
- They don't see the big picture.
- They are too picky about small things.
- They are not as analytical as men.

On how women can be emotional:
- Women can't focus on essentials.
- They can't handle criticism.
- They have larger emotional swings than men.
- They can't "roll with the punches."
- Their crying makes everything traumatic.

On women being bosses:
- They're much tougher on other women than on men.
- They're prone to pettiness and jealousy.
- They criticize each other too much.
- They ruin the spirit of teamwork.
- They have to prove themselves too much.

On the matter of marital status:
- Single women are resented by married women.
- Married women can't work as hard as single women or men.
- There is too much resentment between married and single women (not so with men).

On the matter of male-female relationships:
- They trample all over masculinity.
- Flattery will get you everywhere with a woman.
- Women are too concerned about how they look and this gets in the way.

Most, if not all of these judgments have been formed by male prejudices. As with all prejudice, they are based on faulty logic.

A very common criticism made by men of women in the workplace is that "women are not as good as men at concealing anger or bitterness." Now, I ask you, is concealing anger supposed to be a "superior" quality? This complaint reflects the observation that when a man gets angry he doesn't show it, whereas a woman can't help but show it. Could not one argue that it is unhealthy not to be able to express anger when you are angry? Many women complain that it is impossible to tell what a male is feeling. And even when one has proof that a male is angry, he will not admit it. Males often see anger as a sign of weakness, and so deny it. Clearly, at least to me as a male psychologist, the *lack* of male emotional expressiveness is the true weakness, not the common female inability to conceal emotion. Yes, males and females differ in emotional expressiveness, but it is far from certain which sex is healthier as a result.

COPING WITH MALE PREJUDICE

How should a woman respond to male prejudice? Some prejudice is so inbred it cannot be changed, so you are better off moving to another job. If you have some hope for change, or if you are not free to move, don't overreact. Getting angry puts you at a disadvantage and only reinforces male stereotypes of women. Try to formulate a plan of action that comes out of your rational and objective thinking, not your emotions.

Identify the real prejudice. It is very easy to overgeneralize and counterattack with a shotgun blast at all male prejudice. But this won't change anything. Pinpoint the specific prejudice that is bothering you as accurately as you can. We fight wars now with "smart bombs," and this is the way to reverse prejudice as well. Smart bombs go right to the heart of the target.

When you know what the specific prejudice is, challenge it calmly and objectively. Don't be put off by rejection of your challenge. The "brush-off" is the classic male defense. If your challenge is accurate, it will find its way to the heart of the matter and you will have made a small hit even if the male outwardly defends his actions.

When the prejudice recurs, repeat the challenge with the same objectivity. Remember that prejudice has had a long time to "set." One or two challenges will barely make a dent. But just as water can cut a hole in the hardest rock if it drops over and over again on the same spot, so will focused challenges wear away prejudice.

Let me illustrate the above steps. Janet has worked for a large insurance brokerage for twelve years, slowly making her way up the corporate ladder until she was the next most senior staff person in her division below a vice-president. While the division is dominated by males, Janet has not had much problem with male relationships. Overall, the men have respected her, but only because she was kept "in her place" by the VP. The men never felt threatened by her because they had confidence that the boss would keep her in check.

Then one day the VP had a heart attack in the office while he was meeting with other VPs. Janet saw the paramedics wheel him out, maintaining CPR as they pushed him down the office corridor. He was rushed to the hospital but was dead on arrival.

The sudden death of their highly regarded boss was devastating to the staff. He was extremely popular because he behaved like "one of the boys." They could count on him to join them occasionally for a drink or go to a baseball game together. In fact, many "male only" social activities were scheduled in the office, but being left out never bothered Janet because it gave her the freedom to be with her family more.

As the shock of the VP's death began to subside, a thought began to trouble Janet. Clearly she was next in line for promotion to the VP position. But what if male prejudice prevented her from getting the job? After the funeral, she approached the senior VP who would be responsibile for appointing a successor to her boss, and asked him who was next in line. She was already acting in the position and knew she was best for it, so why not seek clarification?

To her amazement, she was told that the men in her division had already approached him to request she not be given the job. Their reasons went something like this:

"It will not be the same to have a woman in charge."

"She will not be able to go drinking with us."

"Our wives won't like it if we have a woman for a boss."

"We are mostly men, so why shouldn't a male be in charge?"

Janet remained calm. She did not overreact. She knew very well that if she did, the man would have confirmation of one of his major prejudices, one that also dominates the business world. "Women are too emotional. They cry at the drop of a hat!" She instantly identified the real source of the prejudice: Her boss was hiding behind the male staff, but the problem was really his own. *He* was the source of the prejudice. *He* had encouraged anti-women ideas and had approached the men in the office about who should be promoted.

"Did the men actually come to see you to ask that I not be promoted?" she asked pointedly.

"Well, er, no, not really," he replied. "But I know the men. They won't like it. One did come and warn me. Said he was sure you would be pushy and ask for the job." He felt smug in the thought that she had done what he predicted she would do.

"No, I am not asking for the job. I just want to make sure that I am fairly considered," Janet replied. Her logical and unemotional response took the senior VP by surprise.

Thoughts raced through Janet's mind. The senior VP had already told a partial truth, which means that he had partially lied! Should she call him on this? Why did he exaggerate about being approached by the men in her division? Why couldn't he admit that he had approached them? It could only be because *he* was prejudiced. So she decided to challenge him.

"Sir," (everyone called him "sir" because they were a little afraid of him), "I can understand why you would not want to destroy the camaraderie in the office that has built up mainly around male activities. But the office is not a social club. We have work to do and more and more women are joining the company and they feel left out by the men. I know I can do the job and build a harmonious office where men and women will feel comfortable together. What you have heard from a few men is just typical of male prejudice. Please consider me for the promotion."

She left the office. She wasn't angry. One week later she got the job. If she hadn't, I would have advised her to go over the senior VP's head, right to the top. But until Janet had given her boss an opportunity to confront his own prejudice, she needed to be patient. There may be situations where prejudice will not change. All you can do is challenge it at the highest level available to you.

Male prejudices are not the only source of problems for female workers. Female workers can be prejudiced against their own kind (or to males) in ways that can be toxic also.

What do women say about other women? Here are some responses from studies:

- It's tougher to work for another woman because there's more pettiness and jealousy than when you work for a man.
- Other stuff gets in the way, like how they look or what their lifestyle is. If they think you are prettier they give you a tough time.

- Women don't always stand up for each other. They want to please the boss too much, so often they are harder on other women.
- Women in sales have a terrible time selling to other women. Other women look them up and down and will often turn them down just because they're women.
- When two women are at each other's throats, it can ruin the spirit of teamwork. They don't seem to be able to set aside animosity as easily as men.
- Women are under too much pressure to prove themselves, so they can't behave normally. They're always playing to the audience.

Sandy was caught in a classic female-to-female prejudice. She worked as a legal assistant to a group of attorneys. The office staff comprised several female clerks and typists, as well as another legal assistant. The office had operated for many years with no one really in charge. The senior partner supervised them as best he could, but he was a softie, easy to manipulate. All the staff had learned how to play the appropriate games with him, to their advantage.

One day, the man appointed Sandy as office manager. No one seemed to mind. It made sense. But the problem was that Sandy knew an awful lot about how the office staff had taken advantage of their boss. Everyone took long lunches, quit work early, and sometimes never even returned to the office if they knew the boss wasn't going to be in. Sandy felt her responsibility was to "tighten up." She insisted that everyone sign in and out of work, that lunch breaks be limited to the agreed-upon times, and that performance be evaluated before raises were given. This was exactly what was needed, but the staff rebelled.

"What are you trying to do to us?" they complained privately. "Aren't you one of us?"

"Why are you throwing your weight around? You're just a woman like the rest of us, so stop turning against us."

Sandy was flabbergasted. Why wouldn't they accept her authority? Her fellow workers were not accepting normal management controls simply because they were coming from a woman. They wouldn't have raised an eyebrow if their male boss had called for these changes, but because they were coming from a woman they felt they had been betrayed.

Several factors lie behind such prejudiced thinking. For a long time, women in the workforce have served under males predominantly. They know the rules of male-female job interactions (they have had a long time to develop) and these unwritten rules have become the "given" in the workplace. Familiarity breeds comfort. You know where you stand, how to react, and what to expect when you work for a man. Women don't have any longstanding rules to guide them when they work for another woman, who is, after all, "one of us."

When many women first get a female boss they feel uncomfortable. The rules for interacting are not the same as for men, or at least so they think. Men generally give women greater respect than other men and treat them with less assertiveness. Some women like this and object when a woman supervisor doesn't give them the same preferential treatment. With more and more women in leadership positions this will change, but for now switching from a male to a female boss can be disappointing because women lose a little advantage. New rules for interacting will continue to emerge until these become the "given" and the prejudices are resolved.

Women are also threatened by female bosses because women understand women better than men understand women. What this means is that a woman supervising another woman can see through the ploys and gamesmanship (or should that be gameswomanship?) that operate in many male-female interactions. Sexuality is a factor that cannot be ignored in the workplace. Like it or not, males are very responsive to sexual stimuli and many can be manipulated, quite unconsciously, by some women. A female boss spells an end to this manipulation.

This manipulation is not only sexually based, but presumes upon male courtesy toward women. When women are confronted by another woman as supervisor they lose this advantage. Regrettably, this leaves many women preferring to work for men because they can take advantage of the male-female mystique.

The fact that heterosexual females and males are more naturally attracted to each other is also a factor in working relationships among women. It is very difficult not to generalize here, but my observation is that both sexes prefer to work in a mixed gender environment because it satisfies basic sexual instincts. Not to put too fine a psychological point on it, but it probably helps to sublimate the sexual drive. I am not at all saying that most women want a 50/50 mix of males and females.

Some women want to be in the minority so they can be the center of male attention. As a psychotherapist I am aware that many women look for jobs with a preponderance of males because it facilitates dating. This agenda feeds women-to-women prejudice. Look out if you are a woman perceived by other women in the office to be more attractive (to men, that is) than they are! You run the risk of having them make life miserable for you.

How do you deal with female-to-female prejudice? The same way you deal with male-to-female prejudice. You identify its precise nature and get it out in the open. Without overreacting, confront it. Keep challenging it until you begin to see it disappear.

IN WHAT WAYS DO WOMEN CONTRIBUTE TO TOXICITY?

While prejudice in the workplace can be toxic for women, the ways women interact with their work can abet a dysfunctional environment, too. The problem may not lie so much in what a woman's job is doing to her, so much as what she brings to her job. The result is the same, however: Her job becomes a place of unhappiness.

Dr. Harriet Braiker makes a very defensible case for the existence of what she calls "excellence anxiety."[3] I like her concept especially as it applies to women. I can confirm its validity because I see so much of it in my own practice. In her book, she describes her own first real attack of excellence anxiety when she was still in high school, before women's liberation. The student body had taken a poll anointing certain class members with coveted titles such as "best looking girl," "most likely to succeed," and so forth. And what did Harriet get dubbed? She received the distinction of being named "smartest girl in the ninth grade."

How did she feel? Like she had just been punched in the stomach. Like her world had suddenly ended. Her eyes burned with anger. She wanted to run away and hide. She felt that her social life in high school was ruined. What boy could possibly want to date "the smartest girl" in the class? Smartness and popularity were about as far apart as the earth's poles.

Now remember, this was in an era when girls were being instructed to keep their brains under wraps around boys. Social popularity was everything. Brains didn't count for much in teenage life. But Harriet was in a quandary. She liked being smart. She had no intention of foregoing her brain-based ambitions. But she also wanted boyfriends and a normal social life. It seemed unfair.

That night she cried alone in her bedroom. Harriet's father, hearing her, came to console her. Harriet told him her story. All he said was, "Honey, any boy who's not going to like you because you're smart is someone *you* wouldn't really like very much anyway," and left her to do her grieving.

She stopped crying shortly afterward. Her father's words rang true.

But what has this got to do with excellence anxiety? Many women are torn between their motivation to achieve and the relational consequences that may flow from it. "If I act like I'm smart, I won't be popular." The discomfort this conflict can cause ranges from vague feelings of apprehension or arousal (of which stress is made) to full-blown phobic reactions. Dr. Braiker calls this "excellence anxiety."

The feeling of anxiety connected to a strong need for achievement at the expense of something else is what excellence anxiety is all about. High-achieving women are often its victims. On the one hand they desperately want to achieve. They know that they can achieve. But they are preoccupied by the cost of achievement. Their conflict causes unnecessarily difficult psychological hurdles to overcome on the way up their career ladders. This, in turn, makes the pursuit of job success more stressful than it is for men. They become overly preoccupied with being perfect and making no mistakes (which is what "excellence" means for most people). When such striving is combined with a workplace that won't facilitate their success, the result often can be panic anxiety disorder or severe burnout.

Complicating the picture is the fact that the link between wanting to achieve and the psychological discomfort this can produce (anxiety) is much more complex in women than men. For many, a host of unresolved feelings surround the relationship between achievement and femininity, desirability, and lovability. Motives become tangled and pull them in a multitude of directions. To overcome this ambivalence and reduce their risk of stress-related disease, women need to understand how they differ from men in the ways they motivate themselves to achieve success.

According to Dr. Braiker, research shows that a woman's motivation to achieve success is virtually fused to the need for what psychologists call *affiliation*, or the need for social approval and acceptance. Women are not driven by status, but by belonging. What women fear if they succeed is rejection. It was Harriet's dilemma: "If I'm smart, I won't be popular."

High-achieving men are not dependent on high affiliation. In fact, quite the reverse. Men, on the whole, are explicitly unconcerned with making and keeping friends (an aspect of affiliation). They want status and power, which are not to be confused with popularity. So deeply ingrained in women is the need for affiliation that they often run the risk of not succeeding in the competitive world of the male if they don't bring this need under control.

The key to resolving excellence anxiety is to disconnect one's need for achievement from the need for affiliation. Succeed in your job but meet your social needs outside the job. If you fear that success will make you an outcast, chalk it up to a cultural myth. It's not generally true. And even if some turn their backs on you, you won't be short on friends for long—others who are succeeding make wonderful companions! And remember, not all men are threatened by high-achieving women.

If you are self-accepting and don't flaunt your success, but try rather to work toward *mutual* respect, not only will your stress level be lower, but your relationship needs will have the best chance for being satisfied as well. Your workplace will certainly become a healthier place.

But what can you do about your internal confusion that drives you to succeed but keeps you awake at night worrying about how you are perceived? First, and most important, is to change how you think about success. Stop thinking that if you just do the right thing you will be accepted by everybody. It's just not true. No matter what you do or don't do, some people will not accept you. Unless you can *be yourself in truth*, you will never be happy, no matter how many friends you have.

Be clear about what you really want out of your life. Be realistic in setting goals. Most people underestimate their potential and don't aim high enough. But aiming too high will only leave you more frustrated. It's better to take baby steps at first and then lengthen your stride, than to take steps that are too large at first. Successful people always know that what they are attempting is within reach. They succeed because that is how they have planned it. Those who act blindly or take ridiculous risks are really gamblers. Like all gamblers, they may win sometimes but lose most of the time. Be intentional about planning your career.

Decide how far you want to go up the success ladder. Success is a never-ending quest. The ladder has no top. Weigh the costs—to yourself, your family, and your marriage—for how far you want to go. Ask yourself tough questions about how much success is enough and give yourself honest answers. You may gain exceptional success but lose that which is dearest and most satisfying. Look around you—is every highly successful person you know really happy? If you are committed to pursuing high achievement, decide what level will satisfy you, and *do not aim higher*. Toxic workplaces encourage you to be blind to the price to be paid for success. Make sure you are willing to pay this price.

Only you can set the limit on what you will pay for the achievement *you* choose—not your job, boss or company. Make sure you keep control of this decision. It's like going to an auction. What is the cardinal rule for all experienced buyers? Set the limit on what you will pay for something *ahead of time*. If you don't set limits, you will get caught up in the heat of activity and lose perspective. In the end you'll find out that you've paid too much and what you hold in your hand is not worth the price.

Concentrate on building a *balanced* life. Being a high-achiever entails putting up with a certain amount of stress and frustration. Balance this by developing interests outside of your work which will give you something else to enjoy besides your job. Distractions will help you to lower stress and keep your perspective. A good play, moving music, a rich spiritual life, caring and supportive friendships, all help to rejuvenate the mind and the body and keep you sane, *if* they are regularly enjoyed. Neglect of the balanced life will spoil whatever success comes.

We are all controlled by expectations of one sort or another. Some are laid on us, others we lay on ourselves. Some are reasonable. For instance, I expect to get up in the morning, to get paid for what I do, and to be treated fairly. Others expect me to serve them to the best of my ability, to be honest, pay my debts, and treat them with respect. But not all expectations are reasonable. Many, especially those we lay on ourselves, go beyond what one should expect of a normal human being.

What are some of the unreasonable expectations women lay on themselves?

- I must never be seen to be difficult.
- I must never make a mistake.
- I should be able to do unlimited work without ever feeling tired or stressed.
- In order to be liked I must do everything others ask me to do.
- If there is any conflict it must be my fault.
- I have to prove myself before I will be valued.
- I must never show any weakness but prove I am always strong.
- I must never ask for help, otherwise people will think I am weak.

These unreasonable self-expectations, and many others as well, are particularly stress-producing because they are often tied to a woman's self-esteem. And anything tied to self-esteem can lose its objectivity and become irrational. There's just too much at stake. These unreasonable expectations strike at the very core of a woman's identity because they are impossible to meet. Any woman (or man) is doomed to fail at every one of them.

What makes these expectations irrational? They reflect extremes. They are arbitrary and childish. Take each in turn and ask yourself: "Is this really possible? Can I achieve this all the time?" If your answer is "no," then work at removing it from your internalized belief system. It can be helpful to write down a reasonable counter-expectation and keep it handy so you can remind yourself of it often.

For instance, against the irrational expectation that "I must never make a mistake," write "I am human and I will inevitably make a mistake. If I do make a mistake I will learn what I can and not punish myself for it."

Against the expectation, "In order to be liked I must do everything others ask me to do," write "No matter how much I do what others ask me to, they are not going to like me all the time. So I might as well stop trying to please people and do what I need to do."

Go through the list and write out your own counterpoints, then regularly remind yourself of them. You will be amazed how quickly you can begin to restore a more reasonable set of self-expectations in your life.

Two unreasonable self-expectations on the above list warrant further comment. I have encountered them so often that I believe that nearly every woman in the workplace has trouble with them.

The first concerns the expectation, "I must never be seen to be difficult." What a trap this expectation sets for you. If you don't fall into it, chances are you will stand out from the pack. You know how to speak up for yourself and how not to be pushed around. But there is a dreaded five-letter word that can devastate you. They can either say it to your face, or more likely, behind your back. In polite language it refers to a female dog or wolf, but for some reason it is used primarily by males in our culture to describe the ultimate evildoer. The words shrew, vixen, and witch don't do it. Only the dreaded "B" word does. It is often used by men to intimidate women, which is why I want to comment on it here.

Why is it so dreaded? It's only a word. Yet it is an insult that cuts deep. "Queen of mean" or "hard as nails" hardly fazes anyone these days. But b____ cuts to the bone every time.

Maureen Dowd, in a magazine article on this topic, suggests a plausible explanation for why this word has taken on such power to punish and frighten women.[4] When a man is called a "bast__d" (again, excuse me for not being vulgar and spelling out the whole word), it is an insult alluding to his mother, not his sexual prowess. So men don't feel as deeply hurt by it. But when a woman is called a b____, the arrow is aimed directly at the core of her sexual identity. The menacing implication is that she is not feminine, that she is not behaving in the way a woman is supposed to behave.

One way you can defend yourself against this word is to "desensitize" yourself to it. Write out a hundred times, "I am a 'B' and that's OK." Another is to redefine what it means for you. Redefine it to mean "He thinks I am smart, and can stand up to him, so now he is upset and is trying to hurt me." This can help to ease the hurt. After all, it is true, isn't it? Don't apologize for being direct and effective. The sooner you stop showing you are afraid of the word, the sooner men in your workplace will get the message that it doesn't have the power to hurt you anymore. If they get this message they will abandon using it.

The second unreasonable expectation worth commenting on is the belief that your self-esteem is determined by what you achieve. Nothing is further from the truth. I know that many people believe this, but it is quite erroneous. The truth is that many successful, competent people have problems of low self-esteem. Success does not build self-esteem. It never has, nor ever will. All the accomplishments of highly successful people, no matter how great, have not been able to reverse low self-esteem when their low esteem has been around a long time.

In a publication put out by the American Psychological Association on self-esteem, this is labeled as "the great paradox."[5] Citing quotes from John Quincy Adams to modern-day heroes, the theme is the same: "All my success does not convince me that I am a worthy person." More recently Gloria Steinem, the famous feminist, admitted that she has had to battle feelings of incompetence and self-doubt.[6] Low self-esteem assails her constantly. What is the explanation for this paradox? There are several. First, the foundation for low self-esteem is laid so early in life that it often operates irrationally. In other words, logic cannot undo it. Second, most people tend not to believe the positive feedback they receive in later life. They discount their successes, believing that what they achieved was not their own doing. Third, while every human being should expect to receive regular amounts of negative feedback, most people don't know how to handle it. They expect success 100 percent of the time. Since no one can get a perfect score, low self-esteem is inevitable.

So don't look to success to cure you of low self-esteem. Instead, you might want to see a psychotherapist to help you deal with the distortions in your thinking patterns that usually underlie low self-esteem. By and large, most of us can work wonders in our self-esteem simply by not paying that much attention to how we think about ourselves. Self-acceptance is the key to self-esteem, not self-enhancement. Those who stop worrying about how they feel toward themselves often show a dramatic reduction in self-hate. Self-transparency (not being preoccupied with how you look, feel, or react) helps in becoming more self-accepting. Work at self-acceptance and you will slowly undo the damage that low self-esteem does to your self.

DENYING YOURSELF SELF-CARE

You contribute a great deal to the toxic interaction between yourself and your workplace if you deny yourself appropriate self-care.

Most working women carry enormous pressures. Mothers, particularly, have to juggle several roles, work longer hours, and push themselves closer to the edge of exhaustion than men. Trying to be a "power hausfrau" while juggling a fast-track career with family needs can take its toll in depression, panic anxiety, and eating disorders. And unless *you* take care of yourself, no one else is going to. It doesn't matter whether you are married or not, you will only survive and enjoy a quality life if *you* take control and design into your life adequate self-care.

For many women, not just those in the professions, the conflict between work and family dates at least from the emergence of feminism. But it is not just a feminist issue. Economic circumstances have forced many women into the workplace so the family can enjoy a higher standard of living. For many, their very survival mandates that mothers must work at least a few days a week. Forty-five percent of the American work force is now made up of women. And with the labor force getting older, more men are retiring at one end, while more women are entering at the other. It is estimated that by the year 2005, women will make up two-thirds of the net gain in workers.[7] Clearly we are seeing a change in the gender makeup of the workforce.

What will be the impact of this? With three-fourths of women in the workplace becoming pregnant during their working lives, something will have to change. Industry will have to provide better child care. Men will have to take a greater role in parenting and housekeeping. And rigid nine to five hours and forty-hour weeks will have to be modified by both companies and workers.

But why wait for the year 2005 to see change? If your life is hassled, if you feel over-stressed or depressed, now is as good a time as any to begin a program of improved self-care. The direction corporate America is taking in order to accommodate women in the working force points to some important changes *you* ought to be making in your own life *now:*

Consider working less than full-time during periods when you are burdened with small children or ill health. A married attorney I know, quite a fast-track lawyer, cut back her work week to three days in order to become a full-time mommy the other four. She finds this schedule maintains her mind and body and meets her need for being a good mother, while keeping her hand in her career. Some sacrifices must be made if one is going to live a balanced life. The sacrifices, it is to be hoped, are only temporary.

Investigate more flexible work hours, or the viability of "flex-time." A new workforce is evolving right in front of our eyes, so why not join it? It goes to extraordinary lengths to balance job requirements with family or other priorities. With computers, fax machines, and electronic mail becoming commonplace, technology is making it possible for some people to work at home. One can do all one's work at home or combine time at the office with some at home. That's what "flextime" is all about. The work flexes to suit the worker. While some people have to be where they work, many don't. Proof of work actually completed is easy to obtain, so it is an option worth considering.

The downside of flextime or home work is the lack of social contacts. A disciplined work environment is heavily influenced by peer pressure. With flextime, that pressure is gone. You are on your own. However, many report that they get more work done without the distractions that are typical in an office. There is also reduced turnover, absenteeism, and tardiness. Even if you don't feel well enough to go to work, you can get some work done at home. The morale of flextime workers is usually way above that of regular workers. I think it is here to stay, and as communication technology progresses (with video phones for instance) more and more workers will work at home.

If you work for a large company, begin to push for a company-sponsored employee-counseling program. The workplace is full of personal problems from alcohol abuse to depression, from difficult employees to juggling child care, from job insecurity to marital problems. Everyone in the workforce benefits from having an in-house program for assisting employees. It reduces work-site accidents, raises morale, and nips serious problems in the bud. It exposes worker-to-worker abuse, helps women deal with sexual harassment problems, and genuinely empowers people to be more self-caring. Employee assistance can be helped with as little as a workplace library of books, tapes, videos, and other resources. For instance, Focus on the Family, a Colorado Springs-based family resource agency headed by Dr. James Dobson, makes available at minimal cost a complete library of resources for workplace use. CEOs who have put these libraries in place report a dramatic improvement in the quality of life for workers, who readily use the resources.

What troubles most women these days? A lot of problems have to do with the finances and economy. Job security is virtually nonexistent. Many keep asking themselves: "Will I be the next to be laid off? What effect will this have on my family's well-being?" If you are a single mother, this fear can strike at the heart of your security. Also, about 40 percent of female workers who seek help at an EAP (Employee Assistance Program) do so because of marriage or family problems.[8] Two other concerns come up repeatedly: prior sexual abuse which is causing problems dealing with particular authority figures, and infertility. Modern-day working stress seems to be taking its toll on the body's ability to procreate.

Problems like these cause a lot of depression in contemporary working women. A caring and concerned supervisor usually notices it first and is likely to draw attention to it on a performance evaluation. But by that time, damage has already been done. A work record has been tarnished. The problem, therefore, needs to be caught by a woman before it impacts her work record.

WOMEN AND DEPRESSION

Women tend to be the "bluer" sex. While there is no difference between the sexes in major depressions (i.e., severely incapacitating), most women tend to experience mild depressions ten times more often than men, according to a recent study at Johns Hopkins University.[9] Women don't start out the bluer sex. Up until puberty, boys have more depressive symptoms, but entry into womanhood sends female moodiness way above that of males.

Why? A web spun of biological, psychological, and sociological factors traps most women into frequent, low-grade depressive experiences. Hormonal factors are *not* the only reason. Not measuring up to societal standards of beauty and performance, especially in a male-dominated world, contributes greatly to the higher incidence of female depression. Many women are caught in the powerful jaws of this "cultural crunch." If you have an unhappy marriage, problem kids, or stressful job, your depressive tendencies will be very high.

If you are having memory problems, difficulty in concentrating, trouble making decisions, are fatigued often, have difficulty getting up in the morning, cry a lot, or feel sad, you need to get help for a possible depression problem. With depression, the earlier the intervention, the less intensive the treatment has to be and the quicker you will recover. Often, antidepressant medication is a necessity. Not all depressions warrant professional help. Some are mild and transitory.

How can you deal with these milder depressions? Here are some suggestions. Work at identifying *when* you are in a funk. If you can recognize when you are down, you've won half the battle. Be willing to admit it—this increases your control over it. Watch for signs like sadness, fatigue, sleep problems, weight gain or loss, decreased sex drive, and extra aches and pains. These are all associated with mild "down" periods. Talk to close friends. Ask them what they see. Solicit their help in flagging your funks. You can do the same for them.

Identify the *cause* of your depression. At bottom, the cause is usually a "loss" of something you either had or sought. The loss can be subtle and abstract, like a friend moving away or a child graduating from high school, or it can be concrete, like being broke or having your car break down. Get the cause into the open where you can be fully aware of it. This helps the grieving process. You'll get over it more quickly if you don't fight your depression.

Try getting some *distraction* from your problems. Dwelling on negative thoughts feeds depression. Try giving a tea party (English-style, of course), do some gardening, learn to play a musical instrument, or go to the movies. A change of routine can provide distraction that helps restore perspective. You will lighten your mood. The TV doesn't quite qualify here, however. You need to get a change of environment for the distraction to be effective.

Write down your unhappy thoughts so you can review them. This gives you a closer look at what's going on in your head. If you're too negative or defeatist, challenge these thoughts and substitute positive and upbeat ones.

Exercise has been shown to be an effective way to fight depression. It rids you of tension and helps you sleep better. A lot of research has shown that exercise improves certain brain chemicals that control mood. Try very moderate exercise at first—like taking a walk. Don't exhaust yourself; this will only make your depression worse.

Try some moderate *carbohydrate loading*. This is a recent discovery. Carbohydrates include the sugars, starches, and celluloses that supply energy to the body. When you're blue, carbohydrate intake often goes up—for a reason. You are instinctively "medicating" yourself. Carbohydrates increase brain levels of the "good-mood" chemical, seratonin. So, while keeping the fats away by omitting cakes and cookies, try a low fat diet (cottage cheese, carrots, tuna fish), so as to leave calorie room for the carbohydrate mind-boosters like baked potatoes, bread, rice, or even bagels.

If none of this helps, consider a brief period of psychotherapy. The sooner you get control of your minor depressions the better. Left unattended, they can grow into major depressions. Self-help cannot repair deep-seated trauma such as childhood abuse or anxiety caused by abandonment or crazy-making parents. And the therapy doesn't have to go on forever. In fact, I would warn against becoming too dependent on psychotherapy because it can prevent you from becoming self-healing. It's like the overuse of antibiotics—the body stops producing its own healing resources. Overdependence on a psychotherapist or counselor stops your mind from taking control and solving its own problems. A 1989 National Institute of Mental Health Study found that when patients with depression were treated with cognitive therapy (focusing on improving negative thinking), sixteen weeks of treatment was sufficient.[10] So search out a cognitively-oriented psychotherapist and get your thinking back on a healthier track. Your life can be more fulfilling and happier if you do.

STOP WANTING IT ALL

At the outset of this chapter, when asking the question "Are women that different from men?" I stated that while I can see no difference in how the sexes are fundamentally motivated, there are differences in how success and achievement are viewed. Let me close this chapter with some comments about this.

Harriet Braiker accurately describes how success has a different meaning for women than for men by pointing out that men confine their achievement criteria to the arena of work, money and professional or corporate status.[11] Women, on the other hand, define success as achieving in both realms of their life: career and personal. They apply a double standard. They want to achieve success in the workplace *and* in the personal arena as well. The result?

Enormous frustration and exhaustion. You cannot be everything to everybody and hope to survive. We are now seeing the results of this double standard. Panic anxiety disorder is now the number one mental health problem in women, as is ulcer proliferation, addictive tendencies, depression and sexual dysfunction.

The solution is not an easy pill to swallow, but it is simply this: stop wanting it all. Some compromises are essential. Don't rest your self-esteem on your ability to be competent in every area of your life. Choose where you want to place your priorities so that you juggle fewer balls. Work hard at achieving a high degree of competence in managing stress. And know when to quit. Quality of life needs to take precedence over quantity of achievement. That most men don't understand this is a fact to be pitied, not emulated or surpassed.

10 Sex, Power, and the Workplace

> *Common courtesy, common sense, and a habit of close observation of others' reactions to what is said and done go a long way in achieving a friendly environment where both sexes can enjoy each other's company in an atmosphere free of sexual harassment.*
>
> Ellen Wagner
> *Sexual Harassment in the Workplace*

A NY BOOK ABOUT toxic workplaces that didn't address sex and its companion, power, would be woefully shortsighted.

On the one hand, sex is a normal part of being human. Whether we admit it or not, we relate to those we are attracted to in sexual ways. On the other hand, sexuality has become distorted in our culture. We are far more preoccupied with it than people in more primitive cultures. It dominates our thinking to such an extent that it can be described as obsessional. Many otherwise normal men are virtual obsessive-compulsives when it comes to sex. The thriving pornographic industry gives evidence of this.

Many reasons account for the distortion of sexuality in our culture and it is not my purpose to explore them here. Suffice it to say that distorted sexuality overpowers some individuals, making them self-serving, manipulative power-abusers as they try to satiate sexual needs. Workers have a right to be protected from the intrusion of sexuality into the workplace, whether it's blatant coercion or subtle harassment.

Sex is nature's beautiful design not only for procreation, but for intimacy. But of all creatures, human beings have the distinction of misusing it. Gruesome and bizarre serial murders, for example, are usually tied to an insatiable hunger for extreme sexual excitement, obtained in the act of killing.

"Libido" is the name Freud gave to human sexual energy. And according to many psychologists, libido fuels much of our effort to get through the day. In other words, many people who are in dull and unfulfilling jobs may use sex in some way (fantasy, for instance) to help them survive. A client of mine put it this way: "I sit at my desk for long hours at a time. My work is boring; I have trouble keeping my mind from wandering. The hours drag on forever because of the tedium of what I do. If it were not for the women in my office who help to distract me with sexual thoughts I think I'd go crazy."

Do only men function this way? Perhaps a little more than women, but I've heard pretty much the same story from both sides. It's not that fifth or sixth cup of coffee that charges many workers' batteries and keeps them going, but the charge to their libidos, obtained by whatever means possible and available.

If we could confine our need for a recharge to our minds we would not be offending anyone else. But too often sexual needs overstep appropriate boundaries. Then unfortunately, someone always gets hurt.

Crazy-making workplaces include those that tend to allow individuals to recharge their libidos in unhealthy ways. Nude pinups, sexual jokes, flirting, extramarital affairs, and blatant use of sexually-oriented foul language, while not explicitly encouraged, are nevertheless tolerated in such a way as to make the workplace toxic for women. In the long run, such a workplace becomes toxic for everyone.

POWER, SEX, AND TRANSFERENCE

Margaret is frustrated and angry. She is a junior vice-president and the highest-ranking woman at her bank. She is on her way to work on one of the many busy Los Angeles freeways. It's stop and go. She tries to keep the gas fumes out of her car by shutting off ventilation controls and tightening windows. It's stuffy. She almost feels claustrophobic. But this isn't what's really bothering her.

What's on her mind is, "What are they going to do to me today?"

Margaret was married but it didn't work out. For the past five years she has been single. She was hurt so deeply by her first marriage that she has avoided dating and thinking about matrimony. So here she is, attractive, eligible, apparently available, and certainly desirable to several of the also divorced, single males in her place of work. Should that be a problem? It shouldn't, but it is.

Margaret has made it perfectly clear, many times, that she doesn't want to date. She has never been sexually harassed per se, if you take the strict legal definition of harassment as meaning "the persistent, unwanted sexual advances of another." Margaret is thankful she has never had to put up with that. But here she is ruminating again over "What are they going to do to me today?"

Her health has started to deteriorate. She is unhappy in her job, and worst of all, she is beginning to really hate men. She doesn't want to. But she is being forced into it by the behavior of the men who work with her.

What's the problem? Three men in her office, one being her immediate superior, are playing a game with her. The men are not conspiring in any way. But it is a game nevertheless. She senses that they are very attracted to her. Two are single and have tried to date her but she has declined. The other is married and doesn't want to date. He wants something else. All three are playing a game in which they use power of one sort or another to force her into relationships with them. Without realizing it, they have transformed their sexual desire for Margaret into a struggle to dominate and control her. It's nothing about anger directly. It is classic male domination. They all want her to admire them, even if they can't have her intimately.

Every day they "play" to her and try to get her attention. Their goal is to get Margaret to stroke their egos. They give her a lot of attention. They constantly tell her jokes; not always dirty jokes but mostly fun jokes. They tell her about their escapades and ambitions. They regularly check to see if she notices them. And every now and then they try to dominate and control her. They give her advice. They offer to take her home when her car is in for repairs. They seem to take turns as if they are in a competition to see who wins.

And so Margaret is once again asking herself, "What are they going to do to me today?" If one of them would overstep the boundary of sexual harassment she would have a legitimate complaint, but their behavior is always just within boundaries. Furthermore, they are all rather nice men in their own ways. She really doesn't want to offend them or turn them into enemies. But something has to be done because the pressure is taking its toll on her.

What is going on here is both a power and sex issue. Three men are obviously attracted to Margaret. They see her as an "ideal" woman and transfer their need to be affiliated with such an ideal person onto her. Their unmet personal needs may even cause them to over-idealize Margaret: to attribute qualities to her that are not real. "Transference" is very common because many people have a lot of unmet emotional needs. A layperson's label for transference is "infatuation," an attraction to another person that causes you to lose your senses and to be carried away by shallow affection. You can easily make a fool of yourself when you idealize another.

Now you might well ask: But isn't this a sexual issue anyway? Yes, it is. But it has more to do with sexuality than with sex. These men may want to go to bed with Margaret, but their greater need is to be connected with someone who meets the standards they have dreamed up for themselves. Each of us has created such a standard, determined by our personal history of emotional deprivation, which makes us seek closeness and intimacy. The more we have been deprived of these needs, the more we are likely to "transfer" them onto someone who appears to be our "ideal."

It then becomes more than just an issue of sexuality, or being drawn to a particular type of person we unconsciously perceive to be our "ideal." It becomes a matter of power. Unfortunately, most men don't understand how power and sexuality are linked. The need to dominate, inbred in the male so powerfully in our culture, takes over quite unconsciously. The greater the obstacle in the way of getting what you want, the greater the urge to get it. If, for instance, Margaret turned the tables and began to pursue one of her admirers, she might see an interesting reaction. By taking away the power to dominate, the man might well turn tail and run. As long as the male is the pursuer, the need to dominate is his. When he is being pursued, the ability to dominate is reversed and the game changes.

The abuse of power in the workplace, usually by males and directed toward women, shows itself in two ways in the context that I am discussing it here: *first*, in the misuse of power to achieve affiliation or sexual gratification, and *second*, the frustration of one's needs (for love or sex) produces the need to use power to dominate and control the object of one's desire. This is why so many who have examined the phenomenon of sexual harassment have concluded that it is not so much a need for sexual gratification that drives it, or even of sexual attraction toward the object of the harassment, as it is an abuse of power. The male wants to dominate.

What about Margaret? What can she do to stop her discomfort? She quickly understood the phenomenon of transference when I explained it to her and this helped to relieve her guilt. She had begun to believe that she was doing something to encourage the men.

She came to accept that for whatever reason, these particular men were idealizing her and transferring their unmet and even neurotic needs onto her. Since she could not demand that they all go into therapy to resolve their hangups, and since confronting their behavior would probably create an impossible work environment, she decided to ask for a transfer and put a healthy distance between herself and the three men.

One of the problems with the type of infatuation I have just described is that it can readily turn to hate and vindictiveness. When the one who has been infatuated suddenly comes to his or her senses, the passion can turn to vengeance. To some extent, therefore, Margaret's best interests were served by her decision to move on to a new work setting.

TRANSFERENCE PROBLEMS AND THE WORKPLACE

Transference-type problems abound in the workplace and are little understood by managers, who too quickly assume that workers' feelings reflect what's presently happening. Transference doesn't always have to do with infatuation. When someone hates another's guts, the cause may be not what the person has done, but a transfer of negative feelings. Someone, for instance, whose childhood was dominated by an authoritarian father, may well "transfer" the fear or resentment created by the father onto an authoritarian supervisor who behaves like that father. Many people who don't like being bossed by an authority figure suffer from a transference problem. Similarly, someone who was raised by a passive and co-dependent mother, who kowtowed to a brutish husband and told her children to "hush" and not upset him, may have no respect for passive-dependent people. That, too, is a transference of feelings that have no direct connection with the present person. Have you never felt afraid of someone you've just met? What accounts for this? It is probably a transference, even though you may not recall who this person represents from your past.

What this means is that some sexual harassment is an expression of hostility and not attraction. The harasser is projecting anger or hatred that belongs to someone in the past, onto someone in the present. So when you are experiencing feelings about someone else, positive or negative, consider whether you are "transferring" feelings from your past. If you can pinpoint the origin of your feelings you will find greater freedom to remove them from the one to whom you are transferring them.

SEXUAL HARASSMENT

Perhaps no greater source of toxicity for women in the workplace exists than sexual harassment. It's bad enough to be the target of transference by males, but unwarranted advances of a sexual nature can be extremely upsetting to women.

And let me make it clear I am not talking about the boss who refuses to promote a woman if she doesn't go to bed with him, or the fellow worker who writes a woman seductive notes inviting her to join him in the basement storeroom. These are blatant acts of sexual harassment that hardly need dissection. Less obvious, but equally offensive, to women are:

- unwarranted or unwanted jokes, remarks, teasing
- use of sexually explicit language, even if it is "just" swearing
- touching, leaning over, cornering
- pressures for dates
- offensive references to body parts
- sexual compliments
- offensive sexual comments

Who is most guilty of this sort of harassment? In a study of sexual harassment cases dating from 1986, one researcher found that 79 percent of the alleged cases involved a supervisor.[1] Another survey by a popular magazine found that 36 percent of complaints were against immediate supervisors.[2] Coworkers (32 percent) and other people in power (26 percent) are also frequently cited.

Perhaps the reason supervisors are more frequently cited is that they can have the power to coerce a worker into sexual compliance. The worker feels most helpless against a boss and may have to resort to more drastic action to deal with a boss than with a fellow worker. Often a woman can stop a coworker just by saying "cut it out." Bosses are not so easy to stop this way.

Sexual approaches by people in power are also taken more seriously than those from equal or lower levels. This doesn't make it less serious, it just emphasizes that more harassment is going on in the workplace than survey statistics and court actions reflect.

Courts, however, are recognizing that the "working environment" often encourages harassment by not curtailing such practices as posting pin-ups, telling dirty jokes, and dating in-house when this creates a clear conflict of roles or dual relationships which compromises the primary working relationships. The working environment is increasingly coming under court scrutiny and those in charge are being held responsible for not protecting workers from an abusive setting.

Standards and sensitivities have changed. Teenagers are more sexually active. Sexual innuendo that used to be funny when expressed as a joke loses its humor because it is reality. Also, sexual innuendoes offend because often their motive is an ulterior one. Men and women, regrettably, view harassment differently, even when the men are educated professionals. Education and breeding can make harassment even more subtle.

For men especially, allow me to describe how sexual harassment debilitates women. Their typical feelings are revulsion, violation, disgust, anger, and powerlessness. Harassment rattles a woman's confidence. It forces her to face someone who believes he owns her or has a right to her. Often she sees the man as repulsive. Even though he may not be coming on directly and saying "Have sex with me," that is the message she hears behind the compliment, touch, or look. His love letters become her hate mail. She may get headaches, ulcers, asthma, or other stress-related disorders. At home she becomes short with her husband. She's had to defend herself against sexual innuendoes all day, and finds it easy to transfer her resentment to her sexual partner at home. Bottom line: Sexual harassment is an offensive and demeaning experience. I wish all men could grasp this truth.

Why do smart men who can discern subtle issues in other areas harass a woman, even when repeatedly rebuffed and even threatened? Some suggest it is because our culture trains men to push.

They won't take "no" for an answer—they don't even hear it. "Testosterone deafness," I call it. Many men believe the myth, passed on from fathers to sons, that it is natural for a woman to say "no" the first time you approach her. After the fourth or fifth time she will change her mind. So they keep coming back, not realizing what damage it is doing emotionally.

Why do so many women tolerate harassment? Why does it go on for such a long time before being reported? Because women are often in a catch-22 situation. It's a matter of survival. When women complain, they are ignored or they are told, "If you're going to work here you have to put up with it." This is particularly true of workshops or factories where men predominate. So women wait and hope it will stop but it doesn't. Battling it takes the courage to face the fact they may lose their jobs and be marked as troublemakers.

Why are institutions so slow to respond? Employers have enough problems, without also having to teach appropriate behavior to employees. It's just too costly and inconvenient for managers to deal with. Mostly they want to sweep sexual harassment under the rug and hope it goes away.

Is sexual harassment always male to female? Yes, it is mostly, though men are also harassed, both by other men (an increasing problem) and also women to a lesser degree. Fourteen percent of men in a 1991 British survey said they had been harassed.[3] Sometimes lesbians are making the accusations; sometimes heterosexuals are accusing gays. To what extent these accusations reflect the discomfort some feel with gay people in the workplace is not clear. What is clear is that sexual harassment is becoming more complex and now involves same-sex harassment as well as opposite-sex. And because the workplace is where much harassment takes place, the problem must be dealt with there. Everyone has the right to work in an environment free of harassment. Management's responsibility is to ensure that such an environment is created and maintained.

WHAT ARE A WOMAN'S RIGHTS?

In 1964, Congress enacted Title VII of the Civil Rights Act which prohibits all forms of discrimination in all aspects of employment. But the term "sexual harassment" did not emerge in the courts until 1975 when it was prohibited, with some reluctance, as a form of sexual discrimination. Judges feared that "flirtations of the smallest order would give rise to liability."[4] Their feeling was that the attraction of males to females and females to males was a natural phenomenon and that this attraction played a subtle role in most personnel decisions.

The tide began to turn after 1976, when the well-known case of *Williams vs. Saxbe* was considered. Williams, a Justice Department employee, claimed her supervisor terminated her employment because she refused to have sex with him. She won the case. The court upheld her right to employment without having to give sexual bribes to her employee. While sex may be a natural phenomenon, no one had the right to demand it as a favor for employment.

Finally, in 1980, the Equal Employment Opportunity Commission issued its guidelines on sexual harassment. This now-famous document defines sexual harassment as "unwelcome sexual advances, requests for sexual favors, and other verbal or physical conduct of a sexual nature," when it is made a condition of employment, is used as the basis for employment decisions, unreasonably interferes with an individual's work performance, or creates an intimidating, hostile, or offensive work environment.

Can the work environment itself be blamed for harassment? For example, cases have been dismissed where a supervisor pestered a female worker to spend afternoons with him in his apartment, and another where a supervisor begged an employee to go on a Bahamas trip with him. These cases would seem to exemplify behavior deemed unacceptable in the guidelines. Yet they were dismissed. It wasn't until 1986 that the Supreme Court ruled on the case of a bank employee who had been harassed by a supervisor with whom she had felt coerced to have sex forty or fifty times. The bank was held accountable because it had provided a hostile environment that had tolerated such coercive behavior. This finding was a turning point which sent a clear warning that workplaces would be held responsible for what goes in them.

WHAT, THEN, IS SEXUAL HARASSMENT?

From the Equal Employment Opportunity Commission's definition there are two criteria for "formal" sexual harassment charges: the conduct must be of a *sexual nature*, and it must be *unwelcome*.

But when is the conduct unwelcome? When it is unsolicited, the victim has done nothing to invite it, and the victim views the conduct as undesirable or offensive.

Furthermore, just because a victim acquiesces to sexual advances doesn't mean they are welcome. The Supreme Court has made it clear, as in the case of the bank teller who had sex forty or fifty times with her supervisor, that involvement may still be unwelcome. The victim, the court ruled, agreed to the sex out of fear of retaliation and losing her job. Though she acquiesced, she did not welcome the involvement.

It is absolutely imperative when women experience behavior that makes them feel uncomfortable that they clearly, and preferably with a witness, tell the perpetrator that the behavior is *unwelcome* and *offensive* at the outset. Otherwise, coworkers and former lovers may well claim they were entitled to assume that previously welcomed behavior *was still welcomed*. Specifically, women should give notice to those with whom they have ended relationships that *any* advances will be unwelcomed.

Now let me play devil's advocate for a moment and address the problem from a man's point of view. Women are also responsible for what they say and how they behave. Both speech and behavior can have far-reaching effects on how much harassment a woman will experience, and whether or not she can defend a charge she may bring against a coworker or boss. Women would be wise not to give grounds for "come-ons" or allegations that they encouraged sexual advances by their own behavior.

I know a happily married family man who has never been tempted to stray sexually, but a young woman who was recently added to his office is unsettling him. She dresses seductively with low-cut blouses and short skirts that rise when she sits in a meeting. All the male executives, including my friend, are distracted by her.

Try as he may, he can't keep his eyes from wandering to this woman's exposed features. The harder he tries to control his eye-wandering, the more compulsive it becomes. He doesn't like what he does and fears that the woman will take his uncontrolled glances as a form of sexual harassment. He knows that if anyone dares tell her not to dress the way she does she will become offended. She will protest that she is not intending to be sexually provocative, just attractive.

"How can someone persist in being so provocative, and yet hope to be protected from inappropriate advances?" he pleaded to me.

He is absolutely right! Men deserve protection also! How are males supposed to react to blatant sexual stimuli? Walk around with ultra-dark glasses? Go home several times throughout the day and take cold showers? I have heard *many* respectable men voice this frustration. Some have suggested that there is a double standard: women can be as sexually provocative as they want to be, but men are not supposed to react. No amount of sexual provocation can justify inappropriate or unwanted sexual advances, but it does make working a strain.

What advice did I give my friend? I suggested that he talk the problem over with the personnel officer, who happened to be a woman, and have her give the woman in question some feedback on how she was being perceived. It worked. She immediately began to dress more appropriately and the problem was solved.

OFFENSIVE SEXUAL BEHAVIOR

What constitutes offensive sexual behavior? One thing is clear: it doesn't have to be confined to providing sexual favors. In one court case, three female construction workers had their lives made difficult by male workers who were trying to get rid of them. The men locked the restroom at the job site, refused to stop on the road so one of the women could go to the bathroom, and even urinated in the gas tank of one of the women's cars. These acts are not explicitly sexual, but they are based on the gender of the victims. The plaintiffs won their case. Sexual harassment can go beyond sex to humiliating someone of the opposite sex. This has more to do with power than sexuality.

So there are two types of conduct that will not be tolerated. The first is the *quid pro quo* (getting something in return for something) arrangement, and the second, the hostile environment condition. *Quid pro quo* can take the form of advice: "If you really want to succeed in this job you need to keep close to me." Or it can be exchange of favors: "It's very easy for me to fix up that promotion for you, but what's in it for me?" Usually the perpetrator is in a position of authority over the victim and is, in effect, abusing his or her power. And since one's job, salary, and promotion prospects are always at risk, damages can easily be claimed in a court of law.

Hostile environment allegations are a little more difficult to prove. Here the harasser can be anyone in the workforce, including fellow workers, as we saw in the construction site example. One isolated incident is not enough to prove a hostile environment. It has to be continuous, deliberate, and part of an overall pattern. This can be difficult to establish, unless one keeps careful records and gets statements from witnesses.

Furthermore, the hostility must interfere with one's job performance or the job itself must be abusive. It is important, therefore, if you feel thus violated, that you keep records, and even get photographs or videos of the abusive behavior.

Those in management positions need to ensure that adequate policies are in place *and enforced* against sexual harassment. Employees need to feel that it is not difficult to lodge a complaint, and that complaints are acted upon. Common courtesies and respect for the opposite sex (for women *and* men) need to be encouraged.

And for those who fear that harassment concerns are being taken too far, let me say that sexual harassment has nothing to do with normal, pleasant, friendly interactions. As long as good communication exists between the sexes in the workplace, even mildly flirtatious or appropriate compliments between the sexes will not offend. We all enjoy being told we look good or that a new dress, hairdo or tie suits us. A friendly work environment is essential to good morale, but both sexes can enjoy each other's company only when the atmosphere is free of harassment. Anyone suspected of being a sex addict or deviate should be required to get help. It may also be necessary to monitor the behavior of such a person. Sexual addictions are powerful controllers of behavior. Such an afflicted person should have a close friend or work colleague who can help him (and occasionally her) monitor behavior.

WHAT SHOULD YOU DO IF YOU ARE HARASSED?

If you perceive that you are being sexually harassed at work you can do the following:

1. File a complaint with your local, state-run Department of Fair Employment and Housing (DFEH) office. You have to file the complaint within one year of the harassment—this is the statute of limitations for such charges.

2. If the DFEH judges the complaint to be valid, you could receive up to $50,0000 in damages (in California, that is; check on your own state regulations).
3. If the DFEH cannot resolve the case you will receive a "right-to-sue" letter, acknowledging that you have followed the normal administrative procedures. You can then see a lawyer to file a civil lawsuit.
4. Another option is to file with the federally run Equal Employment Opportunity Commission (EFOC). Since federal law is almost identical to state law, there are only minor differences in the way they handle cases. However, the statute of limitations is only three hundred days (about ten months) under federal law. Also, whereas the state (again I am referring to California; it may be different for your state) can file against both the employer *and* the employee, the federal EEOC files only against the employer.
5. There is yet another approach: You can file a worker's compensation claim. This is used when the victim needs disability payments for medical treatment for emotional stress suffered on the job as the result of the harassment. The claim is made against the employer's insurance carrier.
6. Finally, you can lodge a grievance complaint with your company or organization. Staff policies will spell out what you should do.

It is sad that one has to resort to taking legal action to deal with sexual harassment. One hopes that in time the need to do this will gradually diminish as men, particularly, learn to respect the rights of women and, more importantly, come to understand how vulnerable women feel in sexual power plays. The power differences between men and women place women at much greater risk for abuse in the workplace; in such situations, women always suffer more.

A CLOSING WORD TO MEN

The average male today has been detrimentally affected in his sexual development by many unsavory influences while growing up. In a powerful 20/20 TV program (ABC January 29, 1993) a large group of young men at Duke University were interviewed about their sexuality. Every single male interviewed admitted that his attitude toward women had been detrimentally influenced by his exposure to nude magazines and pornography. This exposure occurred at a very early age for most of them. They had learned to masturbate to pictures of pretty women with perfect bodies. Their understanding of sexuality had been influenced by the portrayal of women as sex objects, both in the pictures and stories. In these magazines, every woman is portrayed as a nymphomaniac just waiting to be seduced. According to the young men at Duke, this is the mind-set of the average young male entering the workforce today.

The result? They expected *all* women to be sexually ready at all times; women who say "no" don't mean it and are only wanting to be pursued further. Even more disturbing, these young men reported that they were having great difficulty relating to real women because sex was not seen as a very intimate or personal relationship, but more like an action to achieve release from sexual tension. In a nutshell: these men wanted sex, not a relationship.

Is this true only for young men today? No! I can assure the reader that I believe it to be true for a high percentage of males of all ages. All of this has led me to this conclusion: The sexual development of males in our culture has gone off the rails. It's not just that sexual matters dominate the male psyche—this has always been true and is determined by hormones more than anything else. It's that the only way many men learn about sex and women is through distorted portrayals of women in that branch of the media that serves the male's warped interest in sex. As a consequence, the average male thinks about sex for a larger part of the time than he would otherwise. This high degree of preoccupation with sexual matters can get in the way when men are trying to focus on work.

Many men also experience a high degree of sexual frustration. Testosterone in the normal male sees to this. There seems always to be more appetite for sex than can reasonably be satisfied and the media plays off this frustration by using sexual stimuli to get male attention and sell their wares. Often this only creates more frustration and makes men more open to sexual stimuli in the workplace, with the potential for harassment behavior.

For some, and for more than we realize, the perpetual state of frustration combined with early exposure to pornography or sexual experiences can set up an "addiction" to sex. Sex becomes a "fix" that is as powerful as any drug. The urgency to achieve sexual satisfaction can become overwhelming, and when it reaches the proportions of an addiction, it lacks control. Even the most moral can slip into inappropriate behaviors, as evidenced by the frequency with which clergy fall into sexual sin.

What can a man do about this obsession with sex? He may find it an interesting exercise to keep a log of his thoughts through a typical day, or examine his thoughts about the women in his working life and see how much of what he is thinking is sexual in nature.

He needs to better understand his sexuality, and the extent to which his obsessions and compulsions are out of control. If he has a sexual addiction he needs to get professional help, or at least seek out an effective self-help group such as *Sex Addicts Anonymous.* (Check your local telephone directory for the number.) If such men don't get help now, they may face serious legal and civil problems later.

Of course, there are men out there who merely want to abuse power or who are angry at women and want to hurt them by being sexually explicit, using filthy language, or making lewd suggestions. There are plenty of such men. They usually don't seek help.

My concern here is not with such men. They deserve what they get when they abuse women. Their actions need to be dealt with to the full extent of the law. My concern is, rather, with the average male whose offensive behavior is without malice and whose sexual development has been so distorted that he sees women only as sexual objects. Most of the men I have worked with in therapy who have been accused of sexual harassment fall into this category. They honestly believed that their feelings were being reciprocated; that the women involved were open to their advances and that they were only doing what was natural. The men erroneously believed that women are as preoccupied with sex as they were. Such men *can* change their attitudes. There is no excuse for their behavior. Stepping out of line is no longer permissible, no matter how innocent the motive.

The workplace will never be free of sexual feelings, because wherever there are humans there will be these feelings. But it *can* be free of distressing pressures and distasteful sexual suggestions. We will be the healthier for doing our part to make our workplaces safer and more congenial for all. No workplace can be healthy until it is free of sexual harassment.

Are You Being Exposed to Harassing Behavior?

It is very easy to get used to sexually harassing behavior. When it's all around you and everyone seems to put up with it, you settle down and ignore it. Soon you don't even notice it—but it is still there and sooner or later, it is going to get to you or hurt someone else.

Here is a checklist of workplace behaviors considered to be inappropriate. The behavior is either blatantly distressing or it sets the stage for harassment. Check if it is present.

CHECK

_____ 1. One or more workers tend to tease women more than men, or they carry the teasing too far so that it becomes annoying.

_____ 2. Jokes are frequently told that have sexual innuendoes or are demeaning to women.

_____ 3. Men frequently touch women or physically confine, lean over, corner, or sit close to women.

_____ 4. Women are pressured for dates even though they have already declined, or are subjected to flirtatious behaviors even though they have objected to it.

_____ 5. Privileges (like going to lunch early or taking the afternoon off) are made conditional upon certain social favors (like "if you will have lunch with me").

_____ 6. Men flaunt pin-up posters around the workplace even though they know they are offensive to the women present.

_____ 7. Men often initiate conversations about your sex life or probe for information about dating relationships.

_____ 8. Men show a willingness to discuss their own sexual experiences or want to discuss their own sexual disappointments with their spouses.

_____ 9. Nude or pornographic magazines are deliberately displayed so as to be seen by women.

_____ 10. Language is offensive with frequent use of sexual expletives, or drawing attention to parts of the body.

_____ 11. Sexual propositions are made a part of normal work banter, so that the perpetrator can always claim, "I was only joking—don't be so serious."

_____ 12. Certain men frequently expose themselves by failing to close a toilet door, or assume sexually provocative postures while standing or sitting.

_____ TOTAL

The more checks you have, the greater your exposure to a sexually harassing environment. I have not mentioned overt sexual advances or sexual propositions linked to threats or promises because these are blatantly harassments and need to be reported immediately to the highest supervisor you can get access to.

Ways Women Can Provoke Men

There are many ways in which women can unwittingly provoke, or even harass, men in the workplace. While no behavior on the part of a woman can ever justify a male's harassment, inappropriate behavior can sometimes reinforce male tendencies that might create unpleasant tensions in the workplace. Here are some inadvertent or inappropriate behaviors that can provoke men:

- Enjoying being "office wives" (making/serving coffee to their coworkers or superiors; running errands as if they were substitute spouses, etc.).

- Wearing suggestive clothing (low-cut blouses, tight clothes, short skirts, etc., in a work setting).

- Playing therapist to males, especially feeding into what they perceive as unhappy marriages.

- Allowing men to discuss their sexual escapades, thus providing a feminine audience that is arousing.

- Inadvertently sharing your own sexual escapades or frustrations with men, believing that they are genuinely concerned about your welfare, when they are just being voyeurs.

- Being flirtatious or overly friendly with a male whom you don't intend to date, thus sending a false message.

Changing Your Job

The key to the ability to change is a changeless sense of who you are, what you are about and what you value. Stephen R. Covey
The 7 Habits of Highly Effective People

Decide now what you want on your tombstone: "He had a job that paid well but he hated it," or "He enjoyed his work." Wes Smith
Welcome to the Real World

A MONG THE MANY CHANGES predicted for the next century, one really stands out: People will change careers two to three times over the course of their lifetimes. Not just change their jobs, but change their careers.

This prediction fascinates me because I changed careers about fifteen years into my working life. My first career as a civil engineer was a good fit with my gifts, and I quickly became a senior executive. So why did I change? Because a need wasn't being met.

In my late twenties I was responsible for supervising a staff of engineers, architects, and planners. I also had to deal with contractors, consultants, and the public under stressful conditions. Being so young, I felt out of my depth in dealing with the "people aspect" of my work. Show me where you want a bridge. Tell me how many people you want to house in a suburb, or give me responsibility for designing a water supply system or a major highway—and I was in my element. But people-managing was another matter, and I soon knew it. How was I to select the best person for a particular position? How could I fire someone who was incompetent without getting emotionally involved? More important, how could I manage people and stay sane? These questions vexed me.

So I devised a plan. I persuaded my boss to let me take a few courses in psychology. My specific interest was industrial psychology. I wanted to be a better executive engineer, to know how to handle job analyses, personnel selection, in-service training, worker stress and, most important of all, retain my soundness of mind.

My boss was enthusiastic. He didn't like dealing with people much either. Maybe some of what I would learn would rub off on him. He even agreed to pay for my courses.

As soon as I began to delve into psychology I found myself more attracted to its clinical aspects than to its industrial or engineering applications. I began to see that many of the people I had to deal with had underlying emotional problems. People could easily become dysfunctional in their work because their personal lives were in a mess. They became crazy-making because they felt crazy. Problems with alcohol and post-war traumas began to take on a new meaning for me. Because I was very active in my church, I began consulting with pastors, teaching seminars on how to be a better parent, how to cope with depression, and how to relieve anxiety.

I never thought I would quit engineering. I figured I could function in both professions. Why not? An engineer with a degree in psychology might be a better engineer! But that idea was to change. The years rolled by and before I realized it, I had completed a master's and doctoral degrees. Now what?

Early in my career transition, I met a group of students from Fuller Theological Seminary and helped to found an organization to help churches be more vital and relevant. They told me about the plans taking shape for a school of psychology at the seminary. What a fantastic idea, I thought. Could I possibly take some time off the dual career lifestyle I had developed and do some post-doctoral study in a school of clinical psychology based in a seminary setting? Relating psychology to theology had become a strong interest.

So I wrote to the dean of the newly-founded graduate school of psychology and asked whether I could be a visiting scholar. He invited me. I packed up my family and we went to Fuller. I fell in love with the place and found the perfect outlet for my talents. So we stayed and my new career became my passion.

TILL DEATH DO YOU PART

I grew up believing that success was measured by whether or not you stuck to your job all your life. People who changed jobs were suspect. Work was like marriage. Once you make your commitment, you stick with it, like it or not. That's what most people believed when I entered the workforce.

Those who changed their jobs regularly were considered unstable and even immature. When I hired staff in my engineering days, a resume that showed several job changes always raised my eyebrows. Stability is what I looked for, "because it breeds maturity." We all believed that.

Now I'm not so sure. Changing jobs, even changing careers, may be a sign of maturity, not sticking with the dissatisfaction your whole life. And those who are stuck in toxic workplaces with no prospect of it getting healthier may be wise to consider whether the time has come for them to move on.

But first, some reflections on how things are changing, because they are. The greatest social changes ahead will be in the workplace, as companies struggle to keep up with a workforce that is undergoing a major overhaul of values. I will refer to how we are accustomed to thinking as the "old model." What is emerging and will certainly be in vogue in the next century is the "new model."

Characteristics of the "old model":
- Career moves were always upward.
- Fitting into the company was more important than personal ambition.
- Job prestige was important to feed ego needs.
- Loyalty to the company was rewarded more than quality of service.
- Promotions came regularly and usually at predetermined intervals.
- Job security was paramount, not what you did or how satisfied you felt.
- Success was measured by the size of your check and the status of your position.
- You put up with job stress whether you liked it or not.

Characteristics of the "new model":
- Career moves are often to the side, not upward, if they better suit personal needs.

- Job satisfaction is more important than security.
- Interest and challenge on the job are more important than salary.
- Many will opt not to advance into high stress positions, choosing to stick with less stress.
- Advancement has no schedule—one may stay in the same job for many years, or be advanced every few months.
- Employee aspirations are as important as the company's interests.
- Success means having a job one enjoys and grows in, regardless of status or amount of the paycheck.

Evidence of these changing attitudes and values came out in my counseling with a top executive recently. Now in his early fifties, Ron has felt for some time that he needed to simplify his life in order to feel more at ease and contented. A man of tremendous talent, his company literally "eats him up," as he puts it. Consequently his responsibilities have grown tremendously, along with power, prestige, and a salary package that could make almost any heart skip a beat.

But Ron is struggling with a crucial question: Is it worth it? He has little leisure time. His work intrudes into his church life. He is constantly under tension. He can't find time to enjoy his family. And his wife complains about his frequent absences on business trips or the chaotic deadlines that keep him away on weekends.

Believe me, Ron is successful by worldly standards. But now he is realizing something very important: his life is out of balance. What he is forced to do isn't what he wants to do. So we talked about how to restore equilibrium in his life. As he shared his plan for the future, I could sense where he was headed.

"I want to downsize my job," he said. "I don't need prestige and power any more. My sanity is more important."

He proposed that he request a demotion. He didn't want to change his company, just his job. He wanted to move downward to a level where he could feel comfortable and achieve enough income with less responsibility. He had it all worked out. All he wanted from me was a listening ear and an honest response if I thought he was crazy.

I told him he wasn't crazy. He was doing what many would like to do—get rid of the surplus in their lives so that they can feel happier and more at peace. We're moving into an era when this will become more and more common. People have a growing new determination to control their destinies as employees.

I saw Ron again several months later—contented and much less stressed. Life is worth living once again.

But not everyone has the luxury of changing a job to suit one's needs. Experts are warning everyone to make an inventory of his or her skills, to add to them regularly, and always be ready to answer the question: "What would I do if I lost my job tomorrow?"[1] People ages fifty to sixty, though still energetic, are being pushed out or shot with the silver bullet of early retirement in extraordinary numbers. Moving to a new job may not always be your choice. But if it is, some very important principles should be followed.

For many, it's easier to put up with the crazy-making than to move to another job. Most of us find it somewhat threatening to contemplate moving to a new company or organization. A few may be fortunate enough to be pursued or wooed to a better job, but for most, the initiative has to be their own.

How can you tell if you need to change your job? This may be easy to answer in some circumstances. If you are extremely unhappy in your job and see the cause not in yourself but in your toxic work surroundings, or if you are bored out of your mind with what you do and cannot apply yourself consistently to your work, you need to consider changing.

Being unhappy may not always be an adequate reason. Keep in mind that nobody is ever happy at work at all times. Studies show that most people rate their job-satisfaction at about 60 percent.[2] So if you are happy for less than that, you may well be in the wrong job or career. If your satisfaction is over 60 percent, perhaps you just need a vacation.

In other circumstances it is more difficult to decide if you must change. You may be bored, but get paid well for that boredom and your company really appreciates you. Prospects for promotion may soon move you away from your present unpleasant circumstances. Or the economy may be so bad that leaving your job will put you out of work for a long time. What should you do?

This raises what I consider to be a cardinal rule in all job changes: *never leave one job until you are sure about another,* unless you have very good reasons or prospects.

I have worked with many people in therapy over the years who were unhappy and quit their work without knowing where a new job was going to come from. I have never seen it work out without much pain. Finding a new job when you are unemployed is always more difficult. Besides, why not continue to earn wages while exploring the prospects for a new job?

There are exceptions, of course. If a job is so abusive that you are harming yourself by staying, you may need to take courage and leave before you've found another placement. If you are moving to a new locality, you may be forced to resign your position and take your chances on finding another. But, generally speaking, a bird in the hand is worth two in the bush, so keep the job you have until you are sure of a better one.

Just being unhappy in your work by itself is not enough reason to change a job. Are you sure it is the job that is making you miserable? The unhappiness may not be job-related. You may be depressed and projecting the negativity that comes with depression on your job. Your depression may have a biochemical cause or you may be suffering from a disorder like chronic fatigue syndrome. Or upheaval in your home life may be depleting your energy so you don't have enough to give to your job.

Emily is a good example of how causes outside one's work can make one unhappy. Her job was to find companies or other institutions to buy her bank's money. The job took Emily on a business trip at least once a week. Her kids were in their late teens and quite able to care for themselves. Her husband was another matter!

A bit of a playboy, he resented Emily's absences. She was never gone more than three nights and made up for this by having a flexible work arrangement so that she could do some of her work at home. But hubby didn't like it. Selfish and hedonistic, he didn't like being alone. He wanted to live it up. So he started going out with the boys the nights Emily was away. He made sure she knew about his escapades so she would worry. And worry she did. This was her second marriage. She had met her present husband while he was still married and here he was repeating his previous behavior. She knows, because she was the one he dated while he was still married. *Déjà vu!* How long will it be before he takes up with someone else?

Emily became very unhappy. While traveling, she would worry about her husband, wondering what he was doing. She would make repeated phone calls home to check up on him. And most of the time he wasn't there! She began to bungle her job. She wasn't paying attention to the needs of clients so they began to complain to her boss. Unhappiness at home was making her unhappy on the job. Her work performance began to decline, and made her even unhappier.

When I met Emily, she was an emotional wreck. Her job, she felt, was the real problem. If she didn't have to be away so much her husband wouldn't be so unhappy and would stay home. She had come to hate her work. But as we began to explore her circumstances in depth, it became clearer that her unhappiness wasn't with her job at all. Slowly Emily began to realize that her husband was merely blaming her job absences to justify having a good time. So we arranged to change her work arrangements temporarily so that she would be away only once a month. Did her husband stay home? He didn't. He was playing out some old habits.

Emily took a "tough love" stand, confronted her husband, and demanded that they get counseling. If the job was contributing to the problem, it was doing so only peripherally. With some changes she was able to restore her job satisfaction. I am sorry to say that while there was a temporary improvement in the marriage, it did not survive. Hubby had already taken up with someone else!

For unhappiness, then, to be a reason for job change you must be certain that it is truly the job that is causing it and nothing else. Some people will be unhappy wherever they go. Here are some pointers for evaluating whether or not your unhappiness is based in your work. Your answers to the following questions should help you decide:

- Have you had a long history of being unhappy? If so, are you sure it's your job that is making you unhappy?
- Have you ever been in a job that has made you happy?
- Do others see you as basically an unhappy person?
- Are you unhappy at work but happy at home?
- Are you happier when you are on vacation and away from the job?
- Have you tried to change your attitude to your job to see if you can be happier?

Having worked through these questions, if you are still convinced that your job is the problem, begin planning for a change.

IS IT ENOUGH TO BE BORED?

Job boredom can take many forms. Some jobs are so simple and repetitive that boredom sets in very easily. One cannot remain interested doing the same thing over and over again. Factories, therefore, try to provide ways to reduce boredom. Music can be a distraction. Changing job assignments at regular intervals can minimize repetition fatigue.

Other jobs that are more complex can also cause boredom. I know a surgeon who specializes in one type of surgery. Since I've always been fascinated with surgery, especially the more complex surgery that he does, I commented one day, "Your job is most fascinating. It must keep you most interested."

His response at first surprised me, then I realized it was consistent with what I have repeatedly told my clients when they complain of job boredom. He replied, "I am bored out of my skin. It was exciting at first but when you've done the same procedure over and over again, it becomes tedious. I wish I could do something else." I told him what I have told scores of clients: *Every job becomes tedious with repetition*. No matter how interesting a job is when you just start doing it, it becomes boring when you've done it a zillion times.

The problem is with human beings, not with jobs. Humans thrive on novelty. We want newness, originality, innovation. We don't like doing the same thing over and over again. Sooner or later, with very few exceptions, whatever we do will become monotonous.

Is boredom, then, enough reason to change a job? Not if you are mature enough to accept that everything you do can't always be thrilling and exciting. Work is work, not play. Work means service, not pleasure. Games are for leisure time.

Yes, I know there are some jobs that seem all pleasure—or are they? Whenever I can, I check out reality with someone I think is having a ball. In Hawaii I saw a man taking care of a beachfront rental booth for watercycles, surfing gear and the like. He looked well-tanned and healthy, about forty. I thought he must be one of those really happy workers I think about when I'm bored. So I went up to chat. I did my rapport-building thing (we psychotherapists have it down pat) and asked him how he enjoyed his job.

"Hate it," he replied. "Wish I worked in a bank or something." He explained that the first year was great. He loved the beach, the girls, the surfing, the fun. But five years later, he is bored out of his skin. "And now I'm not trained for anything else! What am I going to do when I'm older?" he asked, with what looked like tears in his eyes.

I strolled across the street to a small golf practice range. I thought I would try my hand at some driving. The girl who rented me the club and bucket of balls looked a little pale for anyone native to Hawaii. I thought, "She must enjoy her job. Let me check it out."

"Yes," she said, "I am ecstatic about my job. Love the people. Little stress. Evenings are fantastic—parties and things."

I must have looked skeptical.

"It's true," she insisted. "This is a fantastic job. Wish I'd come over from the mainland sooner. Been wasting my time in Dallas."

"How long have you been doing this job?" I asked, still suspicious about her untanned skin.

"Oh, I just arrived last week. My uncle owns this range. I've come to help him out. Don't know how long I will stay here—years, I suspect."

Should I disillusion her? No—let her have her fun. She's in the honeymoon phase of a new job. Wait till the tourists get on her nerves. Wait till the novelty fades. I don't have to be a genius to predict her future. I could make my own projections and know I would be correct. All work, even if it seems like a lot of fun at the beginning, will sooner or later become routine. If it isn't yet, one day it will be. Let's just accept this and get on with the one certainty in life, next to death: We all have to work, but the mature person knows how to turn routine into meaningful activity.

How can you tell if your boredom justifies a job change? Here are some questions for you to work through. Answer "yes" or "no" to the following:

- Are you the type of person who always wants to be kept interested?
- Do you regularly seek out excitement or stimulating activities?
- Do you find it uncomfortable just to relax and do nothing?
- Do you become impatient whenever you have to wait in line?
- Do you often buy something, no matter how small, just so that you can feel better?
- Do you complain about being bored at parties, picnics or other recreational activities after only a short while?

If you answer "yes" to more than two of these questions, chances are you will become bored with any work. You may need to examine why you find routine unpleasant and ask yourself whether you are addicted to novelty or excitement. You may be better off taking up an exciting hobby to give you your fix, than to leave your job.

If you are convinced that your boredom lies in your job and not in yourself, then perhaps you should consider a job change. I'll have more to say about how to prepare for that later in the chapter.

OTHER REASONS FOR MAKING A JOB CHANGE

Besides feeling unhappy or bored, what are some of the other reasons that can prompt a job change?

Many workers are trapped in jobs with bosses who make life hell for them. Sometimes the boss is just plain sick. Sometimes it is a personality clash. But moving to a new job may not be the best solution. The questions you must face are:

- Am I in any way responsible for the conflicts I am having with my boss?
- Is there anything I can do that will improve our relationship?
- Even if I decide to move on, can I resolve my present boss conflicts and feel better about myself?

Boss conflicts are such a problem that I devoted chapter 5 to a more complete discussion of this topic. Now may be a good time to review it.

If your job doesn't fulfill you, the reason is more difficult to analyze because "job fulfillment" is almost impossible to define. Part of the problem is connected with the boredom factor already described. Furthermore, you may be in the wrong career, not just in the wrong job. You need to consider several important questions before rushing to change your job:

- How long have you felt unfulfilled?
- Did you feel fulfilled at first but lost your sense of satisfaction later?
- Are there reasons for the change (boss turned sour, overlooked for promotion, etc.)?

- What got you into this job (only one available, parents forced you into it, etc.)?
- Do you feel you have changed or matured since starting this job and may have outgrown it?

Honest answers to these important questions should give you some clues as to why you feel unfulfilled. Many people are trapped in jobs that were forced on them when they were younger. I grew up in a mining community and practically everyone I knew was connected with gold mining in some way or other. So it was natural that most young people felt coerced into taking up a profession connected with mining—assayers, surveyors, metallurgists, geologists, mining managers, and the like. Fortunately, I resisted and did what I wanted to do. Many of my friends did not, and ended up doing what their parents told them to do. Today many feel unfulfilled.

Sometimes when we are young we take up work that doesn't draw upon our talents. As we grow up we may realize, "I can do better than this." If that's your case, now might be the time to consider a change.

One last point. Why is it that some people stay in a job longer than they should, feeling unhappy and unfulfilled? For some, it is a form of learned helplessness—they don't believe they have the power or resources to change their job. For others it is a matter of security. They don't want to take risks. But there is a further reason worth challenging: Some stay in a job out of a sense of loyalty. Admirable? Perhaps.

Some organizations capitalize on worker loyalty. They try to inculcate it as a virtue. Churches and religious organizations can sometimes be guilty of this, as can almost any group that has a noble mission. But when such groups capitalize on a worker's sense of loyalty and refuse to pay decent wages or provide respectable working conditions, these groups are toxic, no matter how noble their cause. Franklin Delano Roosevelt said, "No business which depends for existence on paying less than living wages to its workers has any right to continue in this country." Some of our charitable organizations could do well to listen to FDR!

But loyalty does not get in the way only when misused by companies. I recently heard of a manager who was trying to negotiate with a worker to move to a new position within the same company. The change would bring a slight promotion and pay raise. The worker, however, felt reluctant to accept the change. She had been offered an outside job for considerably more pay. But the new job prospect wouldn't be available for several months. In taking the assignment in her present company, she feared she would get used to and come to like the staff in her new office. "Loyalty can get you into a lot of trouble," she said to her manager. She's right. It can keep you stuck in a job that isn't in your best interests. It can keep you underpaid and unfulfilled. Loyalty to an organization is a virtue only when that organization plays fair with you. Furthermore, loyalty to a job or even fellow workers should never take precedence over loyalty to your own needs and the need to provide adequately for yourself and your family.

When is loyalty a virtue? When should you have the guts to stick out a bad job situation? A lot depends on your value system. Here are a few circumstances that *might* warrant your sticking it out, at least temporarily:

- The mission of the organization may be worthy enough for you to overlook the discomfort of a bad work environment.
- You may have an ethical or legal responsibility to fulfill a contract—even if this contract is only a verbal agreement.
- Your departure may significantly harm the well-being of others (for instance a medical doctor abandoning a clinic for the underprivileged or on the mission field, before a replacement has arrived).
- You may have a strong sense of calling to be in a place of work even if the work is dangerous or very unpleasant. Our world would be a sorry place without heroes or those who are willing to sacrifice their own comfort to make life better for others.

The important principle is that you should *know the reasons* why you are being loyal, that you should be certain you are *not being manipulated* by an appeal to loyalty, and that you have the *freedom to choose* to stay or go.

These are tough times. Not everyone has the luxury of choosing when to make a job change. Some are forced to change; people get fired, laid off, or become incapacitated. Job change is very often forced on us, not freely chosen.

When an economy is in trouble, companies are forced to restructure, reorganize, tighten their belts, and play it safe to survive. You can't blame them for this. Cost cutting becomes a cold, hard fact of life. Unfortunately, labor costs are nearly always the major part of any company's expenses, so workers feel the impact of retrenchment.

Being laid off can be devastating. It undermines confidence and self-esteem. Often it leaves an emotional scar, especially when a replacement job doesn't come easily or quickly. Panic attacks, depression, and generalized anxiety problems are quite common in those who have been dismissed.

MAKING A JOB CHANGE

What should you do if you want or need to change your job, whether you choose it voluntarily or it is forced on you? My suggestions follow.

Stabilize your expenditures. Trim your spending to conserve your resources. If you receive a severance package, bank it. It may take months and months to find a new position. Cut out expensive entertainment and nonessential purchases.

Be honest with your family. This is especially important if you've been laid off. I know of one situation where the father and mother conspired to keep the father's job layoff a secret from their teenage children. They invented elaborate explanations to cover details of daddy's missing company car by saying that "it's in for extensive repairs." The deceptiveness put unnecessary strain on the family— and the teenagers couldn't understand the restrictions placed on their activities. They continued to make financial demands. I encouraged the parents to "come clean." The kids would understand, I assured them, and rally around helpfully. And they did. The older son found a part-time job to help cover his personal needs and dad's reputation was not diminished. If anything, the family become closer as the teenagers took on greater responsibilities, feeling that they were really being valued by their parents for their mature response. Kids are remarkably sensitive and empathetic when given the chance.

If you are making a voluntary job change be honest with your family also. They deserve to know what is going on.

Review the circumstances of your job loss. If you have been let go, it can be cathartic to face up to certain realities. But more than this, you need to ensure that your legal rights have been protected and defended. Are you sure that the company's retrenchment wasn't a guise for your dismissal? Take a look at the details. Was there some action that could constitute an unfair labor practice? If so, you may want to get legal counsel. After all, a workplace that is toxic is not likely to have dealt with you fairly.

If it was a genuine retrenchment, then try to resolve the emotional consequences of your loss quickly. This means allowing yourself some time for grieving. Ultimately grief is resolved when you "let go." Look to the future. The depression of your grief will only get worse if you fight it and refuse to release yourself from what you might be holding on to in your old job.

Don't rush your new job search. Take a little time to reorient yourself, review your job choices, and even consider whether you want to make a career change. Plan your job search. Make finding employment your full-time job for now. Be clear about what you want. Look for opportunities for change and growth. Consider how you might revitalize your skills, perhaps through continuing education. If it looks like you might be out of a job for a while, consider going back to college or university to improve your marketability. Perhaps this is the time to get that extra qualification or degree you've always wanted.

Find someone to talk to. This is especially important if you are between jobs. You will need a confidence boost, yes, but you will also need to keep your thinking straight. Counseling can be very helpful to keep you from getting lost in a maze of confused thinking and emotions. If you've been laid off, you will be experiencing a loss of self-esteem and will need to deal with such issues as denial ("This can't be happening to me"), self-depreciation ("This just proves that I am no good"), and anger ("If only I can get my hands on the so-and-so who said I had to go"). You risk eroding your self-esteem further if you don't talk these issues out.

Let me hasten to add that while a spouse can be a very helpful listener, it is not constructive to keep dumping your emotions on any one person, including other family members. A spouse, by the way, tends to feel blamed for much of what has happened.

Stick to a work routine. What typically happens when someone is laid off? There is a temptation to sleep in, take a vacation, or quit job searching in the early afternoon. You feel down, so you retreat into sleeping or watching television. The soap operas hook a lot of the unemployed because they provide escape into a fantasy world.

Resist stagnating. Set up a regular workday for yourself. Get up at your normal time, plan the day as if you're working, then quit at your normal time. Don't become lazy. Make a schedule and stick to it. There is a lot to do: Apply for unemployment benefits, prepare a top-notch resume, mail applications, search job boards, and so on. Treat your job search as it if were itself a job. This will not only improve your chances of finding a new job, but will keep up your morale and preserve your dignity.

Be assertive in your job search. Don't accept rejection meekly. Fight for the job you want. Ask questions. Insist on explanations for rejection.

A very common excuse for rejection is that "you are over qualified for the job." If it is what you want to do, what is wrong with being over qualified? Explain that you are choosing a job that is easier to handle; you want to enjoy your work more, or that you intentionally want to step out of the rat race and do work that is less demanding. No one is ever over qualified for a job these days. The employer is getting a bargain and should jump at it. Sometimes job interviewers want to see that you really want the job, that you are a determined person who is not afraid to ask questions. Anyway, what do you have to lose?

Whatever you do, *don't become angry* during an interview if you are rejected. Most people can't handle anger—nor should they have to. If you can't be assertive without getting angry, get some assertiveness training before you go job-hunting.

Be strong and take courage. Job searching is not fun, so be prepared for down times and frustration. Avoid allowing yourself to feel self-pity or helplessness. Sooner or later this phase of your life will pass and you might even look back on it with thankfulness. Many people report that they are stronger because of it. They may even go so far as to say, "It was the best thing that could have happened to me. I was in a rut. I didn't appreciate what I had. I needed to change but didn't have the courage to do it!" If you have a personal faith, you may find comfort through exercising spiritual disciplines, such as prayer. Change *forces us to grow*. It helps us clarify our values so that the *really important* things of life become our primary focus.

WHEN YOU'RE FIRED

So you were fired? You goofed and they didn't like it. Or, someone else goofed, but they blamed you. You are bitter, your pride is hurting, and you have the pain of rejection to live with.

Though you may feel that you have been unfairly treated, there must have been some reason for your getting fired, so allow me to be frank. A good shot of reality can be therapeutic! Somehow you are responsible for something connected with the dismissal. Maybe you transgressed or overstepped the company's rules, trampled on too many toes, insisted on doing it your way, or made the mistake of telling your boss what you think of her or him. The sooner you face up to the fact that something needs attention, the better your performance in your next job.

Retrenchment is different. You are not held at fault. It merely reflects the company's inability to stay in business. But when you are fired, someone is saying *you* are faulty. No one handles such an experience with equanimity.

I have yet to meet someone who has been fired from a job who said to me, "I was in the wrong and deserved to be fired." Human nature is always defensive. We usually see ourselves as victims.

Of course, there are cases of unjustified firing. A normal person deserves a second, third, or even a tenth chance. Bosses take out their pathologies on workers. People get fired without just cause or because they are not liked. But my concern here is with those who have been fired for cause, even if the cause is relatively minor.

Your responsibility is to face up to this cause honestly and courageously. It is almost essential that you get counseling. Most people are not able to do it on their own. The more openly you own up to your inadequacies and take corrective steps, the greater you will benefit from this experience. Denial and blaming others will only serve to entrench your weaknesses further. Hiding from yourself never brings growth.

CHANGING YOUR CAREER

Whether you are bored, unfulfilled, or fired, the question arises: Should I consider changing my career?

Changing a career is a much more drastic step than changing a job. It requires a lot more preparation and careful planning. You will need to carefully review the following issues and work them through to your satisfaction:

Explore the real reasons why you want to change.
- Are you by nature easily dissatisfied?
- Evaluate your motives for wanting to change—do you merely want more prestige?
- Are you sure you won't make the same mistakes twice?
- Are you the one desiring the change?
- Will your new career give you different challenges?

What alternative careers are reasonably available?
- Consider your age and what is reasonable in terms of preparation.
- Consider your unique gifts.
- Consider your financial resources.
- Consider the sacrifices your family will have to make.
- Consider opportunities that newly created careers offer.

Prepare the way for change.
- Your financial needs must be carefully planned.
- Consider retraining while you are in your present job.
- Choose the right time to change. A recession is never a good time because opportunities are too limited. Wait until you have enough openings available to give you a wide choice of jobs.
- Seek competent career counseling or consult with someone you trust.
- Be willing to go back to your old career if things don't work out.

DISCOVERING THE RIGHT JOB FOR YOU

The primary question confronting the job seeker is: How can I discover the right job for me? Millions of people change jobs every year, but not many are very successful in finding the right job for themselves.

This is not an easy task. There are no magic formulas. The best I can do is point you toward a *process*. You need to take careful stock of your values, interests, abilities, skills, and goals. The following books will provide clear guidelines and exercises that can help you clarify who you are and what type of job suits you: *Discover the Right Job for You*,[3] *Where Do I Go from Here with My Life?*,[4] *The Three Boxes of Life and How to Get out of Them*,[5] and *The 1993 What Color Is Your Parachute?*[6]

Most people end up in the wrong job because they have failed to plan their careers around their major strengths and motivations. These usually drive us without our awareness. If the books cited above don't help you enough with your self-awareness, try consulting a career counselor.

A second and closely related task is to research the careers that are reasonably available to you. Gather as much information as you can about jobs that interest you and match your major strengths. You can do this by reading, visiting locations where people do what you want to do, and by talking to informed people. I have a son-in-law who is very interested in law. He has spent several hours talking to various lawyers to get a clearer picture of what the work entails, its different specialties, and especially the down side of the profession. When he finally decides on his long-term career, he will have a more realistic notion of what he is getting into.

Perhaps the most frustrating part of finding the right job is in matching what you enjoy doing with what you know you do well. When there is a match, you are bound to feel more fulfilled. Other vocations, however, can look a lot more attractive when you are on the outside. You may think you enjoy a task, but when you have to do it as a job you may not be so good at it. Furthermore, it can be deceptive to think that something you do well and enjoy as a hobby will make a great career. I have several friends who have turned successful hobbies into businesses, only to discover that what they enjoyed as a hobby was miserable as a job.

THE ALL-IMPORTANT INTERVIEW

All job changes lead to one critical event: the job interview. Since this is a crucial step, let me close this chapter with some suggestions on how to handle it.

I am fully aware that my main focus in this book is on the ways a workplace can be crazy-making—so what am I doing talking about how to conduct yourself on a job interview? Bear with me. If your present job is killing you, you may need to make a change. Good interview skills can get you a better job, but more important, they can prevent you from making the same mistake twice and ending up in another crazy-making workplace.

Keep in mind at all times the purpose of the interview: To see if there is a match between you and your potential employer. You need to check it both ways: do you match the job *and* does the job match you? Take an active part in the interview. Ask questions about the company, policies, worker turnover, and job training. A job is more than a paycheck, so make sure you know all that you need to know. If the interviewer doesn't respect your right to know, the job isn't worth having. Toxic workplaces try to hide their toxic ways. Healthy workplaces show off their good qualities.

Do your homework ahead of time. An interviewer is impressed if he or she can see you know what the company is about. Knowledge here can also uncover unsavory aspects of the company and protect you from getting into a company that you later find you despise. Check out what the company makes or does. Look at the product in a store. Does the company have a good reputation? Do some background research—is the company in bankruptcy? Nearly broke? In legal trouble? Having the answers could save you a lot of hardship later.

Find out the company hierarchy. If it is large, check out how instructions are given, teams organized, etc. Who will be your boss? Can you talk to this person personally, before accepting the job?

Most interviewers want to see seven things in a potential worker:

Knowledge. Be prepared to answer questions about your areas of competence.

Enthusiasm. No one will hire you unless you show some enthusiasm for the company and your work. Show your enthusiasm.

Confidence. Uncertainty, vacillation, negativity all turn interviewers off. Leave your cynicism at home.

Energy. Employers are buying your work output. Energy, or vitality, can make up for many weaknesses. Be animated. Show your vitality.

Dependability. This is difficult for an interviewer to assess, so help out. Give examples of your dependability. Make a strong statement about your loyalty to the company you work for.

Honesty. Don't mislead or exaggerate your competencies. Being honest about yourself communicates an ability to be honest in all your dealings. At the same time, don't hesitate to mention your true abilities.

Pride in work. Talk about what you do with great respect. Don't put down your profession or trade, and don't try to minimize what you do. A proud worker is a good worker.

How you present yourself is crucial. Dress appropriately. Don't apply for a janitor's job in a three-piece suit. And don't show up for an interview for a VP position in jeans and sweater. First impressions are crucial, so the best rule of thumb is "be conservative." Looking businesslike shows that you care enough to dress well for the interview. It is a sign of respect.

Be on time. Being late for an interview always leaves a bad impression. And always send a polite post-interview note. It shows good manners—and opens your file one more time!

Be ready for the "killer question." What is it? Every interviewer I know asks it: Tell me about yourself. This can unnerve you unless you've done your homework ahead of time. Be brief, like one or two minutes. Be to the point, no long histories. Highlight your main accomplishments. Emphasize your strengths. If your interviewer wants to know more, he or she will draw you out further.

A terrific way to present your qualifications is in a portfolio format. Put together a file of work samples you are proud of, copies of references, photographs, sample reports, and so forth, to leave with the interviewer. This also communicates that you are an organized person.

If asked about your weaknesses, talk about them positively and show that you are working at correcting them. You walk a tightrope here. Interviewers want you to be forthright. Lies and distortions can come back to haunt you. Yet you should never be excessively self-critical either. Pitch yourself somewhere between honesty and a constructive attitude toward becoming better at what you do.

Happy hunting!

STRETCH YOURSELF AND GROW

As I close this chapter on changing your job, there is one last thought I want to leave with you, my reader. Finding a new job will not fix all your problems if you don't change. Moving to a new desk, office, workshop or city won't change who you are in and of itself. Getting a bigger paycheck or more authority won't turn you into a nicer person or take away your boredom for very long. You'll still be the same person. So don't look to changing your job as a solution to any personal problems you might have.

I say this because too many people I have known through the years have naïvely thought that just doing something different or moving to a new job would change them fundamentally. But it never does—by itself. The reason is that we all continue to behave and feel in the way that gives us the most comfort. We talk, walk, relate and work in ways that give us most satisfaction and coziness. Anything new makes us uncomfortable. Any change disrupts our habits and makes us feel overwhelmed, even fearful. So old habits will die hard. We will settle back into our old ways in our new job, and it will just be a matter of time before the old feelings, whether of boredom or discouragement, will return.

So, if you want or need to change your job you should seriously consider making some personal changes as well. Now would be the time to stretch yourself and grow a little—or a lot. A new place of work, or even a new career, is the ideal time to effect change because the slate is clean. You can start writing a new story on it.

I cannot tell you specifically how to change because I don't know you. But I can leave you with one helpful thought: If you want to change, then tell yourself the truth. Tell yourself the truth about your fears, your guilt and your insecurities. Be honest with yourself about your weaknesses and face up to the reasons for your failures. Speak the truth to yourself—in love. Don't speak it brutally or in revenge, since this never heals, but speak it gently with encouragement and hope. Then the truth about yourself will set you free and your new job will be a springboard to a happier and more fulfilling life. I know. That's what I did when I changed from engineering to clinical psychology.

Crazy-Making Work and Your Family

When companies hire employees, families and all of their home life headaches are taken on as well. Time *magazine*

It would be unrealistic to suggest that managers can become personally involved in the lives of each worker. But a sense of intimacy and mutual trust can be instilled in the workplace when managers show genuine concern for the individual employees.

Chuck Colson and Jack Eckerd
Why America Doesn't Work

"THE FAMILY TAKES MORE HITS than the job. There is more spill over from job to family than vice versa." These are the words of Arlene Johnson, vice president of the Families and Work Institute, a research and consulting firm, after surveying 2,399 employees of a large corporation.[1] Speaking at the 1992 convention of the American Psychological Association on the theme of "Work-Family Spill Over," she made two very important points: What happens at work directly affects the family, and a family-friendly work environment plays a major role in helping families to be healthy and happy.

I can verify the truthfulness of these statements firsthand from the scores of families I have seen in therapy over the years. Take Cedric, for example. He was proud of the fact that he never took work home with him. "I leave my job in my office. I deliberately don't own a briefcase, so I can't slip a file or two into it on my way out of the office, and I have hardly ever in my working life taken work home for a weekend. Sometimes I have had to work late in the office, but I have never wanted my job to get in the way of my family."

Yes, it's true. Even though Cedric is a senior vice-president of his company, no files or documents, memos or reports, contracts or negotiating papers have ever crossed the threshold of his home. But this isn't the whole story. His family is miserable, and they blame his work.

"When he comes home from work we all split," his teenage daughter told me. "I go and hide in my bedroom or make arrangements to visit a friend. All he wants to do is talk about his problems at work."

"I don't like it when my dad comes home from work," his ten-year-old son complained. "He's grumpy, jumps on me for just little things, and if I try to talk to him, he ignores me. After a while he may calm down a bit and then it's OK."

Cedric's family experiences no fun, no laughter, and no family friendship. Cedric's wife had stopped trying to get him to change and had begun to build fun time with her children outside of Cedric. Confidentially, she told me, she was considering leaving him. Married life was too unpleasant. Just a few months previously she had discovered that she has an ulcer and her doctor warned her that if she didn't do something to deal with her rage—mostly the consequence of Cedric's behavior at home—she would need to have surgery.

"I am destroying myself by staying with him. And what is it going to do to my kids? My son is becoming a nervous wreck. He's overly anxious already. I hate to think what sort of man he'll become if this continues."

And here was Cedric, pridefully telling me that he never takes work home with him. I politely reminded him that while he never took work home, it seems that he always took his job home. Finally, he got the point.

It turns out that for some years Cedric had been having major problems at work. He carries more responsibility than anyone else in his office, but this is not the whole story. His company is dysfunctional. "They," meaning those at the top, often engage in "crazy-making" activity. There is no communication from the bottom up, only from the top down. Decisions are made and handed down to be implemented without regard to how they affect those who must act on them. Anyone challenging company policy is severely punished, often by getting fired, so that an atmosphere of fear and distrust prevails. And whenever something goes wrong and a decision handed down from above backfires, scapegoating takes over. Someone else is always to blame, never those who made the decision. No one is allowed to make a mistake. Accidents are supposed to never happen. Nonsuccess *has* to be someone's fault.

And given the specific nature of Cedric's job, he often ends up taking the rap for these failures, or at least having to face the bewildered and emotionally battered employees who feel like they are going crazy.

He is always having to defend himself or someone in his unit. It's not that those at the top genuinely want to know how to correct a problem so that it won't be repeated. It's more a need to blame and fault-find. So at no time has anyone suggested that Cedric is incompetent or that he should find another job. In fact, upper management would be devastated if he ever left the company. He is the perfect scapegoat—compliant, loyal and gullible. He accepts blame too easily and his defensive attempts usually can be shot down without much ammunition, much to the glee of those who do the shooting and blaming. It's a totally dysfunctional work situation.

And its effect on Cedric is deep and becoming long-lasting. While he prides himself in being able to leave his work at the office, the emotional garbage from his job gets packed in his "mood-bag" and taken home almost on a daily basis. The "mood-bag" can be larger than any briefcase. It is as large as the mind itself and can hold a lot of emotional turmoil, yet elude recognition. He is nearly always rageful but doesn't realize it. He is preoccupied with office affairs but is oblivious of it. Given to fantasy, and he is an expert at it, he replays his mental tapes daily, over and over, trying to figure out ways he could have answered back or given a better explanation for something that went wrong. He doesn't comprehend that this preoccupation disturbs his ability to function as a husband and father. The same can be true for working mothers.

Cedric's son is quite accurate in his description of his dad. "He is irritable from the moment he comes home. Some evenings he settles down to a mild grumpiness, but only after he has had a few beers," a habit that his wife has come to resent. But even more troubling, Cedric had begun to do to his family precisely what "they" were doing to him at work. He was blaming them. If anything went wrong, someone had to be to blame. "But dad, it was just an accident," became rebuffed with, "You know very well that ..." So communication had become nonexistent, along with love, tenderness, and understanding. Cedric's toxic workplace had contaminated a beautiful family. The office warfare had become a home battle as well. Without some quick intervention this family is headed for a breakup.

The equation works both ways: when family problems are not resolved, stress is certain to follow and this family-induced stress will affect one's work. When workers have problems at home, they start to arrive late, leave early, become unproductive, and get sick more often. When work problems are not resolved, the stress of the job is carried home, where it then infects everyone in the household.

An executive assistance firm that helps organizations with employee difficulties confirms a fundamental change in the nature of the issues they now deal with. Initially, the firm dealt primarily with executives who were having problems with substance abuse. Now the predominant issues are family-related and job-related stress. The workplace is having an impact on the family as never before.[2]

Where are we headed? Some interesting changes are taking place. *Fortune* magazine has been interviewing twenty-five-year-olds for thirty-five years to keep track of trends. They have found some interesting changes. In the 1950s, twenty-five-year olds quietly and confidently looked forward to a secure work future. One found a job, settled into it, and contented oneself with it for a lifetime. By the 1980s, this had changed. Twenty-five-year olds had become impatient, arrogant, and materialistic. The most recent group, interviewed in the 1990s and representing those who now are taking over the workforce, were found to have totally different attitudes from those of their predecessors: They are concerned about leisure, family, and lifestyle pursuits and saw these to be *as important* as work itself.[3] The up-and-coming workforce wants to live a balanced life. Work is important, but it is not everything.

So business and industry have to change their attitudes and expectations and have already begun to do so. Employers have to place a higher priority on accommodating the needs of workers *and* their families if they want to develop an effective workforce.

Child-care during sickness is now available in many organizations. A Tucson law and accounting firm, for example, pays medical aides to sit with the children of sick employees to help speed their recovery. Another firm hires employment agencies to help spouses of their employees find jobs. Solving work-family problems in these ways helps firms to attract and keep valued employees. They get the best and the brightest because they show that they care. No company in the future will survive unless it makes these sorts of changes and sets a high priority on balancing family needs against job responsibilities.

Younger workers, particularly those who are better educated and in the professions, are also extremely concerned about personal growth and the overall quality of their lives. Work is just one component of their existence and no longer the most important. Work is there to make living possible! Today's workers are not willing to sacrifice family and personal interests to achieve something elusive called "success." Often they are content to forego promotions and even high salaries in order to achieve a balanced and satisfying lifestyle. They want equilibrium and stability. They put a priority on being happy, on being with their families, having hobbies, going to church, and taking vacations. Such a work ethic is going to bring many toxic workplaces into the open and reveal their unhealthy pressures.

ARRANGING WORK/FAMILY TRADE-OFFS

Not everyone is at the place I have just described. Older workers are still caught up in the career mode and having difficulty in re-adjusting their attitudes and priorities. Many baby boomers or even busters are locked into an older work ethic. Progress has bypassed them. Many spouses and children are being sacrificed on the altars of workplaces, which are certainly not always "family friendly."

Who is to blame when a worker's family is destroyed by work-induced stress—the worker or the job? Often it is a shared blame. The solution lies with both the worker and the workplace. While there is much that those in charge can do, each worker also can do much to prevent work from contaminating family well-being.

Trade-offs between work demands and family needs are inevitable. It is a fact of life that most of us have to leave the family and go to work. The family cannot claim 100 percent of all our time and energy. Conversely, work cannot claim 100 percent of our lives either. We contract with our employer, or with ourselves if we are self-employed, to give a certain amount of attention to our work. Every time we give more than we have contracted for to our work, we sacrifice what should go to the remaining aspects of our life.

The big trade-offs are obvious. You might relinquish caring for your child during the day so you can earn a better living for your family. You may refuse a promotion that goes with a transfer to another location because your spouse cannot afford to change jobs, or because your spouse is in graduate school finishing up a degree. The big trade-offs are difficult to negotiate but don't usually cause the problems I am addressing here. The real bugaboos are the smaller trade-offs.

For instance, working on a Saturday and missing a child's birthday party may seem like a small trade-off. It can be rationalized so easily: "Honey, there'll be so many kids there that Cynthia won't even notice I'm not there." Believe me, Cynthia will notice. And the reason she will notice is because these small trade-offs seldom come alone. They are symptomatic of a larger problem—that of priorities. The damaging effect is cumulative.

Take another instance. You know your wedding anniversary is coming up soon. Your spouse is rather sentimental and likes celebrating this event at a favorite dinner-theater. But you have been invited to present a paper at an important conference and the trip will take you away on the date of your anniversary. What do you do? A small trade-off? No big deal if you miss this anniversary dinner, you think? Is it no big deal? Well, it all depends, doesn't it? How often does your job interfere with important family celebrations? How critical is it to your career that you jump at every invitation to present a paper? One small decision... with lot of consequence. These small trade-offs are no small matter, and if allowed to multiply, can spell trouble for your private life.

Trade-offs, of course, are not all negative. A healthy one might be deciding to skip an executive meeting or even asking your boss to delay an appointment, so you can visit a sick mother on her birthday. A friend I know refused to stay home from work when he felt sick after some food poisoning, because he wanted to save his sick days for when one of his children is ill (a company policy allows this). Admirable behavior, assuming, of course, that he wasn't terribly sick. These are positive trade-offs.

And since trade-offs are inevitable, balancing them between

work demands and family or personal needs is the way to serve both best. How can one align one's trade-offs so that they are balanced? By giving forethought to where you want your life to go, by prioritizing the demands in your life. Once you have clarified your priorities, *be true to them.* It can be very helpful and stress-relieving to assign your priorities a ranking. This will relieve the tension you feel when too many are contending for your time and energy.

The three big contenders for our time are work, family, and play. A few people can prioritize in their heads and recall their priorities at will. They have probably been working at it subconsciously over many years. Most of us, however, need reminders and charts to keep the emotions of the moment from overtaking our decision-making. It's useful to list the demands contending for our attention and then assign them an order of importance. Take three sheets of paper. Head the first WORK, the second, FAMILY, and the third, PLAY. Draw a column down the right side of each sheet and head it "score." Now list on each sheet the *demands* that contend for your time in that category. For instance, under WORK you might include:

- developing new skills
- working evenings to please the boss
- achieving promotion more rapidly
- making sure I earn my next raise
- winning the sales award for the year
- relating better to fellow workers

Under FAMILY you might include:

- being available for outings
- having a regular date with my spouse
- helping out with family chores
- giving time to resolving problems at home
- going to counseling with my spouse
- developing shared interests or hobbies with the family
- taking regular vacations with the family

Under PLAY you might include:

- developing a hobby to distract me from work
- going to school to develop other interests
- buying a boat to keep family activities together
- going to baseball games with friends

- planning work travel to include my spouse so it can also serve as recreation

When you have recalled all the contenders for your time, give each a score, using a scale of zero to ten. Zero means it is *not* important to your overall life. Few items on your list will score a zero otherwise you wouldn't have put them on the list. A five would represent moderate importance, and a ten, absolutely important. Use your emotions, rather than logic, in scoring each item.

Then rearrange your lists, so that all tens come first, followed by nines and so on.

Now you have separate priority lists for work, family, and play. Using a pen of a different color, compare your tens across the three lists. Does, for instance, gaining the next promotion rate higher than being available for family outings? Give each a second score of zero to ten, as before, but this time comparing them across the lists for each of your top "ten" scored items. If you like, you could continue down the lists comparing the nines, eights, and so on *across* the lists.

The final step in developing your priority plan is to take a clean sheet of paper, write down on the left side the numbers one through ten leaving space between them. Then, using the work sheets you have used thus far, write down in order of importance the ten top priorities for your life, combining all three categories. One will represent your highest priority. It might be "Having a regular date with my spouse," from your FAMILY list. Two is your next highest priority and it might be, "Achieving my next promotion" from your WORK list. This is second because you feel the family would benefit from the extra pay. Work on down the list until you have clarified your top ten priorities.

Then stick this plan where you can see it regularly, and, assuming it is a healthy list, *be true to it.* Make all your trade-off decisions according to this list, not according to emotions or pressures of the moment. Don't be sidetracked. Don't deviate one inch. Say "no" to anything that weakens your priority plan.

As indicated earlier, work contaminating families is not a problem just for the worker. Managers can be insensitive to how families are being directly affected through the worker, or even indirectly by policies that do not protect their interests. Let's turn now to this consideration.

DRAWING BOUNDARIES BETWEEN WORK AND HOME

Every person has to establish clear boundaries between work life and home life. In some vocations that is harder than in others. For instance, I have done a lot of pastoral counseling and have observed how difficult it is for the average clergyperson to set up boundaries between the church and his or her family. But churches are not the only guilty organizations. Many organizations make sudden changes in schedules, change hours, and call for overtime without consulting the employee or considering how the demand affects the family. And the worker is often as guilty for not speaking up and protecting family commitments.

Andy takes care of his family's physical needs as well, if not better, than most fathers. His one weakness is that he doesn't see how important his emotional support is to his sons, aged nine and seven. Both have great sports talent. Most of their events take place on Saturday mornings. As a key member of an advertising agency, Andy often puts in extra time every weekend. After all, he rationalizes, clients are not very patient. When they decide to move on a project, they want quick action and Andy is always willing to oblige.

A family crisis developed when Andy's younger son started playing basketball. For his first few games Andy made a point of being there to watch his son play. This was the first sport that the young son felt he was really good at, so it was important that his dad be there for him in the crowd of cheering parents.

Then one Saturday morning he told his son he would be a few minutes late but assured him, "I'll be there, don't worry." He wasn't. He promised to be at the next game, but again broke his promise. "My work was just more important," he explained. "I'll be there next time."

But the next time he didn't show up at all. His excuse was: "Something came up at work. I couldn't just walk out. What would they think of me?"

By now his son was deeply hurt. He intuitively knew that his father's priorities, not real crises, had kept him away. Furthermore, his father's unreliability with promises had been the source of friction to his mother as well.

"He always breaks his promises," the young boy complained. He wasn't referring just to his father's not showing at basketball games, but other family outings also. The father was betraying his family's trust by not maintaining appropriate boundaries between his work and home. The family didn't understand why he gave more priority to his work than to them, and rightly so. Families come first. That's all there is to this argument.

How can one draw a clearer boundary between work and the family? How can one strengthen one's resolve to give the family the commitment it deserves?

Learn to recognize the early signs of stress and overwork (such as headaches, ulcers, rapid heartbeat, overeating, alcohol abuse) and take steps to deal with them *before* they start to affect your family.

Make working evenings or weekends the exception rather than the rule. If the job can be done in regular business hours, confine it there. Be sure that emergencies are *genuine* emergencies, and not the consequences of trumped-up crises or incompetent management decisions.

Demand that decisions at work be made in timely fashion and that resources be available *when you need them*, to accomplish your tasks.

This last point is worthy of elaboration. A legal secretary I know often worked late at night because her lawyer boss couldn't make decisions about how to handle his cases in a timely manner. At the last minute he would ask her to work overtime or weekends to get typing done for him in time to go to court. He had a serious problem with decision-making. I taught her how to be assertive. She wrote him a note asking him to give her work in a timely manner. In the future, she wrote, she would decline to work after hours when he had given her nothing to do all day. It was unfair, she went on, for him to so waste her time all day and then expect her to work at unreasonable hours. (Incidentally, she had to be assertive in a note and not face-to-face because he was away all day, usually attending court.)

The first day after receiving her note, he returned to the office at about 4:30 in the afternoon and sheepishly asked her to stay and do a rush job. As she had indicated she would in her memo, she declined and went home. That was the last time he pulled that stunt. He began to make decisions in a timely manner, and always allowed enough time for her to prepare his documents. Sure, there were occasions when she stayed overtime, but because they were for genuine rush jobs, they did not bother her.

In sum, learn to say "no" to colleagues who try to dump extra work on you. This keeps your own work load manageable. Respect your right to take coffee breaks, lunch breaks, and paid holidays without feeling guilty so that you can relax and spend time with your family.

If you are a workaholic, examine the reasons. A work "enthusiast" can do as much, if not more, than a workaholic, and not be as toxic to the family as the workaholic. Are you afraid you will lose your job if you don't put in long hours? Discuss this with your boss to clarify expectations. If you are escaping from a painful home situation, get help. Working long hours won't fix the problems at home.

Try to quit work at the official quitting time (5:00 P.M. for a lot of us). Why? The managing editor of *Fortune* magazine offers ten reasons:[4]

1. It will cause you to become a more efficient manager.
2. It will encourage your boss to act like a true manager.
3. It will shape up your subordinates.
4. It will force you to clarify your values.
5. It will help you to establish independence from your organization.
6. It will make those exceptional occasions when you do stay late more enjoyable.
7. It will keep you out of the burnout cycle.
8. It will permit better use of your leisure time.
9. It will enable you to be healthier.
10. It will enable you to be more loving.

If you do not protect your family from the demands or dysfunctions of your workplace, you may see signs such as these very quickly: Young children with discipline problems and poor school performance, rebellious teenagers, a drug-infested home, and an unhappy spouse.

Growing children need attention, supervision, encouragement, tutoring, and boundaries. If you are preoccupied with work, you might gain some success there, but lose out as a parent.

When you are at home, give your family your complete attention. This is especially true when you first arrive home. Create a happy anticipation of your arrival by occasionally bringing a surprise, or just by making it a happy time.

Take an interest in your children's after-school activities such as sports, drama, dance, church, even friends. This will help keep them away from bad friends. If you don't show an interest in such activities, they are more likely to be drawn to problem activities. Drug addictions in teenagers develop in neglected teenagers *more* than they do in those getting parental attention.

Be sensitive to the developmental pains of your children. Growing up can be a struggle these days. Learning how to relate to the opposite sex, socialize, handle conflicts and losses, can be helped by good communication with parents. If you are not around there can never be communication. Three important rules in maintaining good parent/child relationships are: 1) Communicate, 2) Communicate, 3) Communicate.

Except for absolute emergencies, do not cancel your family commitments. Come hell or high water, stick to your promises. Older children may say they understand, but deep down they will feel disappointed. These hurts accumulate and become embedded in memory, to be recalled again in moments of melancholy or loneliness. Few things hurt as much as being let down, especially if you have the expectation that a parent will do something with you. Childhood disappointments stay with us.

DOING A "MENTAL WASH" ON THE WAY HOME FROM WORK

One of the ways you can rid yourself of work worries is to do a "mental wash." Before you step across your threshold and contaminate your home with emotional toxins you have unwittingly carried with you, take time to cleanse your mind. You can do it as you travel home. You will benefit as well as your family, if you do it in a therapeutic way. It's not unlike decontaminating hazardous waste. I'm sure you've seen people on TV news reports dressed in protective gear, with every part of their bodies covered. When they come out of the dangerous environment they start the "wash-down." With shower-spray nozzles poking into every crevice, they remove every trace of toxin. Our emotions need such "decontamination" each day so as to arrive home clean and avoid infecting our families.

If you work in a family business or an office attached to your home, I recommend a long walk *before* you join your family or friends. The exercise (see directions below) will do you good, but more importantly you need the time for your mental wash-down.

- Gather up the unresolved problems of the day that might still be bothering you.
- If you need to do something to resolve the "unfinished business," make a note or dictate an instruction on a portable recorder. The main point is: get it out of your mind and into some other form of memory. If you don't, it can continue to bug you.
- Review the things that have made you angry. Clarify why you are angry, who has made you angry, and what, if anything, you can do the next day. Write it down or record it.
- Resolve that you won't take your anger or frustration out on your family (or the dog, for that matter). By making such a resolve, you reduce the likelihood of scapegoating.
- Many sources of frustration or anger you will not be able to resolve, or avenge. Try forgiveness as an antidote. Believe me, we have neglected forgiveness as a virtue with practical benefits. Our place of work could use some intensive instruction here. But for yourself, try forgiving those hurts you don't deserve, as well as the ones you do deserve. Nobody's perfect! If you ride home with a friend or work partner, sharing this mental wash-down could be mutually beneficial.

WAYS THAT COMPANIES CAN HELP FAMILIES

A forward-looking company can reduce the negative impact of stressful work upon families by establishing a task force, made up of a cross-section of employees, and charging them with the responsibility for looking at how work impacts company families. This task force can:

- Designate a person to look after work-family concerns.
- Foster training on work-family issues, using lectures, readings, and seminars.
- Survey employee needs or problems.
- Organize care for young, sick, or elderly family members.
- Negotiate flexible work arrangements to help workers meet special family demands.
- Organize counseling services (if possible, on the premises), to make it easier for workers needing help.

Companies can also identify and promote practices that support both women and men in meeting work and family demands.

- Conduct surveys to find out what they need.
- Ensure that managers are flexible in approaching employees' problems.
- Ensure communication from the bottom to the top on matters of employee and family welfare.

Supervisors should be encouraged to manage along the life cycle. In other words, supervisors need to be aware that each employee is at a different place in his or her life cycle. What is important to a mother of three children may not be important to the father of a college-aged adult. Someone approaching retirement will have different needs than a newly married employee. Supervisors can manage along the life cycle by using a style that is flexible; allowing variations in working times to meet family needs, commuting times, etc., and by taking life cycle needs into account when making promotions, reassignments, or other job changes.

Companies would be wise to establish a family leave policy that provides workers a minimum of twelve weeks of unpaid leave to deal with family emergencies, including the birth of a child or the sickness of a child, spouse or parent. Such a policy should be available without penalty to a worker who takes advantage of it. Managers should be trained to know how to handle requests for such leave, without making workers feel guilty or uncomfortable. Efforts should be made to help workers feel a part of social activities of the workplace, so no one feels left out.

The family leave bill, now in effect throughout the nation, is a major step toward creating healthier workplaces and protecting families. This bill requires companies with fifty or more employees to provide such leave. Salaries are not paid, but health care benefits must continue. Also, employees must have been employed for one year and worked at least 1250 hours to be eligible. When returning to the job, they must be given their old position or its equivalent.

Admirable as this family leave policy is, it is only the *minimum* a progressive organization should provide. The benefits to an organization for treating its employees humanely go far beyond keeping workers happy; they result in definite financial benefits to the organization as well.

Before the family leave policy was mandated by law, the owner of a small California company of thirty employees (smaller than the number now legally required) found himself with a dilemma: seven of his ten female employees were pregnant at the same time. The owner put his thinking cap on and came up with an ingenious plan. He granted multiple maternity leaves, but kept his business going by "cross-training" every employee to perform multiple tasks. An account manager learned how to drive the diesel truck. A clerk learned bookkeeping. When the babies arrived, the employees moved from department to department to allow the new mothers to take unpaid maternity leave, yet return to their jobs. All this occurred just before the recession hit. By temporarily trimming its payroll before the downturn, the small company survived the impact and thrives today. And it gained another benefit: its workers don't get bored anymore. They can fill in on other jobs, enjoy the variety, and keep a high level of interest going, all evidence that humane staff management pays off in benefits for the company.

But what impressed me the most about this story was the new mothers' respect and loyalty for their boss. They were thankful that they could be real moms while being able to work. And the company has reaped the benefits of low turnover and greater work commitment.

CREATING A BALANCED LIFE

Can you have it all? Can you have a good job, healthy mind and body, a contented family, and time for love and leisure? Several expert consultants in the management field feel that many companies treat these ideas as if they were a myth. I happen to believe you can have it all, because I do! I have also helped many others to achieve a balance between the demands of a highly successful career and the pleasures of home life. Increasingly, workers throughout the workforce, even at upper management levels, are demanding and achieving this balance.

In theory, most of us recognize the necessity for building balance into our lives. We can see the devastating effects on our families as soon as we allow our work to overcontrol us. While I have provided some specific suggestions for how you can achieve a better balance between work and personal life, we are all different. You may need to adjust my suggestions to accommodate your unique style, personality, and needs.

Are You Taking Your Job Home with You?

It's bad enough when you take work home so that the family is deprived of your love and attention. But even more damaging is when you take your job home in the form of stress, tension, irritability, and moodiness. If you value your family, you will be honest and carefully review whether or not, and to what extent, you leave your work at the office but take the worries of the job home with you. Here are some questions that will help you explore whether your job is hurting your family. Score each question as follows: 0 *Never*, 1 *Sometimes*, 3 *Often*.

SCORE

_____ 1. Does the family break into conflict involving you the moment you come home from work?

_____ 2. Do you resent or have unpleasant feelings about having to go home after work?

_____ 3. Would your spouse say (even if you don't agree) that you don't spend enough time with your family?

_____ 4. Do you and your spouse have an ongoing disagreement or argument over some aspect of your work?

_____ 5. Do you tend to want to talk a lot at home about problems at work?

_____ 6. Are you impatient at home when family members want to talk about their day's problems?

_____ 7. Do you lack friends with whom you can share problems or talk about things that bother you?

_____ 8. Do you feel frustrated or angry about how bad things are at work or because colleagues or management won't listen to your suggestions?

_____ 9. Do you find it difficult to relax at home after a hard day's work because there is too much distraction, noise or interruption, or because you feel too angry or down?

_____ 10. When you come home, do you feel that your family doesn't care what sort of day you have had and that they do not want to hear about it?

_____ 11. Do you continue to think about your job for quite a while after you come home so that you can't think about anything else?

_____ 12. Do you find yourself backing out of family activities for no real reason, or that your family says that it is not an adequate reason?

_____ TOTAL

How did you do?

SCORE

Below 5 You are in good shape. Once or twice every few months you come home from work frustrated or angry but you get over it quickly and it doesn't affect your family.

6-12 You may need to take a look at how and why you are taking the emotional consequences of your job home with you. Your patterns of behavior and/or moods are beginning to affect your family relationships. Hold a family conference. Ask everyone to be honest and tell you if you are not keeping the unpleasant effects of your job at work.

Over 12 You need to get some help. You are out of control. Your job is harming your family. You need to learn how to keep your problems at work—or find another job. Your family deserves better than to be saddled with the worries and problems of your job.

How Supportive Is Your Work Environment to Family Welfare?

A healthy workplace extends its influence beyond the office or factory. Those in charge understand that a worker can be more productive if he or she is not burdened with problems at home. How supportive is your company or organization to your family? Here is a simple checklist.

Check

YES NO

___ ___ 1. My immediate supervisor knows the names of my spouse and children.

___ ___ 2. If I have a problem at home (such as someone being sick) I feel I can share this openly with my supervisor.

___ ___ 3. My company/organization is flexible enough to allow me to take time off (even if it is unpaid) to take care of family emergencies.

___ ___ 4. My company/organization has activities that involve my whole family, especially at holiday times.

___ ___ 5. My company provides opportunities for me to grow, learn new skills, and expand my horizons.

___ ___ 6. My workplace is completely safe. Safety is a priority, so my family is not in jeopardy from my getting injured.

___ ___ 7. I am not forced to work overtime or stay after hours without adequate notice and without my willingness to stay.

___ ___ 8. When my child or spouse is sick, I am not made to feel guilty if I take time off to take care of him or her.

___ ___ 9. My employer does not make decisions about my job (change of hours, transfers) without consulting me.

___ ___ 10. My coworkers do not resent it when I insist on giving priority to my family's needs by not participating in after-work social activities (like spending time in parties or at the pub).

How does your company or organization rate? If your workplace rates a "yes" on all items, it is as supportive as it can be to your family's interests, short of paying you a fortune! The incorrect answer to any question flags a concern that you should try to address with your employers. Start by talking to your immediate supervisor.

| # A Spiritual Resource for Work

> *Work hard and cheerfully at all you do, just as*
> *though you were working for the Lord and not*
> *merely for your masters, remembering that it*
> *is the Lord Christ who is going to pay you, giv-*
> *ing you your full portion of all he owns.*
>
> **Colossians 3:23, 24 LB**

I HAVE INTENTIONALLY REFRAINED throughout this book from imposing my own spiritual frame of reference. Doubtless my values nonetheless have broken through and influenced what I have written. However that may be, in this afterword, I want to discuss several issues that I believe are best resolved by applying a Christian perspective on the meaning and purpose of work.

I will be pointing to scriptural passages that can help you in surviving a toxic or crazy-making workplace. If you are struggling to find meaning in your work, or find your job a drudgery, you can be helped by taking a long, deep look into how work figures into God's plan. A "theological shot in the arm" can revolutionize your work habits and protect you from disillusionment.

DOES FAITH MAKE A DIFFERENCE?

Theresa attended a seminar I was teaching on divorce recovery. My topic was "Failure—and How to Beat It." I emphasized that what we commonly refer to as "failure" is very relative. When a great disappointment looms over you, you can't help but blame yourself and believe you have failed. "But," I asked the group, "how do you know if it is really a failure? What if the disappointment turns out to be a blessing in disguise?" I then went on to relate my greatest life disappointment. I, too, had labeled it as a failure at the time.

In my mid-twenties I enrolled in a post-graduate mathematics course to prepare me for advanced structural design in my work as an engineer. At the end of the year-long course, as is typical in the British system of education in South Africa, I was to take an examination. If I passed, I would get credit for my work. If I failed, a year's work would be lost and I would have to start again. A lot was at stake.

I studied conscientiously, taking time away from my wife and young children. It was a real sacrifice for them, but I felt it was essential to my career. When the time came for the examination I felt confident. I tore open the envelope handed to me and began working feverishly on the first problem. But I began to worry after a few minutes. The problem I was trying to solve wasn't going anywhere. So I abandoned the first question and moved to the next. The same result. Slowly it dawned on me that I was going to fail an examination for the first time in my life. I started to panic. Sweat flowed down my face. Finally I threw in the towel and left the examination room.

I walked around the university campus for several hours before getting up the courage to go home. I must have been depressed for at least a month afterward, but I don't remember. All I can recall was that feeling of total failure. I believed that my future was doomed. My wife commiserated. My friends joked about it. Even my boss took it lightly. But I was down and out.

Then for some reason I decided shortly afterward to enroll in a psychology course. The result? I was hooked. That step was the turning point that eventually led to my making clinical psychology my second career. Failing that mathematics examination redirected my life.

"But was it a failure?" I asked the group after I had told them my story. Sure, I felt totally devastated, demoralized, and dejected. "But was it a *life* failure?" My answer was this statement:

In God's economy there is no failure, only forced growth. Failures are to grow by.

And what of Theresa? She had rejoined her church, having renewed her Christian commitment. The divorce recovery group had become her main support. One day as she sat down at her desk she was handed a letter informing her that she had been sacked. Her boss felt she had slackened off. She tried to explain that she was depressed because her husband had taken up with another woman. She pleaded for understanding, but he didn't understand. He wasn't going to put up with personal problems, he said. Too much work to do. Needed people who weren't emotional. Must have workers who can concentrate. A typical boss from hell.

As Theresa walked home (she was told to pack her things and leave immediately) she kept saying to herself, "I am a total failure. God has abandoned me, just as my husband has." For a moment she even thought what a blessing taking her life would be because she could see no hope for the future. But as she strolled home she remembered the words: *In God's economy there is no failure, only forced growth.*

By the time she reached her apartment her healing had begun. She had something to hold on to. Her faith in God was stronger than she had realized. God would not abandon her. She believed it. She knew it.

Several weeks later, work prospects had begun to open up. But most important, her renewed faith was sustaining her. Without it, she told me, she would have been decimated. Instead, she was experiencing a deep, inner peace that she believed came directly from God. I know what Theresa is saying is real because I have encountered many people who have similarly been helped. Furthermore, I have experienced it on many occasions myself. Christian faith can make a lasting difference. It can help you survive even the most toxic workplace; it can sustain you when you change your job. Faith can restore your shattered dreams. It must be at the core of every Christian's resources for coping with the trials of working.

A BIBLICAL PERSPECTIVE FOR WORK

Given the forty or more hours a week that most of us work (and even longer if we are the homemakers), it is important that we derive meaning from our labors. Without meaning, how can we survive the forty to fifty years we are expected to work? And where does meaning come from?

If the truth be told, most of us would not show up for work if the paycheck were taken away. Let's face it. We work to earn money, primarily. We labor in order to put food on our table, drive a car, go to the movies, put our kids through school, have a TV set, take a trip, dine with friends, or just goof off. Work makes living possible. And there is nothing wrong with this. So how far need we go in idealizing the fulfillment that work offers or should offer?

But another purpose can help us tolerate the boredom, repetition, and even crazy-making aspects of our work: we can see it as a part of God's design for our lives. The Bible presents work as essential to the fulfillment of human purpose and existence. Work is not an afterthought; it is intentional in God's design. Grasping this truth can revolutionize your attitude and make you a better employee.

In the Old Testament, work is seen as a *labor shared with God*. It is part of the creative sustaining and renewing of his world. As the psalmist says: "Then man goes out to his work, to his labor until evening" (Ps 104:23, NIV).

God's commission to humans is "to replenish the earth and subdue it and have dominion over all living things" (Gn 1:28). We ought to labor six days and do all our work, and then rest on the seventh (Ex 20:9). And even though human life was brought under the curse (Gn 3:17), God's intention for humans to work is not altered, even in the New Covenant. Work remains a divine ordinance.

All of creation works. Even animals work, except for those we have domesticated, who live off the fat of our incomes. Left to nature, animals have to gather food, build nests, and feed offspring. Humans are not exempt. Of course, not everyone has to go to a factory or bank to be "at work." Work at home, or in raising children, is as real as any. So not everyone who works gets paid in money. But everyone has to work.

My grandfather worked since he was sixteen years of age, operating the huge winches that raised and lowered workers into the great hole of Kimberley in the Cape of Good Hope from which they mined diamonds. It is the largest man-made hole in the world and was the largest diamond mine. For thirty-nine years my grandfather had worked the steam hoists and winches. Dangerous work. One slip on his part and a dozen men could fall to their deaths. Up and down, up and down, for thirty-nine years. And then, because the work was extremely stressful, retirement came at age fifty-five for him.

In anticipation of quitting his job, he and my grandmother planned to move to a little town on the Vaal river in the Orange Free State to start a new life. I remember his letters to us. I had only just learned to read and devoured them as they spoke of their move, since it meant they would be living closer to us.

I spent every school holiday for the next ten years with my grandparents. But my young mind became puzzled right at the start. I have never seen anyone work as hard as my grandfather did after his retirement. The two-acre homestead they bought needed all sorts of improving. The flower garden had to be converted into a vegetable garden. World War II had begun and my grandparents had decided to grow all their own food so they could better survive on their small pension.

It didn't make sense to me as a child that one would retire and then work that hard. I had imagined retirement as sitting around and doing nothing. One day I asked my grandfather why he worked so hard, especially since he wasn't being paid for what he was doing. His answer was simple: "The harder I work, the better I serve God. Besides, your grandmother has worked harder than me all her life and she never got paid for anything she's had to do. Wages have nothing to do with it." His point was this: work is a necessity for survival, but if you render it as service to God, you can do it without drudgery and resentment.

In the New Testament our understanding of work is found mainly in Paul's epistles. His teachings encourage attitudes like diligence, honesty, and faithfulness as well as the stewardship of our gifts. Perhaps surprisingly, much of what Paul has to say about work is directed toward slaves. Unfortunately, many in the workforce, especially those trapped in toxic workplaces, see themselves as "slaves." I am sure Paul's injunctions to the slaves of his day have no less meaning to modern-day employees. "You slaves must always obey your earthly masters, not only trying to please them when they are watching you but all the time; obey them willingly...." (Col 3:22, LB).

"Work hard and cheerfully at all you do, just as though you were working for the Lord and not merely for your masters...." (Col 3:23, LB).

"Christian slaves should work hard for their owners and respect them; never let it be said that Christ's people are poor workers. Don't let the name of God or his teaching be laughed at because of this. If their owner is a Christian, that is no excuse for slowing down; rather they should work all the harder because a brother in the faith is being helped by their efforts" (1 Tm 6:1-2, LB).

Though written to people who must have found their labors burdensome, these words remain relevant today. When someone pays you for your labor, a part of you is owned. Like it or not, you are a sort of slave. That's why so many start their own businesses. They want to be free. But being free doesn't mean you work less, it just means you are accountable only to yourself—and God. If work is seen as a response to the call of God to serve him, then it loses any sense of burdensomeness. Even real slaves can find freedom in this.

What about the employer? Does Scripture have anything to say to bosses? It sure does: "And you slave owners must treat your slaves right, just as I have told them to treat you. Don't keep threatening them; remember, you yourselves are slaves to Christ; you have the same Master they do, and he has no favorites" (Eph 6:9, LB).

Amazing! Human nature hasn't changed in two thousand years. Paul's words still strike as close to home as when they were written. Masters (or by today's nomenclature, employers) are also told to pay wages promptly (Dt 24:15), be considerate of employees (Job 13-14), and deal with workers justly (Col 4:1). One could easily write a code of ethics for employees using just Scripture as the resource, and come up with the ingredients for a healthy workplace.

A THEOLOGICAL LOOK AT WORK

A comprehensive examination of a theology of work would take a book all to itself, and I am not qualified to write it. However, I believe two theological principles are being neglected in our working world today. These principles do not derive from any single verse of Scripture, but are in keeping with the general truths of Christianity.

Work is not to be an end in itself. Work must not become an end in itself. It must always be seen as a means to an end. Even though we render our service as if it were an offering to God, the rewards of it can be personally enticing. Work earns us a lot of material benefits. It offers possessions, power and pleasure. If we are not careful, we can be seduced into worshiping work for its own sake. Humanists hold to the view that work makes us free because it creates a world of opportunity and the means to travel and achieve whatever we desire.

But a Christian worldview opposes this and presents us with a dilemma. Much of what work accomplishes depletes our world's resources. A vast number of jobs are directed at removing natural resources to help us manufacture what we think we need. Regrettably, most manufactured goods satisfy entertainment and nonessential appetites. We are getting rich and having fun at the expense of future civilizations who may have to find another planet because little of this world's natural resources will be left to support them. So while we must "subdue the earth," we must also not neglect to replenish it. We'll be fortunate if we have any living things to take dominion over if we continue on our present worldly course. We must not only master our world through our work, but keep it in balance. Work, when it is an end in itself, blinds us to our need to take care of the future.

On a more personal level, when work becomes an end in itself it also creates a host of social and psychological problems. Power corrupts and those who are corrupted create a dysfunctional workplace. People who love power are given the opportunity to exercise it, often destructively, through work.

Psychologists also point to the impact that work has on the *self-concept*. Often, the choice of an occupation is a way of expressing how we perceive ourselves. As the work is pursued, the self-concept begins to change in response to the work experience. In bygone times, self-identity, which is derived from self-concept, was not determined so much by what you did, but by what you are. Today our identity is almost entirely defined by our work. This dependence on work, and our ability to perform in our work, may be the major cause of our pervasive self-esteem problems.

If a person is unable to compete in the job market, as is true of millions of young people today, the self-concept is damaged and self-esteem problems follow. To get self-identity, inner city youngsters turn to gang activities. They create their own system for self-valuing. The more fortunate, who get jobs or go into professions, are also likely to suffer because only a few achieve a high degree of success and thus escape the erosion of self-esteem. And even these highly successful people will tell you that they still suffer from feelings of inferiority because they discount their successes and can't trust the feedback. What a trap. If you don't succeed, you will most certainly have self-concept problems. And if you do succeed, there is no guarantee you will accept yourself for who you are. Our culture is too tied to performance and competition, the qualities most demanded of every worker. As long as we continue to see work as an end in itself and not as a means to an end, we will continue to have a pervasive self-esteem problem. Our identity has to be based on firmer ground than work, and the only sure rock I know is our standing before God. Work must never be the sole source of our self-concept.

Work can also create *enslavement* to personal ambitions, and even to work itself. Work can be addictive, as I explained in an earlier chapter. Work addiction is a form of idolatry. You worship your skills, performance, and rewards.

To prevent work from becoming a bondage, we must enrich our overall lives by bringing into them as much as we can of all that is wholesome. Hope, love, peace, forgiveness, and compassion can displace the anxiety and fears generated by too much preoccupation with worldly rewards and success. Building up your family, balancing time given to work with that spent in spiritual and recreational outlets, can help create the balance that God intends us to have.

Work must always include rest. Work has to be viewed as temporary and it must be interwoven with periods of rest. Our failure to do this adequately is a major cause of stress disease. I believe very strongly that the need for rest is a spiritual issue. Consider the scriptural injunctions. The seventh day was designated as the day of rest because it was the day "God ceased from this work he had been doing" (Gn 2:2, LB). Likewise, he commanded humans to work six days and rest on the seventh (Ex 34:21). Even for God, work is not the only thing. Finally he calls us to rest (with him) from our labors (Rv 14:13).

Now the interesting thing for me, having worked in psychotherapy with scores of Christians, including highly-driven pastors, is how hard it is to convince them that they need to take adequate time for rest. I had the same difficulty with it myself at one time. And what is the most common excuse I hear from these well-meaning people? They say they feel guilty when they try to relax. Idleness triggers anxiety.

While I don't hold to a legalistic view about Sabbath-keeping, I do fear that many modern believers have adopted too cavalier an attitude toward the scriptural requirement for rest. While the penalty for breaking the Sabbath was pretty severe under the old covenant (stoning to death), many are still dying because of it. I am referring to the high frequency of heart attacks associated with stress and the inability to relax.

The theological mandate for rest is very clear. What should this rest include? Obviously, time for worship. "Be still, and know that I am God" (Ps 46:10, NIV). It should also include renewal and leisure. Oftentimes the only renewal these days is in intensive care and cardiac recovery wards. A close friend recently suffered a heart attack. He was not particularly over-driven, but he tells me that he now notices just how nonrenewing his life had been. He had never exercised, except for the occasional round of golf (driving in a motorized golf cart). Now part of his daily renewal, in addition to personal devotions and prayer, is an exercise regimen.

Leisure and rest go hand in hand. And here we really run into trouble with conventional religion. Almost all religious traditions, including Christianity, raise questions related to the concept of leisure. How can we justify goofing off? How should discretionary play time, TV watching, or even sunbathing be theologically justified? And how can baby-boomers and busters justify to God their indulgence in the pleasures provided in the industrialized world?

Our culture has constructed a huge industry focused on providing leisure and pleasure. But little that is commercially available really meets the true human needs. Recreational play usually involves stimulating physical activities. Sports, motor-car racing, bungie cord jumping, sky diving, speedboats, sports cars. You name it and it is bound to be more stimulation than you get from your work. These tend to be escapes, not renewing forms of leisure. The same is true of packaged holidays, tours, and cruises. No commercially available leisure activities renew both your spirit and your body. To find leisure that serves both, one has to create it for oneself.

Despite the significant improvements that have taken place over the last quarter-century in the quality of work life for the majority of American workers, there is still a great neglect of the "higher" order of needs. We have turned the autocratic management styles into less rigid, democratic ones. We have pinpointed basic human needs and developed ways for satisfying deep cravings through work. We have replaced the so-called "Theory X," the belief that people inherently dislike work and want to avoid responsibility, with the more advanced "Theory Y," the idea that work is as natural as play or rest and that people want responsibility. We now know that the limits of human collaboration and motivation are not set by the nature of organizations, but by the limits of a manager's ingenuity. If an employer so chooses he or she can turn any toxic or dysfunctional workplace into a healthy one. So what is left?

I would suggest that it is the neglect of the "higher" order of needs that I have discussed in this afterword. In addition to personal recognition, fair treatment, a chance to be heard, and a sense of belonging, every person longs to be spiritually fulfilled. Since work takes up such a major part of life, people long for a greater integration of their work life into their total experience. They no longer want to keep their faith, leisure, and work separated. Christians especially want work to be an expression of their Christian service, not an addendum to it. At least, that's what I want and I know many who feel the same way. Someone has said, "Most middle-class Americans tend to worship their work, to work at their play, and to play at their worship." This is very true, but many want to change this convoluted way of living.

The current wave of interest in the quality-of-life of workers is no passing fad, but unless it seeks to address the spiritual needs of all workers, not just Christians, the most revolutionary of workplace transformations will fall short of helping the total person respond to the challenges of the workplace of the future. Only attention to these deeper needs will bring out the best in all of us. And only those companies who bring out the best in us will survive the competition of the next century.

Allow me to close with a quotation from one of the wisest of men. It comes from the book of Ecclesiastes and is actually a sermon in print by King Solomon. It is his attempt to convince us of the vanity or emptiness of this world as well as our work, and the utter insufficiency of both to make us happy without God.

So I hated life, because the work that is done under the sun was grievous to me. All of it is meaningless, a chasing after the wind. I hated all the things I had toiled for under the sun, because I must leave them to the one who comes after me. And who knows whether he will be a wise man or a fool?... A man can do nothing better than to eat and drink and find satisfaction in his work. This too, I see, is from the hand of God, for without him, who can eat or find enjoyment?

Ecclesiastes 2:17-19, 24-25 NIV

Notes

ONE
Can a Workplace Be Toxic?

1. Vern Bengston, reported in Pasadena *Star News*, October 22, 1992, Living Section, 1.
2. Alan Hedge, "Are you to blame for getting sick?" Pasadena *Star News*, March 5, 1993, D4.

TWO
What Makes a Workplace Dysfunctional?

1. Edwin H. Friedman, *Generation to Generation* (New York: Guildford Press, 1985), 25.
2. William White, *Incest in the Organizational Family* (Bloomington, Ill.: Lighthouse Training Institute, 1986), 311.
3. S. Menuchin, et al., *Families of the Slums* (New York: Basic Books, 1967).
4. Marjorie Blanchard and Mark J. Tager, *Working Well* (New York: Simon and Schuster, 1985), 132.
5. Blanchard, 132.
6. Ernest Becker, *Denial of Death* (New York: The Free Press, 1973), 5.

THREE
How to Keep Work from Killing You

1. Max De Pree, *Leadership Is an Art* (East Lansing, Mich.: Michigan State University Press, 1987), 23.
2. De Pree, 23.
3. Robert H. Rosen, *The Healthy Company* (Los Angeles: Jeremy P. Tarcher, 1991), 9.
4. Rosen, 2.
5. De Pree, 24.
6. De Pree, 24.

275

FOUR
Are You *Poisoning Your Workplace?*
1. Tori Dé Angelis, "Illness Linked with Repressive Style of Coping," *APA Monitor*, December 1992, 15.
2. Dé Angelis, 15.

FIVE
Toxic Bosses
1. Lawrence J. Peters and Raymond Hull, *The Peter Principle* (New York: William Morrow and Sons, 1969).
2. Mandy Grothe and Peter Wylie, *Problem Bosses* (New York: Facts on File Publications, 1987), 10.
3. Reported in *Working Woman*, December 1991, 69.
4. Jill Hodges, "Lousy Boss a Guaranteed Recipe for Workplace Stress," Pasadena *Star News*, October 19, 1992, 4.
5. Hodges, 4.
6. Grothe, 256.

SIX
Dealing with the Crazy-Makers
1. Donald R. Capp, *White Collar Worker's Survival Manual* (Pacific Palisades, Calif.: January 1989), xii.
2. Pasadena *Star News/Star Tribune*, January 2, 1993, News Section Two, 2.
3. *Star News*, 2.
4. Auren Uris, *The Executive Deskbook* (New York: Van Norstrand Reinhold, 1970), 116.
5. M. Lynne Cooper, Marcia Russell, Michael R. Frone, "Work Stress and Alcohol Effects," *Journal of Health and Social Behavior*, September 1990, Vol 31 (3), 260-276.

SEVEN
Your Job, the Pressure Cooker, and Occupational Stress
1. Carolyn Poirot, "We're Talking Stress," Pasadena *Star News/Star Tribune*, October 28, 1992, Living Section, 1.
2. Jonathan C. Smith, *Understanding Stress and Coping* (New York: MacMillan, 1993), 192.
3. Archibald D. Hart, *The Hidden Link between Adrenalin and Stress* (Dallas: Word, 1991).
4. Susan R. Burchfield, ed., *Stress: Psychological and Physiological Interactions* (New York: Hemisphere Publishing, 1985), 271.
5. Smith, 192.
6. Stephen R. Covey, *The 7 Habits of Highly Effective People* (New York: Simon and Schuster, 1990), 146.

EIGHT
Burnout on the Job
1. Smith, 201.
2. Smith, 201.

3. White, 42.
4. White, 42.
5. Henry Cloud and John Townsend, *Boundaries* (Grand Rapids, Mich.: Zondervan, 1992), 25.

NINE
Women at Risk

1. Tom Brown, "Women in Business: New Thinking?" *Industry*, February 3, 1992, Vol. 241 (3), 22.
2. *Working Woman*, November 1991, 103.
3. Harriet B. Braiker, *The Type E Woman* (New York: Signet Books, 1986), 45.
4. Maureen Dowd, "The Bitch Factor," *Working Woman*, June 1991, 78.
5. Richard L. Bednar, Gawain M. Wells and Scott R. Peterson, *Self-Esteem* (Washington, D.C.: American Psychological Association, 1989), 4.
6. Gloria Steinem, "Hey, I'm Terrific," *Newsweek*, February 17, 1992, 6.
7. Fay Fiore, "Women's Career-Family Juggling Act," *Los Angeles Times*, December 13, 1992, D3.
8. Susan Luce, "Getting In-House Help," *Working Woman*, December 1992, 86.
9. Nancy Wartik, "Blue Moods," *Working Woman*, December 1992, 81.
10. Nancy Wartik, "Bouncing Back," *Working Woman*, December 1992, 8.
11. Braiker, 4.

TEN
Sex, Power, and the Workplace

1. Ellen J. Wagner, *Sexual Harassment in the Workplace* (New York: American Management Association, 1992), 9.
2. Wagner, 9.
3. Jim Abrams, "Sexual Harassment—Global Problem Study Says," Pasadena *Star News/Star Tribune*, December 1, 1992, 1.
4. Wagner, 18.

ELEVEN
Changing Your Job

1. Stratford Sherman, "A Brave New Darwinian Workplace," *Fortune*, January 25, 1993, 51.
2. "1993 Job-Seeker's Handbook," *Working World Magazine*, January 1993.
3. Ronald L. and Caryl Rae Krannich, *Discover the Right Job for You* (Woodbridge, Va.: Impact Publications, 1991).
4. John C. Crystal and Richard N. Bolles, *Where Do I Go from Here with My Life?* (Berkeley, Calif.: Ten Speed Press, 1974).
5. Richard N. Bolles, *The Three Boxes of Life and How to Get out of Them* (Berkeley, Calif.: Ten Speed Press, 1978).
6. Richard N. Bolles, *The 1993 What Color Is Your Parachute?* (Berkeley, Calif.: Ten Speed Press, 1993). A practical manual for job hunters and career changes.

TWELVE
Crazy-Making Work and Your Family

1. Nina Youngstrom, "Juggling Job, Family," *The Monitor*, American Psychological Association, December 1992, 33.
2. Alexander and Dorothy Mikalachki, "Work-Family issues: You had better address them!" *Business Quarterly*, Spring 1991, Vol. 55 (4), 49.
3. Mikalachki.
4. Rosen, 278.

Other Books of Interest from
Servant Publications

Personality on the Job
Kevin Narramore

What are the main personality types? Which one are you? What traits can make or break you on the job? How can you learn to handle difficult people?

These nitty-gritty issues and many more are covered by Dr. Kevin Narramore in *Personality on the Job*. The key to making your personality work for you and not against you, Dr. Narramore emphasizes, is understanding your strengths and weaknesses and making the necessary adjustments on the job. **$8.99**

Me, Myself, & I
How Far Should We Go in Our Search for Self-Fulfillment?
Dr. Archibald D. Hart

Archibald Hart believes it's time to take a searching look at what modern psychology and the Bible say about such topics as self-concept, self-image, self-esteem, self-denial, self-sacrifice, and self-surrender. Surely there is a way through these tangled issues that can bring greater clarity to our search for healing. **$10.99**

Healing Life's Hidden Addictions
Overcoming the Closet Compulsions that Waste Your Time and Control Your Life
Dr. Archibald D. Hart

One out of every four Americans exhibits regular compulsive behaviors which can predispose him or her toward hidden addictions—the obsessive desire for food, sex, exercise, entertainment, relationships, shopping, work, and a host of seemingly innocent attachments. Dr. Hart explores fascinating new research on addictive behaviors and the most effective way to overcome them. **$8.99**